More Than Life

More Than Life

Georg Simmel and Walter Benjamin on Art

✦

Stéphane Symons

NORTHWESTERN UNIVERSITY PRESS
EVANSTON, ILLINOIS

Northwestern University Press
www.nupress.northwestern.edu

Printed in the United States of America

10 9 8 7 6 5 4 3 2 1

Library of Congress Cataloging-in-Publication Data

Names: Symons, Stéphane (Philosopher), author.
Title: More than life : Georg Simmel and Walter Benjamin on art / Stéphane Symons.
Description: Evanston, Illinois : Northwestern University Press, 2017. | Includes bibliographical references and index.
Identifiers: LCCN 2017017807 | ISBN 9780810135789 (cloth : alk. paper) | ISBN 9780810135772 (pbk. : alk. paper) | ISBN 9780810135796 (e-book)
Subjects: LCSH: Simmel, Georg, 1858–1918. | Benjamin, Walter, 1892–1940. | Art—Philosophy.
Classification: LCC B3329.S64 S96 2017 | DDC 193—dc23
LC record available at https://lccn.loc.gov/2017017807

And all those who were standing by were overcome by emotion and tears when they saw the erstwhile bride now in faded and feeble old age and the groom still in his youthful beauty, and how in her heart after fifty years the flame of youthful love awoke once more.

—Johann Peter Hebel, "Unexpected Reunion" (1811)

CONTENTS

FIGURES

ACKNOWLEDGMENTS

First of all I would like to thank Roland Breeur, Arnold Burms, Paul Moyaert, Steven Spileers, and Rudi Visker for continuing to show me what philosophy really is and what it can do.

I would like to thank a number of international colleagues who have encouraged me along the way, invited me for conferences or research stays at their institutions, or given me helpful feedback: Ulrich Baer, Ed Baring, Andrew Benjamin, Colby Dickinson, Eli Friedlander, Suzanne Guerlac, Owan Hulatt, Anton Kaes, Michael Jennings, Nathan Ross, Darrow Schecter, Joseph Vogl, Samuel Weber, and Sigrid Weigel. This much-appreciated help, of course, does not necessarily mean that they will agree with all the ideas and arguments that are put forward in this book.

Thanks are due to many friends and colleagues at the KU Leuven, among others Barbara Baert, Rudolf Bernet, Erwin Blendeman, Mieke Bleyen, Geert Bouckaert, Paul Cortois, Paul Cruysberghs, Andreas De Block, Stein De Cuyper, Evelyn Dehertoghe, Nicolas de Warren, Laurens Dhaenens, Relinde Geys, Rajesh Heynickx, Jiha Kang, Sofie Keyaerts, Rudi Laermans, Anneleen Masschelein, Filip Ons, Bart Philipsen, Bart Raymaekers, Jonas Rutgeerts, Toon Vandevelde, Hilde Van Gelder, Ines Van Houtte, Fran Venken, and Jeroen Verbeeck.

I would like to thank my friends Vincent Caudron, Gerbert Faure, Wolter Hartog, Dries Simons, Willem Styfhals, and Simon Truwant for fun times and so much more.

Laura Smith and Samuel O' Connor Perks helped me prepare the manuscript and Henry Lowell Carrigan, Maggie Grossman, Gianna Mosser, Trevor Perri, and Nathan MacBrien at Northwestern University Press did a wonderful job helping the book get published.

An earlier and shorter version of the fourth chapter has been published as "The Ability to Not-Shine: The Word 'Unscheinbar' in the Writings of Walter Benjamin," *Angelaki* 18, no. 4 (2014): 101–123 (available at www.tandonline.com). I thank the editors of *Angelaki* for the permission to reuse this material.

Infinitely much more than thanks are due to my parents, brother, sister, brother-in-law, and family-in-law.

Last but not at all least, I would like to thank my wife, Tammy Castelein, for walking through that door and therewith suddenly making everything different.

I dedicate this book, with all the love in my heart, to my grandmother, Maria Redig-Larosse, and to my uncle and dear friend, Jo Symons.

ABBREVIATIONS AND TRANSLATIONS

The following abbreviations are used throughout the text and notes:

AP	Benjamin, Walter. *The Arcades Project*. Translated by Howard Eiland. Cambridge, Mass.: Harvard University Press, 2002.
GS I–VII	Benjamin, Walter. *Gesammelte Schriften*. Edited by Rolf Tiedemann and Herman Schweppenhäuser. 7 vols. Frankfurt am Main: Suhrkamp Verlag, 1995.
GSG 1–24	Simmel, Georg. *Gesamtausgabe*. Edited by Gregor Fitzi and Otthein Rammstedt. 24 vols. Frankfurt am Main: Suhrkamp Verlag, 2015.
O	Benjamin, Walter. *The Origin of German Tragic Drama*. Translated by John Osborne. London: Verso Books, 1998.
PhoM	Simmel, Georg. *The Philosophy of Money*. Edited by David Frisby, translated by Tom Bottomore and David Frisby. London: Routledge, 2004.
R	Simmel, Georg. *Rembrandt: An Essay in the Philosophy of Art*. Edited and translated by Alan Scott and Helmut Staubmann. London: Routledge, 2005.
SoC	*Simmel on Culture*. Edited by David Frisby and Mike Featherstone. London: Sage Publications, 2000.
SW 1–4	Benjamin, Walter. *Selected Writings*. Edited by Marcus Bullock, Howard Eiland, and Michael W. Jennings. 4 vols. Cambridge, Mass.: Harvard University Press, 2004.
VoL	Simmel, Georg. *The View of Life: Four Metaphysical Essays with Journal Aphorisms*. Translated by Donald N. Levine and John A. Y. Andrews. Chicago: University of Chicago Press, 2011.

When no bibliographical source in English is given, the translations are my own.

More Than Life

Introduction

✦

Georg Simmel and Walter Benjamin

"The Incapability of Any Actual Pause"

It is 1911. A very hot day in Geneva. Mama, Georg, and Dora are bathing in a pool nearby. Walter, however, does not partake in the summer fun. He spends three quarters of the morning on a bench on the far side of the water: he is trying to read Georg Simmel's essay on religion. Strollers and employees on their break pass by. "I read and look up, fully in tune with the joys of being idle, I, who am only half at work, at times a bit more impatient, observing the half work going on around me" (*GS VI*, 248).

A year later, Benjamin has turned twenty and enrolls in a philosophy program at the Friedrich Wilhelm University in Berlin. He attends the courses of the notorious philosopher and sociologist Georg Simmel. Because he is Jewish, Simmel is only allowed to teach as an *extraordinarius* without permanent status. He is considered one of the most popular and inspiring teachers.[1]

1918. Simmel gives up reading the newspaper and has retreated to the Black Forest to finish his final book, *The View of Life*. As a fierce supporter of World War I and a staunch believer in its capacity to restore spiritual unity to a disintegrated Germany, Simmel has finally grown weary of the endless messages about fighting and suffering. "I know that I shall die without spiritual heirs," he notes in his diary, and adds that "this is as it should be. Mine is like a cash legacy divided among many heirs, and each converts his share into whatever business suits *his* nature, in which the provenance from that legacy cannot be seen" (*VoL*, 160). One of the foremost *Lebensphilosophen* (philosophers of life) of his time "finds his absolute," as his young friend Ernst Bloch puts it, "in the trenches."[2] For the one thing that cannot be interrupted, the dynamic of life as such, has seemingly stopped giving. As the Grumbler replies to the Optimist in Karl Kraus's *The Final Days of Mankind*, "the war did not just take place at the surface of life . . . it has wreaked havoc within life itself."[3] Two of Simmel's most dearly held expressions of the force of life, the landscape and the human face, are silent witnesses of this defeat. The mutilated battlefields of Ypres and Verdun are as much a blow to his analysis of the landscape's dynamic unity as the *gueules cassées* (broken faces) of the returning soldiers are to his descriptions of the individualizing mobility of the human face. Simmel's life ends about a month before the war does.

Almost a century later. Walter Benjamin is by now considered one of the most prominent Weimar philosophers and cultural critics. His collected writings have remained in print for decades without a pause. It has become clear that Benjamin's work does indeed contain little more than a handful of references to Simmel's ideas. In addition, only a few remarks about Simmel can be found in Benjamin's letters to his friends and acquaintances. None of them are conceptually developed and most of them come with a critical undertone. And still. The editors of Benjamin's work in English maintain that Simmel "exerted an enormous influence on the next generation of social philosophers, some of whom were his students: Georg Lukács, Ernst Cassirer, Ernst Bloch, Siegfried Kracauer, and Benjamin" (*SW* 4, 76). In similar fashion, Benjamin's most prominent biographers do mention "some reservations on philosophical grounds" but they emphasize that Simmel "nurtured Benjamin's own nascent proclivities" and argue that his writing was "in many ways the inspiration for Benjamin's later 'sociological turn.' "[4]

The best way to start the analysis of the relationship between the works of Simmel and Benjamin involves a long shot that takes in the entirety of Simmel's oeuvre. Georg Simmel is born in 1858 in Berlin, in a world of rapid change and innovation. Aged thirteen when the German Reich is founded, Simmel's coming of age runs remarkably parallel with the massive social and cultural transformations that allow Berlin to grow from a big city into a modern metropolis. The evolutions and phenomena that are being played out in the city where he will spend the largest part of his life set the stage for an important part of Simmel's scholarly interests and academic legacy. Mostly known for his reflections on metropolitan existence and the philosophy of money, Simmel's work is usually associated with the sociology of modern existence. Simmel's writings, however, combine almost all of the major strands of late nineteenth- and early twentieth-century philosophical thought while adopting none of them without introducing conceptual twists and turns that are of his own making. For instance, Simmel can indeed be regarded as one of the grandfathers of modern sociology, but he argues that the most determining law for our existence is of an individual nature.[5] He is a phenomenologist who rejects the idea that our perceptual faculties are an atemporal given.[6] He is inspired by Marxist philosophy but dares call into question the fixed relationship between value and labor.[7] And he is a Kantian who argues that the subject's perceiving and cognizing faculties make up one inseparable totality.[8] The history of thought, however, is one of idiosyncrasies and intellectual obsessions, and Simmel's impact on the postwar generation can only be gauged through a careful analysis of these very conceptual oddities and philosophical complexities. The most relevant one for our discussion, and for the relation with Benjamin's work, is the peculiar version of *Lebensphilosophie* that he develops in a later stage of his writing and that, in hindsight, was already foundational for his views on the relation between nature and culture.[9] As prominent thinkers like Max Horkheimer and Siegfried Kracauer note, Simmel does not consider life to be a mere given and he refuses to simply identify life with nature, be it non-human or human nature.[10] "Nature," writes Simmel, "is just a continuous interdependent totality," marked by an "indifferent regularity [that] does not grant any part of itself . . . an existence that is objectively delineated off from other parts" (*SoC*, 60). In his essay on landscape, he puts it as follows: "In its deep being and meaning [nature] knows nothing of individuality."[11] What is merely natural cannot, in Simmel's view, be considered meaningful: at most, it can be *made* meaningful through a *culturally* conditioned gaze that projects content onto it. In other places of his work, Simmel adapts some of the vocabulary of the *Lebensphilosophen* of his time (most notably under the influence of Stefan George and Henri Bergson) and finds a novel language to argue for this same line of reasoning. Simmel splits up the main category of life into two subcategories, "more life" (the constant replenishment of life) and "more-than-life" (the birth of something genuinely new). The basic argument is that meaning arises when the continual generation of ever "more life" gives way to the appearance of "more-than-life." This entails that, in Simmel's view, the creation of meaning is a process internal to life since, despite its confusing prefix "more-than," his concept of "more-than-life" denotes an element that is immanent to life.[12] However, to the extent that life is a mere, natural given, its dynamic is believed to be only one of "sheer physiological self-maintenance . . . involv[ing] continual regeneration" (*VoL*, 14). If it is to become meaningful, life is to pass through a process of "self-alienation" in which it brings about something that is termed "the absoluteness of its otherness" (*VoL*, 16). The jargon, hence, has evolved but the argument remains standing. In Simmel's view, a sheer given has to undergo an inner change in order to be introduced into culture and thus, as something that is "more-than-life," acquire meaning. "Culture in general," Simmel notes in his last book, "arises where categories produced in life, and for life's sake, become autonomous shapers of intrinsically valued formations that are objective with respect to life" (*VoL*, 33).[13] Simmel is, in other words, a *Lebensphilosoph* of an altogether awkward breed: he is bold enough to criticize the direct relationship between life and meaning since the latter indicates, first and foremost, an *internal transformation* of the former.[14] This idea that life undergoes an important modification when it produces meaning sets Simmel apart from the majority of the other *Lebensphilosophen*, in spite of fundamental overlaps and shared interests. Unlike Nietzsche and his acolytes, Simmel does not consider the clear-cut affirmation of life itself or the cultivation of an unspoiled will-to-life to be the most crucial component in the quest for meaning. And, unlike Bergson and the French school of vitalism, Simmel is much more interested in the inseparability of life and history than in the relation between life and biology ("élan vital").

Simmel understands the transition of nature into culture and the creation of "more-than-life" as a modification of something that is continuous and flowing into something that is *dis*continuous and interrupted. The continual regeneration of life, that is, is marked by the "incapability of any actual pause" (*VoL*, 103) and a "denial of boundaries" (*VoL*, 124), whereas cultural contents require that life separates from this natural drive for self-generation (Simmel calls this drive, somewhat confusingly, "vital teleology") and allows itself to be grasped as a stable unity: "On the level of the spirit, [life] begets something that is more-than-life: the objective, the construct, that which is significant and valid in itself" (*VoL*, 60). It is safe to say that, in Simmel's entire oeuvre, this view underlies his interpretation of a large variety of cultural practices, be they scientific, artistic, or religious ones. Scientific concepts, artworks, and contents of faith are for Simmel "forms" or "constructs" (*Bilder*, *Gebilde*) that are brought about by human beings who, while reworking life, introduce something new into it. It is, writes Simmel, a "fact that spiritual life can . . . only become articulate in *forms*" or, put differently and more succinctly, "life is ineluctably condemned to become reality only in the guise of its opposite, that is as *form*" (*SoC*, 89–90). Be it a scientific law, a painting, or an image of a divinity of some sort, none of these can be believed to be meaningful without first being understood as the result of the human drive to re-create what is otherwise but formless. As we will see, Simmel's philosophy of culture is for this reason a philosophy of genuine *re*-production: in culture, a sheer given is *produced anew* by human thought, creation, or imagination. Ideas, artworks, images, or, quite simply, experiences acquire meaning to the extent that they succeed in molding the stuff of life's continuity into a product with a content and value of its own.[15]

The emphasis on the tension between the continual generation of "more life" and the construction of "more-than-life" saves Simmel from Hegelian presuppositions that his work is nevertheless at times associated with. Despite the use of terms that might suggest otherwise (e.g., the concepts "objective" and "subjective spirit"), Simmel does not allow for a genuine sublation of the duality between the flow of life and what is constructed in culture. Simmel refuses to project meaning or content directly onto the ultimate dynamic of life and, instead, considers life to be an unceasing force of change that remains at all times in tension with the reworkings of nature by culture. No image, idea, artwork, or experience, that is, can be deemed capable of fully putting to rest the flux of life and the rhythm of perpetual innovation that underlies it. Life's quest for nonstop rejuvenation, for its part, is bound to bring down the value of each and every cultural content at some point. "Because of th[e] basic contrast in essence [between life and form]," writes Simmel, "life cannot enter into form at all—beyond every attained structure it must at once seek out another one, in which the play—necessary structure, and necessary dissatisfaction with the structure as such—is repeated" (*VoL*, 15).

These ideas are undoubtedly among the most characteristic of Simmel's way of thinking. In emphasizing the "restlessness" of life's stream (*VoL*, 14; *SoC*, 76), they bring to the surface the deep influence of not just Schopenhauer, Nietzsche, and Bergson, but Kant as well. The flux of life, that is, is indicative of a realm in which no cognition can claim legitimacy. Simmel maintains that the contents, constructs, and forms of culture are "not something incomplete" since life is a genuine "other" vis-à-vis knowledge (*VoL*, 21). His diagnosis of the "tragedy," "conflict," or "crisis" of culture can only be understood from the perspective of this interest in life's quest to continually renew itself. The notions "tragedy," "conflict," or "crisis" refer both to an essential and insurmountable discrepancy that belongs to the inner core of culture *as such* and to problems that are distinctive to one specific cultural era, namely modernity. At odds with any sense of eschatology, be it inspired by Hegelian, Marxist, or positivist philosophy, Simmel's view is that no culture should lay claim to any eternal and absolute validity since all ideals and contents acquire at most a significance that is transient. Any given culture, that is, remains bound to constructs and forms that cannot possibly contain the infinite mobility of life and will therefore at some point degenerate. The relation between the infinite dynamic of life and the contents and products in which it is made meaningful is one of such "deep estrangement or enmity" that "it is often as if the creative movement of the soul were dying from its own product" (*SoC*, 59). In Simmel's view, modern culture has developed such a succinct feeling for change and interchangeability that it allows for a wholly novel experience of life's unceasing variation and its tragic antagonism with constructs and contents. "Here," writes Simmel, "life . . . aspires to the unattainable: to determine and manifest itself . . . in its naked immediacy" (*SoC*, 90). On account of a variety of reasons (pragmatism, money culture, and metropolitan existence indicating only a few of them), modern man has grown weary of any attempt to crystallize life into form, developing a clear preference for the merely functional and formless (*SoC*, 77). The money economy, for instance, poses a serious threat to our perception of uniqueness and it aspires to an annihilation of the differences between various objects (money is the "great equalizer"). It reduces the concept of value to exchange value and sets up a worldview that is both objective (quantifiable) and highly unstable (disconnected from fixed standards) at the same time. This domination of "objective culture" over "subjective culture" endangers the active and constructive role of individuals in fashioning a system of beliefs for their own. The result of this disconnection between life and form is as paradoxical as it is dangerous: modern man is prone to fall prey to both blind dogmatism and a large-scale relativism (see, e.g., *SoC*, 67 and *VoL*, 58–59). The uncritical identification with ideas and values that have in truth become ossified and obsolete (forms without life) hence is as much a symptom of modernity as the inability to experience any idea or value as potentially significant to one's own existence (a life without form). "The culturally significant development of personal existence," however, "is a condition . . . which can be achieved in no other way than through the absorption and utilization of objective elements" (*SoC*, 66).[16] In Simmel's view, the damage of this disconnection between form and life in modernity is making itself felt most clearly in the spheres of religion (the attempt to spiritualize the flow of life itself, rejecting all predetermined articles of faith), social interaction (the inability to experience the singularity and irreplaceability of each individual), politics (the refusal to believe in values of a supra-personal nature), and art (the mania for originality and the endeavor to do away with form altogether).[17]

However fundamental Simmel's view on meaning as the creation of "more-than-life" may be to his philosophy, he hardly ever *argues* for it. The idea that the creation of meaning entails an internal transformation of life because it is at odds with the latter's unceasing flux is no outcome of a line of reasoning or a carefully laid-out argument. For Simmel, the duality between life and form is no conclusion but a presupposition; this duality does not indicate the end of a discussion but its starting point. If one is to recover the bits and pieces of Simmel's reasoning, however, crucial passages in his writings draw attention to one principle that can bring about the internal transformation that is indispensable for meaning to arise: death. In his final book, Simmel states that he is "convinced [that] death is immanent in life from the outset" and that this "is a stepping out of life beyond itself" (*VoL*, 14). Death indicates a principle of timelessness that is at work within the timely bound realm of life, by virtue of which life "also stretches out toward nothingness" (*VoL*, 14).[18] In Simmel's view, death is internal to life but runs sufficiently counter to life's endless dynamic of rejuvenation to constitute an ongoing force of deceleration. As an internalized "other" that cannot ever be fully appropriated by the flux of life, death and nothingness bring about a drastic slowing down of life's rhythm of ongoing renewal. In Simmel's view, the presence of death and nothingness within life is a permanent one and it indicates the persistence of something that refuses to be swept up by life's movement of endless change. However, the immanent presence of nothingness and death within life does not indicate a clear-cut *antithesis* to this dynamic of endless variation. Instead, for Simmel, death and nothingness might be precisely what allows the unstoppable movement of life to nevertheless be paused again and again and, while being held spellbound as a construct or form, to take on meaning. In his essay "On the Metaphysics of Death," Simmel zooms in on the "form-giving significance of death" (*formgebende Bedeutung des Todes*) and names death the "shaper of life" (*der Gestalter des Lebens*) (*GSG 12*, 83–84). In the essay "Death and Immortality," he puts it as follows: "We die and thereby experience life as something accidental, something ephemeral, something that, so to speak, can also be otherwise. Only thus could the thought have arisen that the contents of life do not indeed have to share the fate of its process; only thus could we have become aware of the meaning—independent of all transience and ending . . .—of certain contents. Only the experience of death could have dissolved that fusion, that solidarity of life-contents with life" (*VoL*, 71).[19]

For Simmel, in other words, the very *resistance* to change and the *im*mobility that mark nothingness and death render them operational as a formative element within the flux of life. His version of *Lebensphilosophie*, therefore, is even more extraordinary than it had seemed at the outset. Not only does he argue for the idea that meaning only results from the *internal transformation* of life, but he even suggests that life can be made meaningful solely by virtue of the presence of an element of "*non*-life." In this manner, in spite of obvious philosophical affinities (and a personal friendship) with Henri Bergson, Simmel remarks that his own version of philosophy of life should not be confused with Bergson's vitalist framework. In an essay that he has dedicated to the work of Bergson, Simmel takes his French colleague to task for insufficiently acknowledging that life cannot ever be separated from death. "It seems as if [Bergson] did not at all understand the tragedy that life needs to transform itself into non-life [*sich in Nichtleben verwandeln muß*], simply in order to exist" (*GSG 13*, 63).[20] Simmel's concept of "more-than-life" does include an important reference to an irreducible "counter-to-life" that is both inseparable from and distinct from life. He maintains that, while life and death are wedded to each other, death cannot be fully absorbed by life's constant quest for change and thereby denotes the presence of an excess or a too-much. For this reason, Simmel appeals to "something higher [that] arises over [life and death]: values and tensions of our existence that are beyond life and death and are no longer touched by their opposition, but in which life first truly reaches itself, and reaches the highest sense of itself" (*VoL*, 70–71). It is this ineluctable presence of death which gives cultural constructs and forms the stability through which they, for a specific period in time at least, are capable of withstanding life's nonstop production of difference and innovation.

A second step in the analysis of the relationship between the works of Simmel and Benjamin involves another long shot, this time taking in the entirety of Benjamin's published writings.

In an important passage in his *Habilitationsschrift* on the German baroque mourning play, *Ursprung des deutschen Trauerspiels* (*The Origin of German Tragic Drama*), Benjamin differentiates the *Trauerspiel* authors from the Renaissance authors in that the former reduce nature to "the overripeness and decay of her creations. In nature, they saw eternal transience [*ewige Vergängnis*]." This "saturnine vision" that "piles up fragments ceaselessly" is the "polar opposite to the idea of transfigured nature [*der verklärten Natur*]": "The Baroque work of art wants only to endure, and clings with all its senses to the eternal" (*O*, 179–81; *GS I*, 355–56). Throughout Benjamin's work, the topos of nature illustrates a realm that cannot be considered as meaningful since the only permanent feature that can be discovered within it is its very impermanence. Dystopic views on a natural temporality of eternal transience underlie Benjamin's criticism of "a conception of history that considers only shallow, causal forms" (*GS I*, 935), his views on modernity as hell (Auguste Blanqui's *Eternity through the Stars*, fashion's repetitive infatuation with novelty), and, of course, his famous reading of Paul Klee's *Angel of History* who "sees one single catastrophe, which keeps piling wreckage upon wreckage and hurls it at his feet" (*SW 4*, 392).[21] In Benjamin's view, nothing meaningful can arise from the dynamic of nature alone, and what is genuinely significant cannot be thought to arise from within it.[22] Benjamin's concept of "mere life" assumes the same role as the natural. In his essay "Critique of Violence," Benjamin vigorously opposes the idea that the sheer biological fact that one is alive could be considered as constitutive of anything truly meaningful. In words that have now become very famous, Benjamin claims that "man cannot, at any price, be said to coincide with the mere life in him, any more than it can be said to coincide with any other of his conditions and qualities, including even the uniqueness of his bodily person" (*SW 1*, 251). In Benjamin's view, therefore, it is vital to counter the tendency to sanctify life *as such*. "The dogma of the sacredness of life . . . is indeed probably . . . relatively recent" and signals but "the last mistaken attempt of the weakened Western tradition to seek the saint it has lost in cosmological impenetrability" (*SW 1*, 251). The reduction of human beings to instantiations of mere life is "pernicious" because it comes together with forms of violence that Benjamin calls "mythic" and associates with the universalizing politics of the state and law (*SW 1*, 252).

Benjamin, however, presupposes the possibility that what is natural or "merely alive" can somehow be *modified* into something that can rightfully be considered meaningful. The "transfiguration" of nature that he deems lacking in the baroque *Trauerspiel*, for instance, denotes a disruption of nature that would thus allow it to acquire meaning. It is this moment of transformation of mere life into what is meaningful to the highest degree that Benjamin, in some of the most crucial places of his work, calls "messianic." In his "Theological-Political Fragment," for instance, Benjamin states that the messianic creation of meaning cannot be separated from "the striv[ing] for . . . the passing away of those stages of man that are nature." This endeavor on the part of man is considered "the task of world-politics" and, because it entails both a moment of annihilation and the concomitant creation of truly novel values, is termed, in trusted Nietzschean fashion, "nihilism" (*SW 3*, 306). Similarly, in "Critique of Violence," Benjamin does not only claim that what is alive "could not be [sacred] by virtue only of being alive, of being in life," but adds the important possibility of "an irreducible total condition of man" (*SW 1*, 251) that can legitimately be called sacred. For Benjamin, that is, sacredness denotes not a natural quality that is always already there but a historical condition that is to be *brought about*. Sacredness indicates the coming into existence of a genuinely novel way of being rather than a quality that is simply deduced from any supposedly inborn condition.[23] In line with the views set forward in the "Theological-Political Fragment," Benjamin connects the task of bringing about such a truly new age with a "revolutionary violence" that shatters all forms of violence that reduce man to his biological existence (*SW 1*, 252).

On first view, Benjamin's use of the concepts of nature and "mere life" brings to the fore a possible parallel with Simmel's work. Both Simmel and Benjamin see an opposition between a natural dynamic of mere self-regeneration on the one hand and the creation of meaning on the other. In Benjamin's view as well, the rhythm of nature's progression can at most be *made* meaningful and this by virtue of something that remains "other" to this dynamic. Both Simmel and Benjamin, therefore, understand the creation of meaning as a transformation of life into a "more-than-life" that cannot be fully absorbed by life itself. However, it is important to emphasize at the outset a fundamental difference between Simmel and Benjamin's views on life. While Simmel understands life as a principle of infinite variation and innovation, Benjamin's views on "eternal transience" and a "total passing away" confront us with the very *antithesis* of variation and innovation. Life, in Benjamin's view, is primarily marked, not by change and renewal, but by empty repetition and endless recurrence. In short, while Simmel replenishes life with the capacity to ceaselessly rejuvenate itself, Benjamin empties life of precisely this capacity for self-innovation.[24]

This opposition between Simmel and Benjamin's views of life results from conflicting ideas on the connection between life, death, and meaning. While Simmel connects the creation of meaning to the inseparability of life and death (death is the "form-giving . . . shaper of life"), Benjamin will connect meaning to the possibility, however implausible it may seem, that life and death can nevertheless be *disentangled*. In the earlier mentioned "Theological-Political Fragment," for instance, the messianic creation of meaning is, as we have just mentioned, described as "the striv[ing] for . . . the passing away of those stages of man that are nature" but not without first describing "nature" itself, again, as "messianic by virtue of its eternal and total passing away" (*SW 3*, 306). When there is a chance that the condition of passing away can itself, however briefly, pass away, this means that, in the eyes of Benjamin, death and impermanence are ultimately not to be considered as irrevocable. Messianic redemption, rather, indicates an operative power that is no longer inhabited by death or, as we will see later on, an *interruptive moment* that has separated from an otherwise all-determining dynamic of evanescence. From a very early stage in his writing on, Benjamin reflects on the possibility of an "interval" in the flow of time and an accompanying "birth of immortal time" (*der Geburt der unsterblichen Zeit*) in which a "present that has been eternally will become again" (*die ewig gewesene Gegenwart wird wieder werden*) (*SW 1*, 12, 8; *GS II*, 98, 93, translation modified). Benjamin associates this redemptive experience that transience might itself be something transient with a feeling for "immortality" (*Unsterblichkeit*), a "worldly restitution," and "happiness" (*Glück*) (*SW 3*, 306; *GS II*, 204). Benjamin thus rejects Simmel's suggestion that meaning can be drawn from the experience of death and shifts the ultimate challenge of philosophy to an attempt to think *against* death rather than *with* it. In the final chapter of the *Trauerspiel* book, for instance, Benjamin describes an "about-turn" that exposes the transience of nature as a condition that can be overcome, thus resulting in the expression of the possibility that "transitoriness is . . . displayed as . . . the allegory of resurrection" (*O*, 232). Similarly, in his essay on Proust, Benjamin is mostly fascinated with a "rejuvenating force [*verjüngende Kraft*] which is a match for the inexorable process of aging" and "consume[s] in a flash . . . things that normally just fade and slumber" (*SW 2*, 244: *GS II*, 320). In the final chapter of this book, moreover, I will argue that Benjamin's rejection of the idea that death is an immanent presence within life underlies his critical stance vis-à-vis the tragic hero and the act of sacrifice. In Benjamin's view, the tragic hero meets death as a "power that is familiar, personal, and inherent in him. His life, indeed, unfolds from death, which is not its end but its form" (*O*, 114). For this reason, however, the actions of the tragic hero remain cut off from the potential for change and intervention that, in Benjamin's view, characterize genuine fulfillment and morality.

Because Simmel considers death to be an immanent presence that opens up life toward meaning, he emphasizes that the creation of meaning (the coming into existence of forms) provides proof for life's "self-transcendence" and that "insofar as life's essence goes, transcendence is immanent to it" (*VoL*, 9). Meaning thus signals in Simmel's view the presence of a "more-than-life," but life's "constant abandonment of itself is precisely the mode of its unity, of its remaining in itself" (*VoL*, 11). For this reason, Simmel maintains that the significance of the constructs, images, and forms of culture is attested to by the manner in which their initial *autonomy* from life is overcome by a secondary *reconnection* with it.[25] According to Simmel, cultural change is an enriching event when the forms of culture, marked by their seeming independence, let go of this primary independence and relate back to their initial context of origination to innovate it from within. "Only when that axial rotation [*Achsendrehung*] of life occurs around [the great spiritual categories of meaning] do they become truly productive; their objectively true forms are now the dominant ones, they absorb the stuff of life and it must yield to them" (*VoL*, 25–26). The creation of meaning is for this reason always a two-sided process: when life gives shape to a "more-than-life" with a meaning of its own, it is the very autonomy of the latter which allows for a genuine renewal of the former. For Simmel, in other words, the "absoluteness of the otherness" and the "no longer vital meaning" that is present in the forms of culture should not be considered their most determinate feature. Unless they belong to a culture in crisis (like modern society in his view), the forms and constructs of culture do not retreat in their autonomous sphere from life:

from this independence, rather, they derive the power to release the meaning they contain into the stream of life.[26] In Benjamin's view, to the contrary, the creation of meaning is *not* a process internal to life. Benjamin's reflections on a messianic separation of life and death result in the idea that the creation of meaning cannot be considered an immanent feature of life. His messianic framework is built on an assumption that cannot be comprehended from within Simmel's philosophy: it presupposes the idea that the "transcendence" that shapes meaning cannot be deemed immanent to life itself.[27] What is truly meaningful, rather, is believed to be charged with an absoluteness and autonomy that cannot be recovered by an overarching continuity of life. For this reason, in crucial places of Benjamin's work, the categories of meaning and expression move into the categories of *justice*, *truth*, and the *expressionless*. These three concepts assume an irreducibility vis-à-vis life that cannot in any way be overcome. Unlike Simmel, Benjamin maintains that, rather than being overturned by a process of overall recovery, the very interruption of life's progression is to be *maintained* and *prolonged* if it is to become the site of an expression of something genuinely truthful. In describing the "mythic" violence that is endorsed by law and driven by the state, for instance, Benjamin returns to both the theme of eternal transience and the possibility that it can ultimately be disrupted by an external power. In "Critique of Violence," he maintains that the "eternal forms" of state-driven and legally endorsed violence can nevertheless be overthrown by genuine justice because they are "open" (*SW 1*, 252). Elsewhere, Benjamin emphasizes that "authentic political experience is absolutely free of . . . the semblance of eternal sameness, and even of repetition, in history" (*AP*, 471). His political views argue in favor of an active affirmation of the incompleteness of all worldly phenomena and for the existence of a type of violence that remains "pure" or "unalloyed."[28] For this reason, Benjamin will not at all associate the capacity of life to restore its own continuity with the presentation of meaning. In his work, the moment of life's self-recovery indicates the very *antithesis* of the presentation of meaning, namely, semblance (*Schein*). Forms that, in Simmel's words "absorb the stuff of life" are in Benjamin's view what "enchants chaos momentarily into world." Simmel considers such forms to be the vehicles of meaning while Benjamin maintains that they establish "mere beauty, mere harmony." For Benjamin, the becoming-visible of truth takes place only on the condition that a "life undulating . . . appear[s] petrified and as if spellbound in a single moment" (*SW 1*, 340). This moment of rejuvenation, paradoxically, cannot be separated from a "mortification" of life (*O*, 182) and an "expressionless" (*Ausdruckslose*) that "arrests . . . semblance, spellbinds the movement, and interrupts the harmony" (*SW 1*, 340).[29]

Simmel connects his insights on life's dynamic of change and renewal with the idea that time subsists, writing that "a time that merely flows away, that is, as it were, devoid of memory . . . is no time [*Zeit*] at all, but rather an undimensional now [*Jetzt*]. . . . Absolute becoming is precisely as unhistorical as absolute non-becoming."[30] As will become central to the analysis of Simmel's views on Rembrandt in the second chapter, Simmel presupposes that life is a "steady stream" that cannot be "further deduced." This view entails that the past survives in its entirety and accumulates with each instant that is added to it (*R*, 6). Because the past is "contained" (*gesammelt*) within each moment, it constitutes the horizon from which every present instant is experienced (*R*, 7). "Life," writes Simmel, "*is* immediately nothing other than the past becoming present" (*R*, 34; see also *VoL*, 6–9). In Simmel's (Bergsonian) view, the survival of the past becomes the very condition of possibility for change and rejuvenation in the present: it is only because the past lives on within the present that the present can be experienced as *different* from the past. On account of his views on the "eternal transience" that dominates nature and life, Benjamin, however, does not emphasize their continuity but the need for a moment of *dis*continuity, herewith bringing into the picture the key concept of "now-time" (*Jetzt-Zeit*). In the fourth chapter, I will zoom in on the importance of such experiences of momentary discontinuity to Benjamin's philosophy at large. His views on the "dialectical image" and "messianic power" will help us understand how and why the "now" is in his mind not at all to be confused with the "undimensional" or "unhistorical" element that is mentioned by Simmel. "Now-time," to the contrary, indicates in Benjamin's philosophy an *interruptive* power that actively *brings about* change and innovation. For Benjamin, as well, this issue of genuine rejuvenation and renewal through the operative qualities of the "now" opens toward views on duration. The "rejuvenating force" of the now indicates the dislocation of transience and runs counter to time's "total passing away." Its interruptive powers, therefore, save the past from disappearing and allow it to become "legible" or, in Benjamin's messianic jargon, "rescued" (*AP*, 463–73). However, it is important to note that, in Benjamin's view, neither this possibility of genuine change nor the subsistence of the past can simply be *assumed*. For Benjamin, the survival of the past in the present is not, as Simmel puts it, "a basic given that cannot be constructed" (*R*, 6). It is, rather, something that one does indeed need to *create*.[31] The duration of the past into the present, therefore, does not signal the essential structure of time but the very *suspension* of temporal progression: "Only a redeemed mankind is granted the fullness of its past" (*SW* 4, 390). In this manner, Benjamin turns Simmel's framework fully on its head. In Benjamin's view, it is not the supposed survival of the past in its entirety that assists in making each given present a site for meaningful renewal, but it is, vice versa, the construction of a true present (the messianic "now-time") that is believed to bring about the duration of the past and thereby save it from vanishing into nothingness. "A redeemed mankind has its past become citable in all its moments" (*SW* 4, 390).[32] Benjamin is fascinated by the existence of a "messianic" power in which a *true* kind of repetition (that is, not a mere, empty repetition of the same) is made inseparable from a *genuine* renewal: "the 'experimentum crucis' of [the] philosophy of history," he writes, is "the question in what sense repetition can become manifest in history—itself an unrepeatable course" (*GS I*, 935). What escapes life's otherwise all-encompassing force of annihilation is thereby granted both an unsuspected duration *and* a sudden rejuvenation.

Moreover, on account of Benjamin's idea that life is haunted by endless repetition rather than driven by infinite variation, he blurs a distinction that is fundamental to Simmel. Benjamin does not consider the distinction between nature and culture an essential one. In his view, both the realm of nature *and* the realm of history are marked by transience. In this manner, Benjamin's concept of "mere life" indicates *both* nature and culture since the latter is believed to testify to the very same incapacities. For him, the entire realm of history needs to be considered as not meaningful in its own right and as a context that can, at most, *become* meaningful. In a short essay that was published only after Benjamin's death, he opposes "fulfilled time" or "messianic time" to "historical time [which is] infinite in every direction and unfulfilled at every moment. . . . For empirical events time is nothing but a form [and] as a form it is unfulfilled" (*SW 1*, 55–56). In the "Theological-Political Fragment," Benjamin puts it as follows: "Nothing that is historical can relate itself, from its own ground, to anything messianic" and no one but the "Messiah . . . redeems, completes, creates [the] relation [between history and] the messianic" (*SW 3*, 305). Likewise, in "Critique of Violence," the concept of "mere life" refers to a *historical* category, that is, to a form of life that only *appears* as nature because it was naturalized by the "mythic" violence through which the state and the law constantly reinstall themselves. To indicate this parallelism between nature and history, Benjamin coins the term "natural history" (*Naturgeschichte*), drawing attention to the manner in which history, like nature, is hollowed out by endless recurrence. In the *Trauerspiel* book, for instance, Benjamin addresses the topic of the "physiognomy of the nature-history" as the "form of the ruin" and, thus, as an indication that nature's cycle of nonstop disappearance has taken over even those constructs that were brought about by man (*O*, 177–78). In the German baroque mourning play, the realm of history is presented as fully sharing in all the elements that Benjamin categorizes under the concept of "the creaturely": "The decisive factor . . . is not the antithesis between history and nature but the comprehensive secularization of the historical in the state of creation" (*O*, 92). In this manner, "history" itself assumes "the form . . . of irresistible decay" (*O*, 178).

The difference between Simmel and Benjamin's views of life casts light on the handful of references to Simmel's writings that can be found in Benjamin's own oeuvre. A third step in evaluating the relationship between their works therefore involves a close-up of some of these passages.

Surprisingly so, Benjamin's rejection of the opposition between nature and history is at play in the most *positive* reference to Simmel's work that can be found in the entirety of Benjamin writings. In a remark that is included in *The Arcades Project*, Benjamin highlights the relation between his own concept of "origin" (*Ursprung*) in the *Trauerspiel* book and *The Arcades Project* and Simmel's concept of "origin" in his book on Goethe. Calling his own concept of "origin" a "rigorous and decisive transformation of this basic Goethean concept from the domain of nature to that of history," Benjamin indicates both the affinities and the differences between his framework and Simmel's philosophy. For, whereas Simmel presupposes "the pagan context of nature," Benjamin names his own context as "the Jewish [one] of history" (*AP*, 462).

Simmel's elaboration of the concept of truth in his book on Goethe is an interesting example of his overall view of life that is developed in other texts. Goethe's theory of primal phenomena (*Urphänomenen*) presupposes the presence of an absolute idea within a natural element on account of which the natural element itself can take on a mediating role in bringing such an idea to expression. These primal phenomena are considered as dynamic entities in that they indicate the organic unfolding of the universal species within a particular natural phenomenon. It is hardly a coincidence that Simmel focuses on Goethe's theory of truth. In his view, Goethe understands "the unity of All" as "the dynamic unity of life, which flows through the diversity of the parts and holds them together in myriad sizes and types" (*GSG 15*, 56). Goethe's concept of truth fits Simmel's own scheme in that it describes how a natural element that is not in itself a vehicle of meaning, say an ordinary plant, *becomes* a vehicle of meaning on the condition that it is transferred to a context that is *not* natural. "From particular parts that are cut out of nature and spirit," summarizes Simmel, "one may not be able to deduce their harmony; but when one considers the totality of spiritual life . . . truth is reconnected with the complete process of this totality" (*GSG 15*, 40). Though an organic element might in fact be no more than a part of nature, it can nevertheless be brought to express its own essence and the totality to which it belongs. The condition for such a modification is that empirical research translates an element of nature into a language that was *constructed*, that is, the human language of concepts and forms. Along with Goethe, therefore, Simmel claims that "all understanding is indeed an act of construction" (*alles Verstehen ist ja ein Schaffen*) (*GSG 15*, 58).

Benjamin's work on the German baroque and Parisian modernity can indeed be considered as a translation of this same line of reasoning to *historical* and *cultural* phenomena. Both the *Trauerspiel* book and *The Arcades Project* are steeped in the perception that historical and cultural material inherited from respectively baroque Germany and modern Paris can be used as vehicles of meaning (in Benjamin's words, they can be "made legible"). Like Simmel, Benjamin claims that such a presentation of meaning requires a strategy of transformation and an act of construction. In Benjamin's view, the seventeenth-century mourning plays and the nineteenth-century phenomena that are being researched need to be *released* from the initial historical and cultural context in which they were conceived. It is for this reason that Benjamin highlights the necessity to fashion "constellations" (in the *Trauerspiel* book) and a "literary montage" (in *The Arcades Project*) that allow historical and cultural material to be reworked. From the first pages of the *Trauerspiel* book on, Benjamin emphasizes that "philosophical writing . . . must continually confront the question of presentation [*Darstellung*]" (*O*, 27; *GS I*, 207, translation modified) and that "that which is originary is never revealed in the naked and manifest existence of the factual" (*O*, 45, translation modified). Similarly, in *The Arcades Project*, Benjamin proclaims the need for a genuine "*construction* of a historical state of affairs" and sharply differentiates it from a mere "*re*construction" that is "one-dimensional" in order to thus highlight the transformative capacities of historiography (*AP*, 470, emphasis added). Moreover, just like Simmel, Benjamin was very much influenced by Goethe's insights on the presence of archetypes and primal images within empirical phenomena. Making use of Leibniz's concept of the "monad," Benjamin claims that a total and essential image of the German baroque or nineteenth-century modernity can be glimpsed from within individual phenomena, say a baroque play or an architectural structure in Paris. In the *Trauerspiel* book, Benjamin writes that, as a monad, "the purpose of the presentation of the idea is nothing less than an abbreviated outline of [an] image of the world" (*O*, 48, translation modified). Likewise, in *The Arcades Project*, Benjamin claims that he seeks to "assemble large-scale constructions [*die großen Konstruktionen*] out of the smallest and most precisely cut components" (*AP*, 461). In both the epistemological introduction to the *Trauerspiel* book (the "Epistemo-Critical Prologue") and the convolute on epistemology in *The Arcades Project* ("Convolute N: Theory of Knowledge, Theory of Progress"), therefore, Benjamin carefully explicates his credo as a historian of culture and a philosopher of history: what was at some point a mere part of history and culture can, at a later moment, be modified into an instrument to understand the overarching totality to which it once belonged.[33] Benjamin's remark about Simmel and Goethe ends with a clear description of the philosophical ambition that runs through *The Arcades Project*: to present "economic facts" as "origins" and the arcades themselves as the "concrete historical forms" in which these "origins" can become visible (*AP*, 462). On a first (Marxist) level of analysis, in other words, the arcades are believed to present an objective and comprehensive take on the social-economic situation or material substructure in the nineteenth century.

However, a further exploration of Benjamin's concept of "origin" brings to light elements that cannot possibly be made to fit Simmel's framework. What is more, this opposition between Simmel and Benjamin's views of "origin" is determined by their conflicting views of life. While Simmel focuses on organisms that partake in the overall "dynamic unity of life," Benjamin focuses on historical and cultural periods that, however different they may be, embody the endless repetition of the same that he associates with a history-become-nature. In Benjamin's view, that is to say, both the baroque authors that figure in the *Trauerspiel* book and the conceptual personae that, in *The Arcades Project*, are positioned in the heart of the capital of the nineteenth century share a marked sensibility toward transience and impermanence. Benjamin carefully brings this shared feeling for an "eternal passing away" to expression in phenomena as diverse as allegory and melancholy or photography and boredom.[34] Benjamin's reference to the "Jewish" context of his concept of "origin," moreover, indicates that the reworking of historical artifacts into presentations of meaning entails an interruptive and messianic moment of genuine truth expression and "redemption." In both the *Trauerspiel* book and *The Arcades Project*, Benjamin emphasizes that the presentation of "origins" involves, not at all, as Simmel would claim, the recovery of a natural and dynamic totality, but a redemptive and interruptive power of fragmentation. In the *Trauerspiel* book Benjamin writes that "phenomena do not . . . enter into the realm of ideas whole, in their crude, empirical state . . . but only in their basic elements, redeemed." This redemptive work of art criticism entails that phenomena "are divested of their false unity so that, thus divided, they might partake of the genuine unity of truth" (*O*, 33). Similarly, in *The Arcades Project*, Benjamin claims that the "historical constructions" which bring out "the indestructibility of the highest life in all things" are inseparable from a moment of "destruction" (*AP*, 459, 461–70; *GS V*, 575–87, emphasis added). The emphasis on the importance of redemptive fragmentation and destruction for genuine art criticism and history-writing once again makes clear that, while Simmel focuses on expressive capacities that are believed to be immanent to life, Benjamin highlights that life can only yield a truth-experience to the extent that its objects and phenomena are exposed to an external and arresting power.[35] It is for this reason alone that, as we saw earlier, the transience of nature that is expressed in the mourning play can be modified into its very opposite, that is, an expression of the possibility of resurrection (see *O*, 232). Likewise, when history-writing manages to rework modern phenomena like arcades, boredom, *flânerie*, and prostitution into genuine presentations of truth, it does not merely allow a more comprehensive understanding of the social-economic situation of nineteenth-century Paris. In Benjamin's view, historiography becomes redemptive when it actively dislodges the transience and boredom that haunted the nineteenth-century mind. In this manner, scholarly work is believed to tap into the interruptive capacities of a genuine "now-time," actively *bringing about* a dimension of the past that cannot otherwise survive. For Benjamin, that is to say, the modern phenomena that are at issue in *The Arcades Project* do not just allow a glimpse of the modern feel for eternal recurrence, but they also entail the sudden actualization of something that is seemingly at odds with such an experience, that is, the survival of age-old wish-images. Throughout *The Arcades Project* Benjamin highlights that the act of reworking the nineteenth-century past into a presentation of truth gives shape to the unsuspected persistence of paradisiacal ideals of a reconciled mankind and a fulfilled nature. "Corresponding to the form of the new means of production," he writes, "are images in the collective consciousness in which the new is permeated with the old. These images are wish images; in them the collective seeks both to overcome and to transfigure the immaturity of the social product and the inadequacies in the social organization of production" (*AP*, 4). In Benjamin's view, the redemptive moment through which modern phenomena are made visible as a materialized "dream universe" saves them from being but a symptom of false consciousness or escapism. From his point of view, the fact that these ideals can be retrieved within the very heart of consumer capitalism grants them an immunity vis-à-vis the realm of history at large and an immortality that they would not otherwise come together with.

In December 1917, Benjamin writes to Gershom Scholem that he has read Simmel's essay "The Problem of Historical Time" and adds what is perhaps one of the most aggressive remarks he ever put to paper. Simmel's essay is "an extremely wretched concoction that goes through contortions of reasoning, incomprehensibly uttering the silliest things."[36] Simmel's view of history is built on the intimate relation between concrete experience on the one hand and historical events on the other in that both are marked by the infinite complexities and continuity of life. "The event as an object of experience," writes Simmel, "transpires in a continuous medium without interruptions at all, a medium which is welded onto time itself without a break."[37] Fostered from the mere stuff of life, however, historical events can only be made meaningful with the help of (cultural) concepts, ideas, and categories that cannot fully capture the continuity and complexity of the former.[38] In Simmel's view, therefore, historical knowledge cannot overcome a relative and approximate value that is essential to the very endeavor to recapture the past and has nothing to do with a lack of information. "The decisive point," writes Simmel, "is certainly not . . . [that] we . . . do not know 'enough' in order to achieve an exhaustive comprehension of the total stream of living reality. . . . Just the contrary. *In principle, historical knowledge simply does not have the form* which would make it possible to reproduce the continuity of experience."[39] Simmel therefore warns against zooming in on the details of a specific event. For such an approach only yields historical *contents* and results in "discontinuous phenomena" that are "analytically fragmented, and thereby de-animated."[40] Since the categories of thought and knowledge cannot ever be a true match for the complexities of historical events, it is vital to avoid the "threshold of analytical reduction" and to keep in mind that the "purpose of history is not knowledge of . . . details but . . . a more comprehensive and abstract structure . . . which is necessarily continuously *extended* throughout an expanse of time."[41] When thus undertaken in a sufficiently "comprehensive" manner, the forms, concepts, and constructs of history retain a sufficient degree of life that does not betray the "individuality" of the event that is being researched.[42] In such cases, the "transformation of life that we call history" shares in the very continuity that characterizes the historical event and thus makes palpable that "in the final analysis, history is also an expression and an act of life, precisely the same life to which it is originally *juxtaposed*."[43]

Benjamin's own views on history, which will be outlined most coherently more than twenty years later (1940) in "On the Concept of History," can be understood as an almost complete reversal of this line of reasoning. As indicated above, in Benjamin's view the realm of history denotes a sphere of mere life that is hollowed out by an endless repetition of the same. "All rulers are the heirs of prior conquerors. . . . Whoever has emerged victorious participates to this day in the triumphal procession in which current rulers step over those who are lying prostrate" (*SW* 4, 391). Benjamin associates this uninterrupted continuity of history with a downright absence of meaning and not with a dynamic of life from which meaning can arise. The experience that historical progression embodies one continuous unity brings him to a conclusion that is the opposite of Simmel's: in his view, this experience yields the insight that no historical truth can be believed to arise from the endeavor to "reproduce" the past. According to Benjamin, no attempt to "enter into" the past can be deemed worthwhile for the quest to make it meaningful. Psychological concepts like "empathy" and the wish to "relive an era" only result in a repetition and extension of its injustices (*SW* 4, 391). For this reason, Benjamin introduces the earlier mentioned concepts of "dialectical image," "messianic power," and "now-time" to denote an arresting power that stubbornly refuses to be absorbed by the continuity of history pure and proper.[44] In Benjamin's view, the procedure of materialist historiography is not "additive" but "constructive": when produced anew, in and as "an image," the past undergoes an essential *modification* with regard to the present it once was (*SW* 4, 396, 390). The "weak messianic power" that Benjamin deems capable of "interrupting" the course of history therefore always also entails the revelation of the latter's ultimate incapacity to interrupt *itself*. Moreover, unlike Simmel, Benjamin emphasizes that historiography requires a level of analysis that focuses on details and seemingly insignificant minutiae. As we will see in the fourth chapter, Benjamin maintains that the belief in the possibility of genuine historical change and intervention presupposes "the following truth: nothing that has ever happened should be regarded as lost to history." The historian is to "remain aware of [the] most inconspicuous of all transformations" (*SW* 4, 390). Benjamin's philosophy of history ultimately presupposes a messianic and utterly non-Simmelian framework in that it defends the viewpoint that historical knowledge does not just make the past *meaningful*. Rather, the messianic force of "arrest" and "standstill" is a power of *redemption* and, while bringing about an unexpected and infinitely brief instant of historical transformation, it turns a given moment into the site of the presentation of an *absolute truth* (see, e.g., *SW* 4, 390, 396).

Finally, the opposition between Simmel and Benjamin's views of life illuminates a remark about Simmel that Benjamin includes in his own essay on Goethe (1924). Benjamin criticizes Simmel's book on Goethe for clinging to the theorem that "beauty is truth become visible" and argues instead that "truth is not in itself visible and its becoming visible could rest only on traits not its own" (*SW 1*, 350–51). Because Simmel takes "more-than-life" to be a category of life, life is deemed capable of producing on its own the beautiful forms that are supposed to bring truth to expression. Based on such a view, the absolute and transcendent originate from nowhere else than from within life itself: while their becoming-visible does require a moment of life's self-alienation, this moment belongs to the very essence of life and shares its unity and continuity. Benjamin, on the contrary, understands the idea that the absolute and the transcendent are immanent to life as testifying to the power of "myth." For Benjamin, endowing life with the capacity to bring about meaning on its own results in the false belief that truth (and justice) are "fated."[45] These views rest on a belief in a "false, errant totality" since they project redemptive capacities onto the very principle that is in need of redemption (*SW 1*, 340). For Benjamin, "the natural condition of the living" is always already one contaminated by the Fall and "guilt," that is, by incompleteness and a removal from truth. Rather than understanding the "life in [man]" as an inherently productive dynamic, it denotes what remains at all times in need of "judgment" (*SW 1*, 204).

The five chapters that are brought together in this book revolve around a relatively simple but fundamental idea that is shared by Simmel and Benjamin: the artwork is a human construct that creates meaning by *re*-producing a part of the world. Wholly at odds with the view that artistic reproduction entails a mere mimesis or imitation of a part of the world, Simmel and Benjamin's views endow the artwork with the capacity to *produce* it *anew*.

In the first part of the book, I will develop the argument that Simmel's philosophy of art is rooted in the feeling that artworks are marked by a way of being that is wholly their own. Artistic expression, that is, results in Simmel's view in the creation of an object with a mode of existence that is essentially *different* from that of other objects in the world. In his essays on realism and naturalism in the arts and on the philosophy of art in general, Simmel opposes "the actual world" (*die Wirklichkeit*) on the one hand and the work of art on the other because the actual world is, unlike the artwork, not "a thing of the senses" but rather "something that we give *to* the senses" (*GSG 8*, 407, emphasis added). The world that surrounds us, that is to say, does not result from the activity of man and therefore retains an exteriority that cannot be appropriated. In Simmel's view, the experience that something physically exists comes together with a "specific tone [which] tells us: this is the actual world" (*GSG 8*, 405). This experience that something actually exists cannot be reproduced: the physical existence of a given thing can only be imitated but never truly replicated since it points toward "something metaphysical," "the ineffable mystery of being," "a value that exceeds the sum of the qualities [of things]" and "something abstract" (*GSG 8*, 407). Because artworks, to the contrary, are not just physical objects but primarily *constructs* or *artifacts*, they inevitably exist in a way that is essentially different from "ordinary" things in the world. In an essay on the picture frame, Simmel emphasizes that the work of art "encloses itself as a *world for itself* against all that exists external to it."[46] In Simmel's view, the artwork is a prime example of the human ability to create a "more-than-life" since it designates a formed reality of its own and not a mere part of the "actual" world (see, e.g., *R*, 14). Artworks, that is to say, are things-in-themselves that *re*work the material of the physical universe and thus change it in a meaningful way. Art is thereby confined to working with "the perceivable contents of things" or the "*qualities* of actual reality." For this reason, an artwork does not derive its significance from the physical reality to which it refers but, instead, manages to give shape to something genuinely new. "Art," writes Simmel, "[has] nothing to do with the actual world as such. . . . [The actual world] [is] foreign to art [since art] brings together novel constructs [*neuen Gebilden*] out of forms and colors alone" (*GSG 8*, 407). A painted portrait, for instance, as we will see in our analysis of Simmel's interpretation of Rembrandt, requires the "real creativity" to "create the appearance anew" and to thereby allow it to "grow once again on the soil and under the specific categories of artistry" (*R*, 29).

In some of his most notorious essays, such as the "Artwork" essay or the essays on Brecht, surrealism, and "The Author as Producer," Benjamin develops a critique of mimesis that seems at first sight to adopt some of these ideas. As is well known, Benjamin describes how the artistic use of the technological apparatus allows for a genuine *renewal* of the world in which we live. Film and photography, that is to say, "exploded" the surrounding world and they give shape to "*another* nature" (*SW 3*, 117, my emphasis). In the second part of the book I will argue that the challenge that underlies Benjamin's philosophy of art is an exploration of the capacity of an artwork to reopen the world toward new possibilities and unexpected dimensions of meaning. Herein deeply influenced by Brecht's concept of "functional transformation" (*Umfunktionierung*), Benjamin argues in favor of an intimate connection between aesthetic value on the one hand and the transformative qualities of constructs and images on the other. In his view, art should, rather than imitate the surrounding world, fashion it anew by "mak[ing] use of elements of reality in experimental rearrangements." In this manner, a given situation is "not brought home to the spectator but distanced from him" in such a manner that it can be truly understood and "discover[ed]" (*SW 2*, 778). Benjamin criticizes artworks that trigger the spectator's "mental absorption" or "concentration" because these indicate a passive stance and install an inability to truly gauge the potential for change. Benjamin's plea for a genuine *re*-production of the world by way of art underlies his influential program for a "politicizing [of] art" that, for its part, runs wholly counter to the dangerous "aestheticizing of politics" (*SW 3*, 119–20). Like Simmel, therefore, Benjamin differentiates between the "actual" world in which we live and the "reality" that is shaped by the artwork itself in order to discover, within art, a wholly novel construct. In his view as well, the artwork can establish a space of its own in which the world "has transcended itself" (*SW* 2, 217–18). Surrealism, for instance, is capable of reworking the most inconsequential materials, thereby transforming them into a work of art with a sharpness and urgency of its own. Likewise, as we will see in the fourth and fifth chapters, photography and film are capable of drastically innovating our experience of the world, "explod[ing] th[e] prison-world [of ordinary existence] with the dynamite of the split second" (*SW 3*, 117). Like Simmel, Benjamin emphasizes that the *re*-productive faculties of art involve a way of being that is not deducible from the "actual" world. The "image-space" (*Bildraum*) of the artwork, namely, denotes in his opinion a "universal and integral actuality" that differs essentially from the ordinary existence of an object (*SW* 2, 217).[47]

Nonetheless, a wide margin divides the first three chapters on Simmel from the last two chapters on Benjamin in this book. While, for Simmel, the artwork gains meaning to the extent that it shares in a *movement of continuity*, for Benjamin, the artistic creation of meaning is inseparable from a *moment of discontinuity*. To understand the nature of this fault line that runs throughout the entire book, it is important to keep in mind the oppositions between Simmel's *Lebensphilosophie* and Benjamin's messianism that are explicated above. From Simmel's point of view, a dynamic of renewal and rejuvenation is inscribed within the very heart of life itself and, for this reason, the constant generation of the new is considered to be an ontological given that the artwork should bring to expression. The very autonomy of artworks is for Simmel always but a precondition for their capacity to replenish our overall experience of life's infinity. Simmel's philosophy, it seems, cannot therefore come to terms with any form of genuine discontinuity: the forms and contents of culture that Simmel, to be sure, *describes* as discontinuous can only be considered vehicles of meaning when they preserve an internal relationship with the underlying continuity of life itself. Simmel's intuition that even the "more-than-life" of formed constructs is ultimately determined by life's immanent dynamic of innovation and variation underlies his philosophy of art as well. In his view, aesthetic value cannot be disentangled from what can only be called a restoration of our faith in life's supposed ability to continuously renew itself. In his text on *l'art pour l'art*, for instance, Simmel argues against the artistic ambition to disconnect art wholly from life. Even art produced for its own sake serves as a revelation of "*la vie pour l'art* and *l'art pour la vie*." Art, therefore, cannot shake off a most "paradoxical and antithetical" status in that it is "wholly enclosed in itself and released from life" while it remains nevertheless "embedded in the full stream of life, which it—on the side of the artist—introduces into itself and—on the side of the spectator—releases from itself" (*GSG 13*, 13).

The first three chapters of the book start from this intimate connection between an artwork and the dynamic infinity of life and render a close reading of Simmel's three most important essays on art, that is, of his texts on Michelangelo, Rembrandt, and Rodin. The main aim of each of these chapters is to analyze Simmel's views on these artists in detail and to situate the main argument within the overall framework of his philosophy. A second aim is to go beyond the immediate context of Simmel's essays and turn to some of the main works of the artists that he deals with. One of the difficulties of Simmel's ideas on art (apart from their overall philosophical complexity) is that he very often fails to zoom in on specific works and details. This renders the gist of his reasoning abstract and, at times, quite hard to understand. For this reason, each chapter seeks to make Simmel's most fundamental intuitions relevant for art criticism and, inserting specific works directly into the discussion, aims at a further elucidation of their artistic value. It is for this reason that each of these chapters concludes with a coda that uses Simmel's ideas to analyze one specific artwork or series of artworks.

In the work of *Michelangelo*, Simmel discovers figures that are seemingly disconnected from the continuous stream of life in that they seek to represent ideals with a *universal* validity. Simmel's essays on Michelangelo revolve around the duality between the "*supra*-actual" reality that is opened up by art as such (an artwork is no mere thing in the world) and the "*super*-individual" world of essences and types that Michelangelo's works refer to. Simmel maintains that Michelangelo's figures are marked by an intense yearning (*Sehnsucht*) to become one with ideals that cannot in fact be properly actualized. In Simmel's view, Michelangelo's figures are not fully individualized because they are "closed off" with regard to the infinity of life's becoming. Replacing this infinity by the eternity of unchanging ideals, they open up a gap between immanence and transcendence that cannot be overcome and they encounter the absolute as a force of Fate (*Schicksal*). The coda of this chapter focuses on Michelangelo's so-called slave series of sculptures.

The chapter on *Rembrandt* makes up the main part of the first half of the book. It brings together the most important issues of Simmel's philosophy of art and focuses on the most extensive and conceptually developed of his essays. Simmel's interpretation of the work of Rembrandt builds on the idea that the "form" or "construct" that is the painted portrait captures the *singular* existence of the model. In Simmel's view, the portrait can be understood as the genuine *re*-production of a "soulful life" since it is marked by a dynamic and irreplaceable unity of its own. Rembrandt is believed to grasp how a human being builds up an intimate self of his own by remaining "open" to the vicissitudes and changes in life. In this manner, Rembrandt introduces the realm of history pure and proper, understood as a series of fates, into the context of art. Because Rembrandt thus bridges the distance between immanence and transcendence, Simmel argues that his artworks express a religious quality that is immanent to life itself. The coda of this chapter focuses on Rembrandt's *Self-Portrait with Two Circles*.

Simmel considered his friend *Auguste Rodin* to be the most important artist of his time and devoted numerous essays to his work. The third chapter starts from the idea that Rodin's work brings to light the *general* nature of life as such. Rodin is believed to recover the continuous flow of life itself since his works are marked by a sensibility for surfaces, fragments, and gestures. For this reason, Simmel maintains that Rodin's works express both the essence of modern existence, that is, an increased identification with anonymous forces, and a contingency that cannot be surpassed in any way. Still, Simmel endows Rodin's sculptures with redemptive qualities. In bringing to expression the infinite mobility of life, Rodin is believed to recapture an openness within the realm of the historical that precludes the possibility of conclusive meaning. The coda of this chapter focuses on Rodin's *The Burghers of Calais*.

The first part of the book is constructed around a thread in Simmel's work that starts with the level of the universal (Michelangelo), passes through the level of the singular (Rembrandt), and concludes with the level of the general (Rodin). This descent into the general puts the finger on a fundamental tension in Simmel's work and prepares the ground for our discussion of Benjamin. While Simmel clings to the Bergsonian view that individual identity is inseparable from a dynamic unity or "continuous becoming" that builds up an intimate self, his fascination with modern society confronts him with contemporary forms of social and psychological fragmentation. In the introduction to the second part of the book, we will look at the locus classicus of Benjamin's encounter with Simmel: his reference to Simmel's text on the metropolis in the essays on Baudelaire and Paris. The outcome of this analysis is that, while Simmel never manages to fully embrace the modern situation of fragmentation, Benjamin's writings include important references to sudden and interruptive experiences of meaningfulness and to artistic personae that are not properly individualized but, for this very reason, are charged with an unsuspected significance.

The second part of the book will therefore revolve around Benjamin's view that innovation and renewal might not in fact refer to a metaphysical given but to a momentary intervention that needs to be brought about. From Benjamin's point of view, one could argue that genuine rejuvenation resists being ontologized: if every ordinary instant would, as Simmel suggests, embody the possibility of something new to arise, the truly new would cease to exist and become a mere "phantasmagoria of what is 'always the same'" (*AP*, 22).[48] As we have seen, for Benjamin life is first and foremost marked by transience and an unending repetition of the same, and life itself does *not* bring about the new. The second part of the book retraces Benjamin's description of art's capacity to *interrupt* this disenchanted pattern of eternal recurrence in life and to thereby even potentially prepare a moment of truth presentation. It is no exaggeration to state that these ideas on true innovation and change are at play in all of Benjamin's most important writings on art. From the *Trauerspiel* book on Benjamin argues for the possibility that "depersonalization" can be "set in an incomparably productive context" (*O*, 140)—a formula that he will reiterate in the "Artwork" essay in the statement that "the representation of human beings by means of an apparatus has made possible the highly productive use of the human being's self-alienation [*Selbstentfremdung*]" (*SW 3*, 113; *GS VII*, 369).[49] Benjamin therefore emphasizes that the experience of possible change always and necessarily comes together with a feeling for life's inability to change *itself*. In his essay on surrealism, for instance, Benjamin writes that "[André] Breton and Nadja convert everything that we have experienced on mournful railway journeys, on godforsaken Sunday afternoons in the proletarian neighborhoods of great cities, in the first glance through the rain-blurred window of a new apartment, into revolutionary experience, if not action" (*SW 2*, 210). Likewise, the capacity of photography and film to rejuvenate our experience of the outside world indicates for Benjamin a brief suspension of the otherwise endless repetition that inhabits life. In photographs Benjamin most often discovers both "infinite sadness" or scenes "without mood" *and* "the scene for a salutary estrangement between man and his surroundings" (*SW 2*, 515–19). In Benjamin's view, therefore, "interruption" is to be discovered as "an *organizing* function" and it does not at all open toward the discovery of a metaphysical principle of infinite change and renewal (*SW 2*, 778, emphasis added).

The fourth chapter of the book proffers a close reading of those passages in Benjamin's work where he describes moments of meaningful interruption with the term *unscheinbar*. Arguing that this concept cannot be reduced to its privative prefix "un-," the chapter explores how moments in time, objects, or images that are not meaningful in themselves can nevertheless trigger an experience that is to be called such. It analyzes Benjamin's ideas on friendliness, melancholy, recollection, *mémoire involontaire*, and photography with the purpose of understanding how a detail or fragment can strike us as significant, despite the fact that it cannot become visible as a unity or continuous totality in its own right. As indicative of a dislocation of endless recurrence, what is inconspicuous can bring about an experience of possibility and change that has redemptive qualities.

In the "Artwork" essay, Benjamin mentions the "historical significance" of Charlie Chaplin and adds to this the remark that it can only be understood against the earlier mentioned idea that the medium of film has "opened up new fields of action" (*SW 3*, 118). The fifth chapter articulates a close reading of Benjamin's views on Chaplin and makes up the main part of the second half of the book. It elaborates on the connection between meaning and contingency in Benjamin's writings and elucidates the close relation between these issues and the genre of comedy. This chapter differentiates between the tragic hero's absorption of absolute ideals on the one hand and a "character's" ability to affirm the seeming chaos of the surrounding world on the other. By focusing on the concept of "pure means," the difference between Benjamin and Bergson's views on politeness is analyzed in detail, as is the political relevance of Chaplin's work and Benjamin's own comparison between the Tramp and Adolf Hitler.

Part I

✦

Georg Simmel

Chapter 1

✦

Michelangelo

Life and the Fate of Mankind

On the morning of September 8, 1889, the readers of the *Vossische Zeitung* find that the Sunday edition of their newspaper includes a long piece on Michelangelo that one can only call remarkable. For, rather than focusing on either the sculptures or the frescoes that made the Renaissance artist so illustrious, the author of the article has decided to undertake a close reading of some of his poems. Barely mentioning masterpieces like Michelangelo's *Moses*, the tombs of the Medici, and the frescoes in the Sistine Chapel, the article is almost entirely dedicated to the verses that Michelangelo wrote in celebration of beauty, the divine, love, happiness, and, the combination of all of these virtues, his beloved Vittoria Colonna. Most remarkable of all, however, is that rather than highlight the humanism and artistic self-confidence that Michelangelo's art is usually associated with, the author instead underlines the "most overt pessimism" (*unverholenste Pessimismus*) and "lack of harmony" (*Mangel an Harmonie*) that gives sharpness to his poetic output (*GSG* 2, 41, 48). For this reason, Michelangelo is believed to hold a special place within the history of the Renaissance since, whereas Raphael, for instance, can rightfully be called "blind to ugliness" (*häßlichkeitsblind*), Michelangelo "experienced ugliness so sharply, since it rose up from the background of his ideal of beauty" (*GSG* 2, 42).[1] The main hypothesis that underlies the article "Michelangelo as a Poet" is therefore that Michelangelo's poetry is situated between two poles, idealization and melancholy, that cannot be separated from each other. "His entire experience of love, to the extent that he has expressed it in a poetic manner," claims the author, "rests on *one* idea: the opposition between his personality and that of his beloved" (*GSG* 2, 40).[2]

The article is signed "Georg Simmel," who was at that moment in time a 31-year-old unpaid lecturer in philosophy at the University of Berlin who was making a reputation for himself as a devoted teacher and all-round essayist. Michelangelo's life and art will remain of interest to Simmel until the moment of his death. Still, it will take more than twenty years for his ideas to crystallize in a more systematic text, the essay "Michelangelo: A

Chapter on the Metaphysics of Culture" (1910–11). In this text, Simmel does direct his attention to Michelangelo's sculptures and frescoes but maintains the earlier duality between idealization and melancholy. Trying to identify why the Italian artist's work is so characteristic of the Renaissance, he draws attention to a "yearning" (*Sehnsucht*) that has as its object something "absolute, infinite, unreachable" (*GSG 12*, 126). Crucial in this regard will be the idea that Michelangelo's works are isolated from any genuine sense of life because they are too much wedded to a longing for stable and eternal forms. In Michelangelo's work, the feeling for what is universal is so overpowering that it cannot come to terms with the contingencies and singularities of this world. As a consequence, the duality of idealization and melancholy is to be complemented with the concepts of Fate and tragedy if one is to understand why Michelangelo's figures express a profound lack of freedom. Since they acquire their particular significance from a reference to the eternity and immutability of a type, Simmel maintains that Michelangelo's works cannot express the infinite potential for change that marks life as such.

Titanism and Loneliness

Simmel's 1910–11 essay on Michelangelo builds on the idea that his figures are marked by a complete reconciliation between body and soul.[3] Despite the expression of the dual nature of every human being, body and soul are "completely interwoven" (*absolut durchdrungen*) (*GSG 12*, 114) and thus attain an "existential completion" (*existenziale Vollendung*) (*GSG 12*, 125) or a "formal perfection" (*formale Vollkommenheit*) (*GSG 12*, 117). This internal completeness is the result of a specific kind of "closure" (*Geschlossenheit*) that pertains to all of Michelangelo's figures. According to Simmel, these figures have entirely retreated from the external world and they seem oblivious to what goes on around them.[4] It is indeed already clear from looking at the most famous of Michelangelo's artworks that what caught his eye was not the flux and change of the outside world but the very emergence from this seeming chaos and becoming in "a higher life" (*ein höheres Leben*) (*GSG 12*, 125). The Virgin Mary's right hand in the Vatican *Pietà* (1498–99), for instance, or God's left arm in *The Creation of Adam* (1511) mark places where an external turmoil is held at bay and fully retreats in favor of an internal equilibrium and order that cannot seemingly be interrupted.[5] Simmel describes it as follows: "What seeks to liberate itself and what hinders this liberation, completely falls together in one point, a point where these forces are not differentiated [*den Indifferenzpunkt der Kräfte*], where the appearance often is held spellbound, suspended in a great moment where the decisive powers of life sublate each other [*sich . . . gegenseitig aufheben*]" (*GSG 12*, 123). For this reason, Michelangelo's figures are to be termed *substantial* unities. Their individuation is vouchsafed by the manner in which they lay bare an unchanging quality that underlies their identity and remains identically present within them throughout their lives. As such, the multiplicity of the events, feelings, experiences, moments, and encounters that mark an ordinary existence have, in Michelangelo's figures, wholly retreated in favor of the clear visibility of a continuity and unified life that entirely rests within the human being and remains fully untouched by the contingencies from without. The human being in Michelangelo's art is a substance on its own and is indivisible in itself because what happens *to* it leaves behind no trace whatsoever *within* it: it is "unmoved by anything human-fragmentary" and its life is always an "entirety" that originates in "a unifying center" (*GSG 12*, 117).[6] Such a human being is lacking in nothing and is moved only by what is fully internalized, which gives its "gestures . . . a clear logical consequence" and its life the "determination of *one* internal lawfulness" (*GSG 12*, 116–17).[7]

Michelangelo's figures have no small price to pay for such blatant "titanism" since they are, according to Simmel, marked by a profound loneliness (*Einsamkeit*) (*GSG 12*, 118). Because Michelangelo's figures have fully withdrawn from the surrounding world, their titanism exposes an inability to relate to anything that is external and a sense of complete self-isolation. Their "meaning" (*Bedeutung*) is "superpersonal" (*überpersönlich*) (*GSG 12*, 132) and "super-empirical" (*überempirisch*) (*GSG 12*, 126) because they have fully dispensed with the many fates and vicissitudes that make up an ordinary existence.[8] Because these figures are moved by an absoluteness that is fully internalized, they have lost the capacity to respond to and connect with what goes on around them: because theirs is an existence of mere acting, they lack the ability to react and relate. One important symptom of this loneliness is the fact that they are both stoic, that is, *un*affected by anything from without, and unfeeling, that is, affection*less*. To such personalities "a wholly subjective reflex does not apply," and neither do "changing circumstances of pleasure and pain" (*GSG 12*, 132). On account of their titanism, Michelangelo's figures have thus taken on a superpersonal guise that obfuscates any reference to the desires and feelings that make up the psychological life of a normal individual. Michelangelo's figures, that is to say, are, in opposition to Greek sculpture, fully individuated because they do clearly exhibit the dual nature that all human beings have in common, but they are not individual*ized*. Neither their bodies nor their souls mark a relation to the outside world since they have seemingly rid themselves of the "stuff" that makes up any existence that can be termed truly singular. As we will see in the second chapter, Simmel maintains that the individuated but non-individualized life in Michelangelo's figures sets them apart most clearly from the human beings that are depicted in Rembrandt's art.

On account of this loneliness, Simmel maintains that Michelangelo's works do not just *depict* fully autonomous and isolated human beings but that they *are*, themselves, autonomous and cut off from the world around them. The loneliness or "closure" of Michelangelo's figures is not merely a *psychological* quality expressed through the human beings that are depicted, but is also an *artistic* quality pure and proper that pertains to the artworks themselves, regardless of what they represent. There is no "contradiction" between the "loneliness of the sculpture" and the "loneliness of the essence that is presented" by it, even though both are "something entirely different" (*GSG 12*, 119).[9] Simmel emphasizes that the entirety of Michelangelo's work, even his painted images, shares in a distinctively "*plastic* essence" which, "as such [is marked by] loneliness, much more than painting" and is even "seamlessly closed off from the world around them" (*GSG 12*, 118–19).[10] It is first and foremost this "closure" which appears to put them at an unbridgeable distance from the realm in which we live our own lives. For, if Michelangelo's figures do not seem to *inhabit* a world this is because they have, themselves, *become* one. Simmel writes: "The borders of the world in which the sculpted figure lives, its ideal space, are nowhere further and nothing other than the very borders of its body, beyond them there is no longer a world to which they can relate" (*GSG 12*, 118).[11] In this manner, the "super-empirical" nature of Michelangelo's figures does not run counter to their presence as physical bodies in space since it is this very physicality that gives them an independence from the world around them ("the borders of . . . [their] ideal space are . . . the very borders of [their] [physical] body"). The fact that they remain unmoved by what goes on around them gives them both a distinct presentness ("they *are* what they *present*") *and* a profound inaccessibility ("The human being of the sculpture and its viewer . . . cannot be surrounded by the same air," *GSG 2*, 118–19).[12]

Universals, Types, and Forms

In Simmel's view, the "closure" that marks Michelangelo's figures indicates that "the religious feeling has turned itself within the earthly" (*GSG 12*, 126).[13] The "yearning" that Simmel deems most characteristic of Michelangelo's figures (in both his sculptures and his frescoes), as a consequence, is not a yearning for a first, immediate, glimpse of the transcendent but a longing for a second, mediated, experience of the immanent. Such a *Sehnsucht* "does not, in fact . . . aspire to anything transcendent." Its object is "an earthly possibility" (*ein irdisch Mögliches*), it indicates a "redemption that does not originate from a God," and it entails a "Destiny that arises from the forces of life" (*GSG 12*, 126).[14] Simmel argues that, while the Renaissance man has seemingly dispensed with religion altogether, his soul is in truth "tuned to the infinite, the absolute" (*dem Unendlichen, Absoluten zugewandten*) (*GSG 12*, 127) in the sense that he longs for an experience in which the very bodies that are at hand radiate with a sense of absoluteness. Contrary to the dualistic, religious *Sehnsucht* of the Middle Ages, which immediately connects the possibility of transformation to an external power that annihilates the body's natural dimension (mortification), Michelangelo's *Sehnsucht* testifies to the experience that nature *itself* has absorbed a kernel of absolute truth. For this reason, it indicates not so much a *gap* between *diesseits* (here and now) and *jenseits* (beyond) as a desire to *reconcile* immanence and transcendence. "It was determined by Fate that his soul would mobilize the entire richness of infinity for the entire richness of what is finite" (*GSG 12*, 129).[15] Whereas the religious *Sehnsucht* seeks infinity by closing off the finite (it is the "closure of a finite path" [*Abschluß eines endlichen Weges*] [*GSG 12*, 126]), Michelangelo is believed to turn to the finite in order to identify an infinite dimension within it. Similarly, while the religious *Sehnsucht* of the Middle Ages disrupts the relation with nature altogether, Michelangelo's *Sehnsucht* aims for a sustained engagement *with* nature that encounters it as *more* than mere nature. "It is," writes Simmel, "the finite itself which prescribes [Michelangelo's longing] its direction" (*GSG 12*, 127).

According to Simmel, the retreat into an autonomous world that marks Michelangelo's figures goes hand in hand with the ambition to universalize the human body: "In Michelangelo's figures," writes Simmel, "a highly personal existence that is undergoing its proper sense of misfortune [appears] . . . expanded toward a most universal Fate that is interwoven with mankind at large" (*GSG 12*, 115).[16] The universalization of the individual is a theme that returns in the most diverse places and contexts in Simmel's work. In his writings, the "conversions of the individual into the universal" can indicate, for instance, not only a necessity that accompanies the "praxis of life" (*VoL*, 49) but also the way people interact in big cities (*SoC*, 184), the quintessence of the money economy, and even the nature of the female sex since, according to Simmel, "the species and the personal elements coincide more readily" in women than in men (*PhoM*, 380).[17] The same concept of universalization underlies Simmel's view of Renaissance art and Michelangelo's works specifically. There it is connected with the opposition between the dynamic of a truly individualized life on the one hand and the universality of types and forms on the other. Renaissance art presupposes "the character of the type" (*R*, 67) and a "self-sufficient, self-statutory, *external form* of life" (*R*, 73; *GSG 15*, 404, translation modified).[18] Such types and forms are to be considered as "super-individual" (*überindividuell*) (*GSG 15*, 404) in that they serve as a bridge between the particular and the universal.[19] In Renaissance art, that is, the human figure is individuated by way of a form that can be *shared*. Simmel therefore stresses that the "substance" of the human being that is depicted in Renaissance art is dealt with from the perspective of "commonalities of form" (*Formgemeinsamkeiten*) (*GSG 15*, 422) or "a *universal* formation" (*eine allgemeine Formgebung*) (*GSG 15*, 396). In this sense, Michelangelo's figures display a grand attempt to derive the very particularity of a human being directly from its universality. There, "an individualistic accentuation of the appearance was substituted . . . for a classical, super-individual stylization that seeks to approach the typical" (*GSG 12*, 115).[20] The conversion of the individual into a super-individual type requires the visibility of elements that are known to be present in other individuals as well. In Simmel's view, the principle of individuation that underlies Renaissance art cannot be separated from a "metaphysical-monist root" in that "[the fact that] a human being is an individual . . . can be assembled from the sum of his perceivable qualities" (*GSG 15*, 422, 395).[21] In his oeuvre at large, Simmel describes these qualities with the German word *Einzelnen* (particularities) and opposes them to what renders the existence of an individual truly unique (the singular or *der Einzige*). In the essay "Death and Immortality," for instance, Simmel states that "the particular identifiable qualitative elements" of someone's personality (*die einzelnen, inhaltlich benennbaren Elemente*), such as "intelligence or stupidity, fascination or dullness, goodness or evil, religious or worldly tendency" have "a *universal* nature" (*allgemeine Natur*) since they are "realized as relatively similar, yet distributed throughout mankind in infinitely manifold combinations" (*VoL*, 94; *GSG 16*, 341). These particularities are contrasted with the "point of uniqueness of the individual" (*Einzigkeitspunkt des Individuums*) that, as we will see in the next chapter, cannot be shared by others even though it is marked by a generality of its own.[22] In Simmel's view, therefore, Michelangelo's figures are fully individuated but not at all individualized; they can be recognized as human beings of a certain type but not as persons with an existence that is truly their own, and their being is a particular one (*einzelne*) but not a singular one (*einzige*). They are, first and foremost, *exemplary* since they serve as a "symbol of mankind" (*Menschheitssymbol*) (*GSG 15*, 442) and relate to their form like "particularities under the authority of . . . a universal" (*GSG 15*, 396).

Fate and Tragedy

For the above reasons, Simmel associates Michelangelo's work with an "abstraction" that does not, however, denote a *lack* but an *excess* of determination. Because Michelangelo's figures derive their very individuation from qualities that can be shared, the life within them is a deeply ambiguous or equivocal one, unable to shake off an "ultimate strangeness" (*letzte Fremdheit*) (*R*, 103; *GSG 15*, 442). In Simmel's view, Michelangelo's figures are always marked by *both* an accentuation of the "unifying center" of a human being (*seinem einheitlichen Zentrum*) (*GSG 12*, 117) *and* an immediate reference to something that leads "beyond individuality" (*R*, 67). Simmel maintains that Renaissance artists portray the human being as having found "its eternal form" (*seine Ewigkeitsform*) (*R*, 91; *GSG 15*, 427) and as drawing meaning only from what is immutable and transfixed within it. Such an existence has, so to speak, absorbed its ideal way of being within itself. On account of the universalization that characterizes Michelangelo's art, his figures cannot be disentangled from a fundamental "timelessness" (*Zeitlosigkeit*) (*GSG 15*, 448). When a human being is portrayed in this manner, however, it is wholly abstracted from any dynamic of change and it remains cut off from any potential for transformation. "The form," emphasizes Simmel "cannot change itself" (*R*, 53). It "is delivered to a specific being-such and it is complete" (*R*, 53; *GSG 15*, 380, translation modified).[23] In Simmel's account, the Renaissance artist depicts the life of human beings as utterly alien to the continuous movement of renewal and rejuvenation that, in his view, characterizes life as such: "On account of their different relation with time and with power, form and life are wholly different" (*GSG 15*, 380).[24] For this reason, the life of human beings is expressed not only as finite but, what is most important, as fully *defined* from within and as having always already found its *definitive* form. Michelangelo's figures do not embody "a life process in temporal development, but a being in a result-like quality—a timeless definitive entity" (*R*, 54; *GSG 15*, 381).[25] According to Simmel, in the Renaissance, human existence appears as the result of a lawfulness and a logic of necessity through which it has forfeited all sense of contingency, thus playing itself out as something that could in no way have been different from what it currently is.

From this perspective it makes sense that Simmel emphasizes, in different places of his text, that the life of Michelangelo's figures is a priori determined by "a metaphysical Destiny" (*ein metaphysisches Schicksal*), however strange this may sound in a discussion of one of the most eloquent illustrations of Renaissance humanism (*GSG 12*, 132). Simmel stresses that "only the individual dies, the type does not" (*R*, 77). For this reason, in Michelangelo's figures, "all elements that can be perceived as [individual] contents have surrendered to the pressure of a universal Destiny." The force of Destiny "weighs down on [these figures] and permeates them as the life in its totality [*das Leben als Ganzes*], the life as Destiny as such [*das Leben als Schicksal überhaupt*]" (*GSG 12*, 131).[26] For Simmel, the lack of genuine individualization reduces a human being to the status of a mere example and thus delivers the life in it to "the fact of Fate" (*die Tatsache des Schicksals*) and to "the mere life that throbs through it" (*das in ihnen pulsierende Leben überhaupt*) (*GSG 12*, 131, 115). The gap between individuation and proper individualization that marks Michelangelo's figures is therefore, first and foremost, the result of a propensity to shift the attention away from the singular existence of the individual and in the direction of a fated and profoundly nonpersonal life that is supposedly at work.[27] In Michelangelo's art, an individual cannot ever become visible *as* an individual because his existence is submerged in an obscure and supposedly predetermined "life as such" (*Leben als solches, Leben überhaupt*) (*GSG 12*, 131, 132). What obstructs the view on the many singular *fates* through which a person builds his own individual existence is nothing but a unified *Fate* that renders an existence, however particular it may be, profoundly nonindividual.

This connection between a "life as such" and the internal necessity of fated time shows how Michelangelo's art is wedded, not just to what is eternal, but also to "a profound, in fact, already tragically colored gravity" (*ein tiefen, eigentlich schon tragisch gefärbten Ernstes*) (*GSG 12*, 120). Simmel deems Michelangelo's art to be tragic to the bone because, on account of the a-priori determination of what is eternal, immutable, and universal, his figures resonate with a "life as such" that can neither be shaken nor be in any way modified. For this reason, the "loneliness" or "closure" that was earlier described as essential to Michelangelo's figures is not just a psychological feature, nor a merely artistic quality, but an ontological one. Michelangelo's figures are deemed tragic because their entire life is governed by a cosmic Fate that cannot in any way be altered by the historical fates that make up an ordinary life. Michelangelo's figures are not privy to "the anthropomorphic inflation of [their] own Destiny to a cosmic Fate" since their identity, vice versa, "flows from and becomes graspable through . . . the brilliant, metaphysical feeling of the essence of the world" (*GSG 12*, 132).[28] As such, in Michelangelo's art there is no room for anything that is of *this* world and for the vicissitudes that characterize a genuinely individualized or singular life. Simmel describes the force of Destiny as it is embodied by Michelangelo's figures as "the air we breathe" and as something which "lies dumb and burning, heavy and all-pervasive over mankind and all human beings. It grabs us like the rotation of the earth, that, with it, spins us around." It "keeps us in its grip as an objective force that governs throughout the universe" (*GSG 12*, 131–32).[29]

Simmel takes our day-to-day existence to be marked by a "lack" (*Mangel*) because this existence cannot close itself off from the external world and because, moreover, it shapes itself precisely *by way of* these various connections and relations.[30] For this reason, lack and longing will always be part and parcel of an individual's existence. However, they cannot be seen as something that pertains to its *structure* and they are nowhere close to being *tragic*. Because the fates that color our existence take place *in* a world and *throughout* history, some of our desires and wishes will inevitably remain unfulfilled, but this has nothing to with any supposed internal necessity or Fate. Lack and longing, in other words, will be forever present in our lives but they are not "eternal forms." To the contrary, they result from the very fact that our existence will always remain a historical one. There is no such thing as a "fact of Fate" or "life as Destiny as such" through which our being is a priori determined. In Simmel's view, however, Michelangelo's *Sehnsucht* is "internal to his being" just like his "being [is internal to] his *Sehnsucht*."[31] As such, it testifies to a lack of being that is *structural* and not just *accidental*.[32] The *Sehnsucht* of Michelangelo's figures, namely, is tragic because it demonstrates that even the longing to *escape* from the eternal, immutable, and universal foundation of their individuation remains fully determined by these qualities. Thus Simmel describes the "annihilating Destiny of his will of life": "From the outset, [Michelangelo's figures] are stamped with this problem and the need of an absolute, [of] something that is released from all earthly standards. . . . The completion of their being is [at the same time] the annihilation of their being" (*GSG 12*, 134).[33] Simmel considers "a struggle without a chance of victory" (*ein Kampf ohne Aussicht auf Sieg*) central to the existence of Michelangelo's figures since the very freedom they resonate with is derived from a power that is fated (*GSG 12*, 122). In Michelangelo, it seems, a newly found autonomy rests squarely on a deeper form of heteronomy. As a consequence, the longing for redemption that can be discovered in some of his sculptures, however "earthly possible" this redemption may be, cannot but be insatiable. Expressed as something universally human, this *Sehnsucht* itself is inevitably tuned to what is eternal and immutable. "The elements of Fate and freedom . . . [have] here [been] put together in a more intimate and unified manner, with a more decisive equivalence, than in any other art" (*GSG 12*, 122).[34] The tragic life of Michelangelo's figures has for this reason nothing to do with a *bad* fate, nor with an *unfortunate* destiny which would render suffering or unhappiness inevitable, but with the mere presence of Fate as such, regardless of whether it is good or bad. Similarly, this tragedy is not at all irreconcilable with the overall "titanic" nature of Michelangelo's figures: on the contrary, their titanism testifies, above all else, to the eternal and never-resolved "struggle" with their non-individualized life.

Coda: The Slave Series

The tragic quality of Michelangelo's art becomes most strikingly visible in those sculptures where he has brilliantly portrayed human beings in the least free and most trying of circumstances: the famous series of slaves. On a purely formal level, these works already illustrate what the concept of a non-individualizing individuation and the structural lack that comes with it truly entails. Quite a few of the works that are part of the slaves series, for instance the *Awakening Slave* in Florence (see figure 1), have remained famously unfinished and some have not been fully released from the raw material out of which they are carved. These slaves are, to some extent, still immersed in the very marble from which they are sculpted, and they have not totally separated from the substance in which they are shaped.[35] Nonetheless, though the work on these figures is to a certain extent unfinished, they do not give the impression of being altogether incomplete. On the contrary, it seems indeed as if the very manner in which they emerge from something that is nonindividual and impersonal truly individuates these figures. It is *because* they "only arise from the marble exhausted and struggling" that they have gained an acute and particularized presence (*GSG 12*, 124).[36] Michelangelo famously claimed that he merely wanted to "set free" the form that was already internal in the stone, and it seems, indeed, that these not fully formed slaves portray, paradoxically, that their form was always already complete

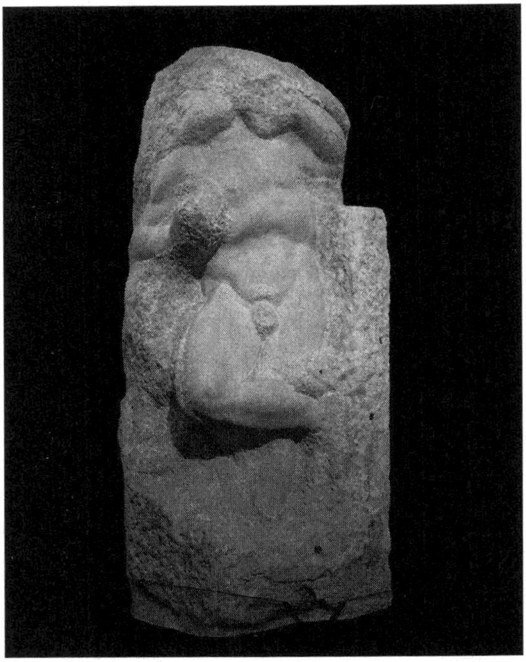

Figure 1. Michelangelo, *Awakening Slave*. 1520–23(?). Galleria Dell'Accademia, Florence.

in its own right. Such forms had, as it were, merely been lying in wait for the moment of their ultimate release, and this for an eternity. In these works, what is unfinished is not at all portrayed as unfulfilled; lack itself has here seemingly become a structure for itself. Little as their lives are to be envied, these slaves nevertheless display the deep "pride" (*Stolz*) (*R*, 62) that Simmel deems characteristic of Renaissance art. Even these slaves echo that their individuation is carried by a superpersonal and universal idea, and even they testify to what Simmel has described as Michelangelo's own embodiment of the Renaissance ideal: "From the earthly-personal human being something absolute is demanded, objective values fill up entirely with a subjective life—but in this very manner it is relieved from the contingent subjectivity of an individualistic state" (*GSG 12*, 132).[37] No less than Michelangelo's sculptures of Greek gods and mythic heroes, these slaves conjure up a life that is fully autonomous from its surroundings and a titanism that no force from without could possibly interrupt.

However, the slave series makes an equally powerful impression in laying bare a *lack* of freedom and an *absence* of self-determination that do not merely result from the ardent and trying circumstances in which these figures are depicted. Near the end of his 1910–11 essay, Simmel returns to the topic of Michelangelo's poems and draws attention to Michelangelo's sensibility for "the eternal perdition . . . that awaits him"[38] (*GSG 12*, 132). In line with his interpretation of Michelangelo's sculptures and frescoes, Simmel repeats that a genuine relation or connection with anything external is foreign to Michelangelo's overall thinking. In the poems about death, therefore, there is "no fear for the suffering in hell, but the purely internal affliction: to be of the kind that deserves hell. . . . Hell is here not a Fate threatening from without, but the logical, continuous development of the earthly condition" (*GSG 12*, 132).[39] In a similar manner, Simmel describes Michelangelo's experience of love as the confrontation with an internalized "*fated moment*" (*Schicksalsmoment*) and as something that is wholly disconnected from the external world (*GSG 12*, 131). Similarly, the lack of freedom that is expressed in the slave series should not be considered the result of circumstances that are, to a certain extent, contingent (that is, as something that "could also have been different"), but as the outcome of a predetermined Fate. Exemplifying the very idea of slavery, the conditions of these slaves are not expressed as pertaining to "appearances that are caused by the This and That of the world" but as submerged in the tragic time of eternal, immutable, and universal ideas and a mere, nonpersonal life. The titanic strength that is embodied by the slaves cannot, for that reason, become visible as directed against an obstacle with an external and empirical nature, obstructing the way to freedom. On the contrary, it only expresses the very condition of being a slave—a condition, that is to say, which is entirely internalized by the slaves themselves and serves as a principle of individuation in the first place. The slave series does not express any genuine fight for liberty but merely portrays, to paraphrase the earlier mentioned quotation, "the purely internal affliction: to be of the kind that is a slave." It seems, for that reason, that the "pride" with which these slaves are endowed is not merely a psychological quality that pertains to the figures themselves. "Pride" has altered, first, into an artistic characteristic (the sculptures are physical bodies that have "proudly" retreated into a sphere that is fully their own) and subsequently into an ontological one pure and proper: the condition of being a slave is here not expressed as taking shape in an empirical world or throughout historical time, but as the exemplification of an internally necessary and eternally "defined" idea.[40] It is, in short, precisely this "pride" which stands in the way of the artistic expression of any genuine struggle for freedom. The difference between both ways of being may seem subtle, but it is enormous: whereas an existence that is played out in an empirical realm testifies to the properly historical time of "things that can also be different," an existence that has retreated into an autonomous world of absorbed universals is submerged in the fated and mythical time of what is believed to be unavoidable.[41] Whereas, from Simmel's perspective, an existence that is perceived as historical is always and irreducibly open to change, the "fated moment" that is expressed by an idealized and universalized life can very well lead to a "struggle," as indeed it visibly does in the slave series, but only to one that is deemed eternal and cannot itself ever lead to any "victory."

Chapter 2

✦

Rembrandt

Re-Producing the Soulful Life of the Sitter as a Portrait

Introduction

In 1916, two years before his death and in the midst of the First World War, Simmel publishes a book—his last monograph—that will have a larger circulation during his life than any of his other works: *Rembrandt: Ein kunstphilosophischer Versuch* (Rembrandt: An Essay in the Philosophy of Art).[1] The text is to be considered as both an important pathway into Simmel's more overarching theories and conceptions and, indeed, a philosophical *essay*. It is an *attempt* to engage, through words and concepts, with ideas that cannot truly be released from the body of work in which they are first expressed.[2] What is more, Simmel's Rembrandt book is not just helpful in understanding what is at stake in his philosophical thinking at large or in Rembrandt's work specifically, but it is also one of the most moving texts of his entire oeuvre. We see Simmel indulge in rich descriptions of the uniqueness and irreplaceability of every individual, while at the same time the first industrialized war in the history of humankind is wreaking its brutal and dis-individualizing violence on the heads of millions of young men. Moreover, it is here that Simmel comes closest to rendering what genuine infinity in his mind consists of, at the exact moment when, in the minds of many of his contemporaries, students, and friends, world history is killing off what was considered valuable, meaningful, significant, or even sacred. It seems as if Simmel's obsession with the singularity of the individual and the infinite variability of life was a final attempt to shield the plausibility of these ideas and intuitions from the reality in which they had first been formulated. Still, what is remarkably absent in Simmel's book is an extended and profound engagement, not with Rembrandt's *work* but with his *works*. Simmel hardly ever goes into detail about the specificities of particular masterpieces. Rather, putting it somewhat disrespectfully, he prefers to *use* them as the raw material through which he can build up his philosophical framework and make it more compelling. It is for this reason that this chapter will not just summarize and explore the most fundamental philosophical ideas that are presented in the Rembrandt book, by focusing on Simmel's theory of the individual and the concept of infinity, but will also return time and again to specific works painted by Rembrandt that, in most cases, Simmel does not even mention.

The Soulful Life of the Sitter

At the very beginning of the Rembrandt book, Simmel describes the life that is depicted in Rembrandt's paintings as a "vital connection accomplished in the stream of time" and contrasts it to an "atemporal logical connection of contents" (*R*, 13). Rembrandt is considered to "practic[e]" his "unifying power" on "that temporal life extended via an infinite/endless continuous variety" (*R*, 36; *GSG 15*, 356, translation modified).[3] A couple of pages earlier, this endless connection that makes up the existence of an individual is understood as that which is "always new in its unity and always a unity in its novelty" and as that which is "at the same time whole and in a state of flux" (*R*, 12, translation modified). The life that is captured in Rembrandt's portraits, in other words, is both unified *and* in continual rejuvenation.

Simmel starts from the idea that the life of an individual cannot be understood without taking into consideration the multiplicity of different events and experiences that the individual in question undergoes *throughout* his life. However, since the life of an individual is itself a *unity* and not a multiplicity, it cannot indicate a mere *sum* or *succession* of fates and feelings. The series of events that an individual undergoes entails no mere "next-to-each-other" (*Nebeneinander*) of different contents of experience.[4] Such contents denote the mere particularities (*Einzelnen*) from and through which an individual constructs his life, but something "additional" seems indispensable in order for such a multiplicity to be called the *continuous* life of an individual with a *unique* (*einziges*) existence. In line with Henri Bergson's views on a *moi profond* (a deep, intimate self, or inner-I), Simmel argues that the life of an individual does not presuppose an atemporal and self-identical I which could be believed to *underlie* the entirety of his course of life. What unifies and singularizes the series of particularities that an individual undergoes is in no way granted an existence *beyond* the life of that individual. "There is no life beyond its individual moments [*jenseits seiner einzelnen Momente*]," writes Simmel, "it is rather, always the one and the whole, however much its continuously alternating forms—according to their conceptually expressible meaning and isolated content—contradict each other, or stand unconnected side by side [*zusammenhanglos nebeneinander stehen mögen*]" (*R*, 161; *GSG 15*, 514).[5]

In his essay "The Law of the Individual" Simmel explains that even though the individual's ego cannot be released from his existence in time, it denotes something "supra-empirical" (*überempirisch*) that "we bring along into empirical relationships as an a priori to form them" (*VoL*, 114; *GSG*

16, 367, translation modified). The idea that our most intimate self is both supra-empirical *and* temporally conditioned introduces a Kantian separation between (a posteriori) contents of experience or thought and the (a priori) formal structure of experiencing and thinking into the phenomenological (and non-Kantian) discussion about the uniqueness of each individual. For Simmel (and Bergson), the singularity of the individual consists in the continuity that links up the many experiences and events that are lived through, but this continuity itself cannot ever become a content of experience or an object of conceptual thought.[6] Therefore, Simmel emphasizes that the "additional something" that unifies and singularizes the life of an individual is a *movement* that exists *between* the many events and experiences he undergoes and *through* which these all hang together: the "deeper formula of life" is "that its totality . . . consists exclusively in the movement through all these opposites" (*R*, 8; *GSG 15*, 317).[7]

Although Simmel calls this singular unity the "soul" (*Seele*) or "soulful life" (*seeliches Leben*) of an individual, the life of an individual is to be considered a *relational* unity and not a *substantial* unity.[8] An individual does not derive the unity and uniqueness or "soulfulness" of his life from the continuous development of deeply rooted character traits alone. According to Simmel, Rembrandt's art makes visible precisely how an individual's life is a "becoming" (*Werden*) (*R*, 35).[9] The life of an individual cannot be delineated or fully grasped through the determination of a set of particularities that are unchanging and ever-present throughout the process of becoming.[10] The statement that an individual has a soul or, to put it more succinctly, that he "lives a soulful life" does not denote the mere presence of a stable and non-changing quality; rather, it presupposes that the experience of an individual's life as a unified continuity with a unique existence can be reconciled with an *ability to change and be changed*. In the same vein, the claim that an individual lives a "soulful life" does not just refer to an autonomous or unaffected layer of being, but rather presupposes a *world*.[11] The concept of "soulfulness" does not so much describe an individual as the *relation between an individual and his surroundings*. In Simmel's view, a genuinely individualized life needs to be considered as "not-closed-off" (*unabgeschlossen*). In one of the most crucial formulas in his book on Rembrandt, Simmel therefore returns to what is arguably the most fundamental idea of his *Lebensphilosophie*, namely, that life resists containment: "Life is that which at all points wants to go beyond itself, reaching out beyond itself" (*R*, 57; *GSG 15*, 385).[12]

Simmel understands a soulful life as a "course" (*Verlauf*) that has not yet reached its temporal end. Rembrandt's portraits do not depict a present moment that lies *beyond* the stream of time since his sitters *emerge from* that stream of becoming itself.[13] In Simmel's opinion, Rembrandt manages to capture an individual life by transcending the reality of the present moment, and he grasps how the past lives on within it.[14] In a move that runs parallel to Bergson's famous example of the inverted cone in *Matter and Memory*

(1896), Simmel maintains that the past of the life of an individual survives into the present and is truly "collected" (*gesammelt*) in or "narrated" (*erzählt*) by it.[15] Modifying time itself into something spatial (a painting) and history into something material (paint), Rembrandt makes visible what has in fact passed as that which has not yet fully ended and thereby endows it with a reality of its own. The history (*Geschichte*) of the sitter is, as it were, layered (*geschichtet*) onto the way he looks in the portrait.

As a consequence, Simmel emphasizes that in order for a specific instant to become of particular value to an individual, the personality of the latter needs already to have been marked by a prior openness to these very moments. In other words, what is of value to an individual are those moments to which the individual was already inclined to respond in a valuable way. In this line of reasoning, when a given moment is considered to yield a meaningful experience, this importance is believed to always already have been prepared by a specific and preexisting receptiveness on the part of the individual. For Simmel, the genuine mark of the value of a moment does not reside in the moment itself, but in the *continuity* that can be built up from it and that can thus be contracted by and within this moment.[16] His framework considers the overarching (and even "supra-empirical") principle of temporal continuity to be ontologically prior to elements of *dis*continuity, and in fact one could claim that it lacks a philosophy of the instant. This will be one of the foremost oppositions with Benjamin's thought, which is, as I will argue in the second part of this book, rooted in a philosophy of "now-time" and momentary interruption. For Simmel, to the contrary, a given temporal *moment* deduces its ultimate significance from the overarching *movement* in which it partakes. Therefore, Simmel's philosophy does not consider an *interruption* of continuity as truly meaningful or individualizing. "The individual," he writes, "can only be imagined through a kind of intellectual conception, insofar as this means the apprehension of a whole through an integrative function. I do not claim that one may not also grasp one element after another in the individual; but then comes an instant in which they combine into a totality that is not juxtaposition—mere being together—but an entirely new construction [*ein ganz neues Gebilde*]" (*VoL*, 128; *GSG 16*, 386–87, translation modified).[17] Although it revolves around change and becoming, Simmel's philosophy does not consider a specific instant, however significant it may seem, to be *itself* a starting point of anything genuinely "novel." The here and now is always at most a "moment of harvesting" and acquires meaning by being integrated into the larger totality that is the individual soul (*R*, 7).[18]

Individuation (Michelangelo) and Individualization (Rembrandt)

Whereas Simmel describes the figures of Michelangelo as "closed off" and sees their "ideal space" as "nothing other than the limits of [their] own body"

(*GSG 12*, 118), the individual in a painting by Rembrandt is characterized as something "*not*-closed-off" (*unabgeschlossen*), which "interacts with, pervades, and melts into the sphere of others" (*R*, 45; *GSG 15*, 369).[19] Because the "titanism" of Michelangelo's figures is wholly antithetical to the structural openness of the portrait and the dialectics of the gaze, it is easy to explain why he indulges in an artistic elaboration of only those body parts that are nowhere directly exposed to the outside world: the musculature of a human being.[20] In this manner, Michelangelo forfeits what Simmel, in an essay on the "Aesthetic Significance of the Face" has called the "uncanny mobility" of the face, and instead focuses on body parts that help make manifest an idea that is of great importance to the Renaissance view of man, that is, that the true impetus of bodily movement is *internalized* by the human body.[21] For Simmel, however, the capacity of the face to individualize a human being denotes at the same time an intimate and irreducible relationship with one's surroundings. Michelangelo's figures, one could therefore say, have the muscle to move and act but they lack the face to *be* moved and *re*act: they are "assembled" (*zusammengesetzt*) as structures that are both unaffected and affectionless, but they cannot in fact become visible as a singular "connection" (*Zusammenhang*) marked by a responsiveness to an "outside." In the majority of both his frescoes and sculptures, Michelangelo renders the faces of the human figures in a detailed manner but, in opposition to Rembrandt's portraits, little attention is given to the specific dynamics that, in Simmel's opinion, singularizes the interplay between the various parts (a nose, mouth, ears, and eyes) that make up a given face.[22] In a large part of Michelangelo's frescoes and sculptures, the overall symmetry of the face is prioritized over the interplay between these particular features, and this gives them a stability that gives way to the universal and the typical.[23]

Simmel deems such a principle of *individuation* characteristic of the medium of "sculpture" (*GSG 7*, 40) and opposes it to the genuine level of *individualization* that can be achieved through the painted portrait.[24] Unlike Michelangelo's figures, the people that are portrayed by Rembrandt do not aspire to the determination by a type or essence that, on account of its "super-individuality," needs to be considered eternal, immutable, and predetermined. Rembrandt, Simmel claims, "gave to [the individual] that which—in a probably rather unclear expression—we call 'necessity' [*Notwendigkeit*], without achieving this at the price of a universalization towards a type" (*R*, 65; *GSG 15*, 394, translation modified).[25] In contrast to Michelangelo's figures, who derive their significance directly from "the brilliant metaphysical feeling of the essence of the world" and "whose life is the life of humankind" (*R*, 102), in Rembrandt the expression of an individual essence reaches its apex, but it comes at the cost of the expression of a cosmic one. While Michelangelo's figures have always already absorbed the "eternal form" of ideas and universals, Rembrandt, on the contrary, exposes the very *gap* that separates the "mere life" from any "absolute calling" or "objective values."[26] As a consequence,

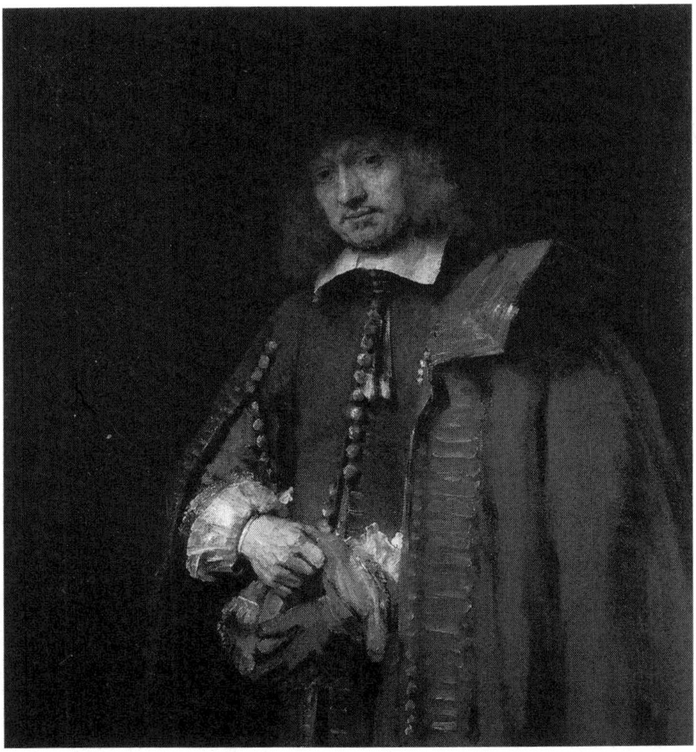

Figure 2. Rembrandt, *Portrait of Jan Six (1618–1700).* 1654. Amsterdam, Six Collection.

even in those cases where Rembrandt was specifically asked by the most prosperous and influential among his fellow citizens to put on display their very prosperity and influence, the human beings that are rendered become visible *as* individuals and not merely as exemplifications of types and universal essences. From almost all of his portraits, we learn that Rembrandt is first and foremost fascinated with what can be termed the "remainder" or "residual meaning" that surfaces when a subject is "caught" in a place that is not just the instantiation of a universal, let alone a pure and absolute ideal. In Rembrandt, writes Simmel, "the form is . . . so completely identical with this individuality that its repetition in another individuality may well be possible by chance, but makes no sense as a universal principle" (*R*, 65–66, translation modified). In the famous *Portrait of Jan Six* (1654; figure 2), for instance, the sitter is shown, not only as the son-in-law of the mayor of Amsterdam and as a notorious magistrate and writer exemplary of the Dutch Golden Age, but just as much as an individual with a life that is irreplaceable. On account of the dynamic rendering of, among other parts, the hands, the sitter seems perpetually suspended in the very movement of entering into the world of the viewer. He seems forever ready to walk out of the atemporal realm of types and into the empirical world that is our own.[27]

Excursus: Rembrandt's *Portrait of a Beggar* as a Self

It is known that Rembrandt had a particular fondness for smuggling into his paintings a figure with facial features that are very similar to his own. A face that bears a striking resemblance to the painter himself is quite easily found in the mythologized history painting *The Magnanimity of Claudius Civilis* (1626) and in the biblical scenes *The Stoning of St. Stephen* (1625), *Samson and Delilah* (1628), and the *Raising of the Cross* (1633) (see figure 3). The effect of this crypto-presence of the painter's face corroborates Simmel's argument on the essential difference between what has been termed individuation and individualization. It results in the sentiment that these scenes are freed from the timeless and unworldly realm in which the depicted mythologized and biblical events are usually imagined to have taken place. On account of the presence of the singular and individualized facial features of the painter, however minimally they are sketched, these scenes do indeed resist being translated into the language of universals and essences that is the only vocabulary fit for the universe that is inhabited by Michelangelo's figures. Rembrandt's own unique facial features prevent these scenes from being enclosed into the fully autonomous realm of ideals and types, and they thus shatter the borders of an absolute universe that is, as it is the case in Michelangelo's art, "seamlessly closed off from the outside world." The interruptive effect of the unique traces of Rembrandt's own face brings these images to the brink of an empirical world that is irreducibly different from the Platonic domain inhabited by eternal types and fully defined ideals, and it taints them, however briefly, with the impurities and heterogeneity of an existence that is not entirely out of the ordinary. Injecting the "uncanny mobility" of Rembrandt's own individualized facial features within a universe that is otherwise peopled by mythological heroes and biblical figures alone therefore results in images that can be considered the reverse of a painting like *Self-Portrait in Oriental Attire, with Poodle* (1631–33) (see figure 4). The mythological and biblical images where Rembrandt's face lives its incognito life do not seek to dress the self up as a type (an endeavor that is not by accident bound to fail in all of Rembrandt's self-portraits) but, the other way around, they *strip the type down to a self*, and they thereby rid it of its universalizing pretense. The movement of singularization therefore establishes a connection between the depicted scene and the world of the beholder that has nothing to do with shared qualities, a universal or an absolute truth.

In a series of etchings where Rembrandt portrays himself as a beggar, the figure in the picture lacks none of his facial features (figure 5).[28] In this way, it makes visually explicit the specific "hanging together" of the potato-like nose, black circular eyes, thick lips, and, if one looks closely at the suggestive

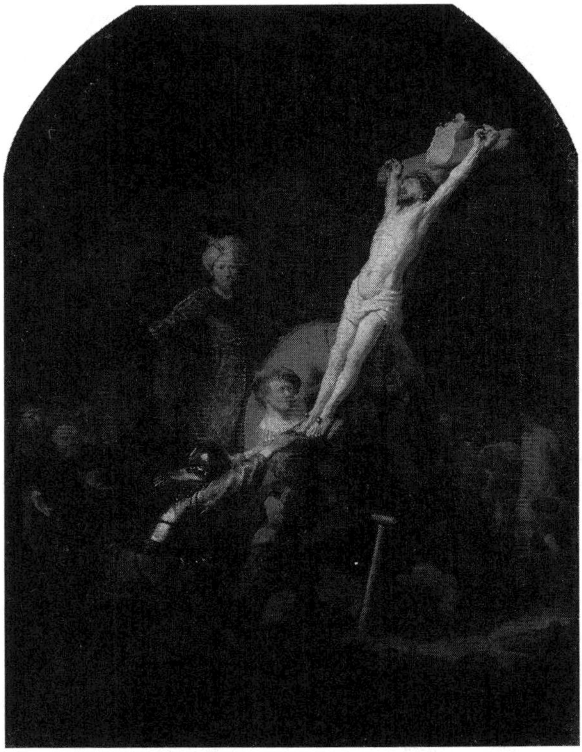

Figure 3. Rembrandt, *The Raising of the Cross.* Circa 1633. Munich, Alte Pinakothek.

manner in which the hair is etched, even the painter's flat beret that renders his looks so very unique. By thus giving him his own recognizable features, Rembrandt frees the beggar from the idealized world in which he would merely exist as an essence or type, and he all but drops him off at our doorstep. Moreover, by setting him up with his own unique features, Rembrandt shows the beggar as the social and economic figure he truly is, since it is but through such a movement of individualization that he can be emancipated from the timeless and unworldly universe in which situations cannot be understood, let alone changed, through empirical elements and historical forces and need only to be accepted as predetermined and unavoidable. Rembrandt's etching is in truth more the image of a beggar-as-a-self than that of the self-as-a-beggar.

The Soulful Life of the Portrait

In various places of his work, Simmel highlights the inherent difference between what we see in an artwork and what we see in the actual world,

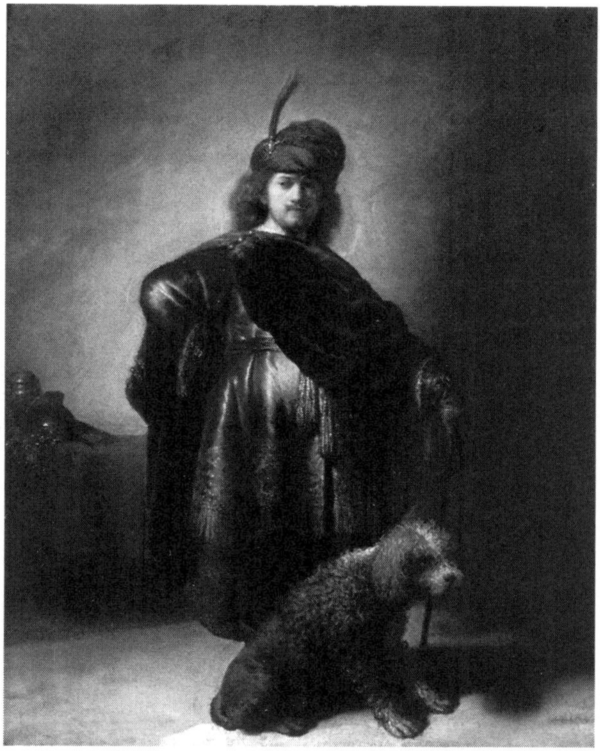

Figure 4. Rembrandt, *Self-Portrait in Oriental Attire, with Poodle*. 1631–33. Paris, Petit Palais.

claiming that the artwork is not just the "record" of something that exists outside of it but that it needs to be considered as a reality in its own right. In the essays "On Realism in Art" (1908) and "On the Problem of Naturalism" (published in 1923), for instance, he describes how a profoundly *anti*-artistic tendency motivates movements of realism and naturalism in the arts.[29] Naturalism reduces the artwork to a "mere means" (*einem bloßen Mittel*) (*GSG 8*, 411) in the quest to imitate what cannot possibly be imitated: the experience that something has a genuinely "actual" existence. Realistic tendencies in art are bound to focus on qualities that "are in a secondary manner inseparable from the being actual of things," that is, on "mere contents" (*GSG 8*, 407).[30] The experience that something is not an image or representation and belongs to the "actual" world, to the contrary, eludes the act of artistic creation and can therefore, in Simmel's mind, be called a *metaphysical* experience pure and proper.[31] It is on account of this intrinsic difference between artistic representation ("a thing of the senses") and "actual" existence ("something abstract [that] lies beyond the surface of things") that a genuine artwork does not

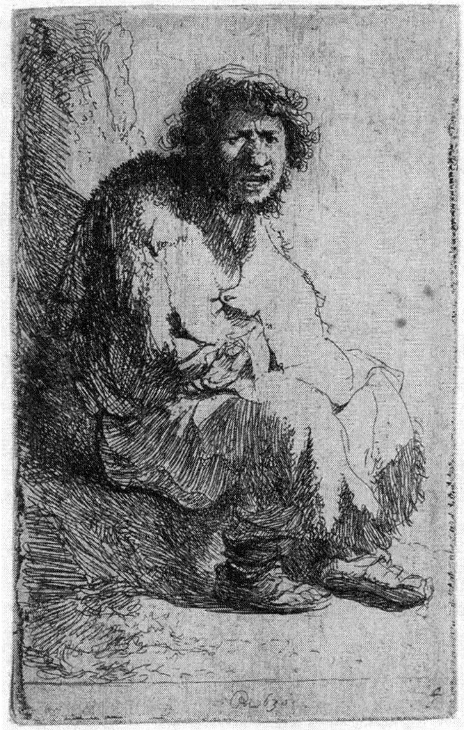

Figure 5. Rembrandt, *Beggar Seated on a Bank*. 1630. Amsterdam, Rijksmuseum.

merely "awaken" in us the perception of the original but *modifies* it into a *novel* reality (*GSG 8*, 407).[32] Simmel suggests that Rembrandt's portraits do not just *depict* the "soulful" life of an individual but, as it were, *create* one. He reverses the commonly held viewpoint that a successful portrait manages to convey the "actual" mental life of a sitter and maintains that the "soul" "that gives meaning and substance to the artwork . . . truly lives *within* it, and not beyond it" (*GSG 7*, 332).[33] Rembrandt's portraiture is for this reason not to be considered as an art of mimesis, let alone one of idealization, but as an act of genuine re-production: in translating the sitter's existence into paint, it modifies it into something altogether *different* and thereby *creates it anew*.[34] Thus, so to speak, the portrait *converts* "the human-being-insofar-as-he-is-an-empirical-reality" into "the human-being-insofar-as-he-is-an-artwork" (*R*, 83; *GSG 15*, 416, translation modified).[35] As a consequence, Rembrandt's art is "*individualistic, without being realistic*" (*R*, 95; *GSG 15*, 432).[36] Whereas the attempt to read emotions, thoughts, and feelings from the facial expressions of an "actual" person is the mark of the *psychological* capacities that assist our daily social life, a portraitist uses such mental concepts as a mere starting point for an *artistic* reworking.[37] "For the artist," writes Simmel, "the examination of the model is only a conceiving, a fertilization, and he shapes the appearance anew [*zeugt die Erscheinung noch einmal*]. It grows once again on the soil and under the specific categories of artistry" (*R*, 29; *GSG 15*, 347).

According to Simmel, the excessive visibility of details is detrimental to this artistic re-production of an individualized life.[38] He maintains that it is precisely the "specific," or the "minutiae," which indicate "that which a large number of appearances have in common" (*R*, 48). Details that are worked out in a clear manner become visible as particularities (*Einzelnen*), that is, as members of a universal class which can therefore be recognized as elements with a possible existence elsewhere. "Only the totality of the human being," claims Simmel, "is singular [*das Einzige*]. Everything that is particular [*alles Einzelne*] to him is a universal [*ein Allgemeines*]" (*R*, 67; *GSG 15*, 395–96, translation modified).[39] It is this law which explains why in some of Rembrandt's late masterpieces the beholder only learns about the true finesse of his genius from the rough residue that it has left behind. In some of his best paintings, nothing testifies as much to the delicate skills of the master as the sheer materiality of the paint itself and the very briskness with which the brush is being handled. This, according to Simmel, points to the "deeper connection" (*tiefere Verknüpfung*) that turns "the oftentimes border-blurring, vibrant, and unclear in Rembrandt's way of painting" into "a vehicle for his propensity for individualization" (*R*, 51; *GSG 15*, 376, translation modified).[40] In the late portraits, Rembrandt captures the singularity of his figures precisely *because* these works were not elaborated in a detailed manner and thus push a great many particularities out of sight: "The singularity of the pure becoming," Simmel writes, "cannot at all be expressed by means of qualities, either [conceived as] being or becoming" (*R*, 69; *GSG 15*, 397, translation modified).[41]

Rembrandt's best paintings famously show that the attempt to deplete the image of a human being of the particularities that refer to his actual existence need not automatically result in the impression that his individuality has dissolved into the sheer materiality of the paint. On account of the direct physicality of their paint and the visible vivacity of the brushwork, Simmel maintains that in some of Rembrandt's portraits our experience of the sitter gives us something that has a "truth but no actuality" (*Wahrheit, aber nicht Wirklichkeit*) (*R*, 109; *GSG 15*, 450, translation modified).[42] Freeing him from his presence in mere "actual" reality and delivering him to the seemingly improvising hands of the artist can very well allow a person to safely land in and become visible as an individual through the secure movements of the brush. Rembrandt's best paintings push the oppositions between work and outside world to such limits that the painterly qualities of the image themselves conjure the feeling that it has become a "world" on its own. It is this process which turns *A Woman Bathing in a Stream (Hendrickje Stoffels?)*

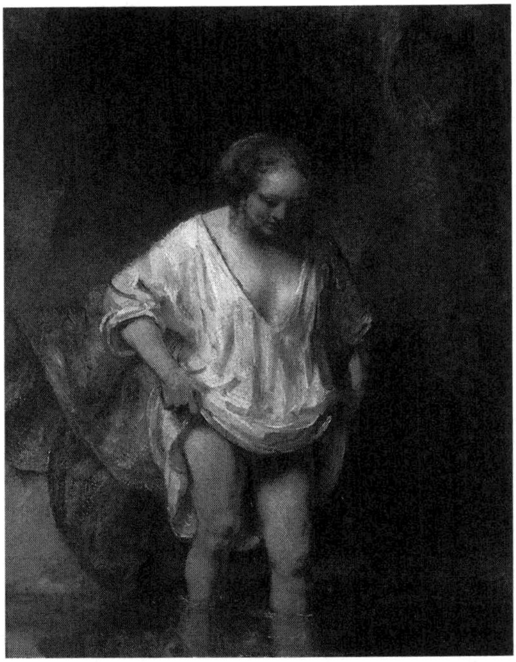

Figure 6. Rembrandt, *A Woman Bathing in a Stream (Hendrickje Stoffels?)*. 1654. London, National Gallery.

(1654; figure 6) into a masterpiece. Rendered throughout in just about the most free and unbound manner imaginable, it seems as if Rembrandt makes visible the brushstrokes as, indeed, *strokes of a brush*: in allowing the mere "stuff" with which he creates the picture of his lover to stay so clearly visible, the brush manifests itself, perhaps for the first time in the history of painting, as a genuine extension of the artist's hand and the various strokes, for that reason, take on the character of a series of caresses. Hendrickje's left sleeve and right hand are "treated so freely and broadly . . . that generations of connoisseurs assumed this to be a damaged passage," but above all, they are witnesses in paint of an affection that is as unspoiled as they come.[43] More aptly called, in Dutch, "penseel-*strelen*" (caresses by a brush) than "penseel-*streken*" (brushstrokes), the act of painting itself actualizes a moment of individualization and heartfelt recognition. This moment is all the more moving because it indicates at its very core an *artistic* gesture and cannot for that reason be deduced from the reference to the mere, actual existence of Hendrickje herself.

Simmel emphasizes that the beholder's experience of "the possibility of failure" (*Möglichkeit des Mißlingens*) is a requirement to encounter a painting as the becoming-visible of an individual. In Rembrandt's best works, the sitter is created anew and caught in the paint itself because the "possibility of failure" that marks all things truly "alive" is not obfuscated. To the contrary, it is this very instability that saves them from perfection and idealization.[44] Simmel writes: "As with [Rembrandt's] human beings, so, too, his works are subjected to life's fate with its possibility of failure, even where this possibility has not in the smallest degree become reality [*auch wo diese mit keinem Bruchteilen Wirklichkeit geworden ist*]" (*R*, 85; *GSG 15*, 419, translation modified). The possibility that an artist fails in bringing about the individuality of his sitter is therefore not at all antithetical to the certainty, experienced by the beholder, that he has nevertheless succeeded. This possibility that the painter fails is part and parcel of the process of producing anything that can be called successful, and it fully enters into it. The portrait is a "creative making" (*schopferische Tun*) that manages to actively "bring about" (*zeugen*) the individual's becoming-visible because it allows the uncertainty of the entire process to remain in full view: the search is here still noticeable in the catch, and the hope that motivated the painter's quest has clearly left behind its traces in the relief of the find.

Excursus: The Self-Portraits

Rather than opposing Rembrandt's portraits and self-portraits to each other, Simmel maintains that the activity of ceaselessly creating his self-image is to be considered as "the school and to a degree the prototype" of Rembrandt's art of portraiture in general (*R*, 27). The self-portraits provide ample proof for the intuition that, as we now know, also motivated the "normal" portraits, that is, they make explicit that capturing the life of an individual as a unity need not entail that any one quality or particularity should be identified as supporting the entirety of his existence. This is attested to by even the most cursory look at the diversity of the images through which Rembrandt has chosen to represent himself. From the scruffy clothes of a beggar to the posh paraphernalia of an oriental king, from the playfulness of a young lad to the wise introspection of an old man, and from the zeal of the man hoisting Christ's body onto the cursed cross to the thoughtful stare of a bohemian painter eyeing his unfinished canvas, these self-images speak of just about everything one can possibly imagine, yet remain silent about anything in particular. The self-portraits constitute a rich variety of different languages, but at no time do they seem to find the words to pinpoint any one trait that has remained the same throughout. Contrary to the self-portraits of Rubens, which can easily be molded together into the flawless and perfectly streamlined picture of a devoted family man, a trustworthy diplomat, and a professional artist, Rembrandt's self-portraits, in fact, need to be edited into a montage of juxtaposed images that, when put together, tell a story of ongoing change and restless pursuit. The ornamentations and attributes, clothes and hats, and symbols and allegories cannot be categorized under the label of mere artifice obscuring the view of a supposed and unspoiled essence but instead illustrate, however puzzling the resulting images may sometimes be, that some individuals can only build up a genuinely unique identity by wearing many different faces. The "pure" truth that supposedly hides behind all surface and appearance may be hard to locate in these images, but it is clear that this existence of trying out one persona after another is one of integrity and, what etymologically speaking comes down to the same thing, *wholeness*. In Rembrandt's self-portraits, writes Simmel, "the unity of the internal and the external was immediately experienced [and] he consistently trained himself in the presentation [*Darstellung*] of this unity, for which he had a matchless talent. In objectifying this unity in artistic forms in ever-new ways, he more and more found, as it were, the general formula for such unity" (*R*, 27; *GSG 15*, 344, translation modified).[45]

It is crucial to Simmel that it is Rembrandt's "*artistry as such* [which] lifted him above [*hob ihn . . . über*] . . . the actual reality of his subjectivity" (*R*, 27; *GSG 15*, 344, translation modified, my emphasis).[46] Rembrandt's self-portraits, that is to say, are to be considered neither as the result of mere introspection, detachment, and spirituality, nor as attempts to look at himself through the eyes of, for instance, his lovers, clients, or children. Simmel emphasizes that the older Rembrandt gets, the more his self-portraits show themselves off *as* objects of art, in the first place by allowing the thick materiality of the paint to stay astutely visible. They thus reveal that it was, before all else, the old but trusted couple of paint on canvas that Rembrandt wanted to bet his money on. He almost literally trusted *art* with his life, since he knew from his own experience that an identity is not a given but a construct and that a true genius for that reason has no choice but to *paint* himself into existence. For Simmel, the later self-portraits show that Rembrandt "retreats from [the] entwinement with the world" and they "bring only himself to expression" (*R*, 96; *GSG 15*, 433–34, translation modified).[47] This entails, however, that he is "indifferent toward the relationship to the outside objects *as such*; that [he] indeed express[es] only [himself], *but as artist*" (*R*, 97; *GSG 15*, 434, translation modified).[48] Whereas the earlier self-portraits still thrive on references to the outside world and actual contexts of meaning (the oriental king, the beggar, etc.), the later ones are to a large extent emptied of such particularities and they thereby allow elements of a merely artistic nature to take over. This means not only that Rembrandt portrays himself before all else as a painter but, first and foremost, that the restlessness with which he sought his self and through which he continuously created and re-created his own images slowly gives way to images that are lacking in detail but rich in physicality. It is as if, through his lifelong practice, Rembrandt's trust in the capacity of the very materiality of paint to bring about and preserve his own most intimate self has grown exponentially with his *dis*trust in the actual world to build up anything that can properly be called unique or meaningful. According to Simmel, the world "became ever stranger [*fremder*], more hostile [*feindseliger*], more meaningless [*sinnloser*] to him" (*R*, 96; *GSG 15*, 433–34). It is this very evacuation of meaning from actual reality that slowly carves out the necessary space for artistic creation to do its mysteriously individualizing business. According to Simmel, the late self-portraits show that "his whole and ultimate essence is completely absorbed into his artistry" and that "his artistry has transformed itself completely into the subjectivity of his life" (*R*, 97; *GSG 15*, 434, translation modified).[49] Rembrandt's late self-portraits, therefore, both express and bring about "a higher ego" (*jenes höhere Ich*) which, "without forfeiting the character of its subjectivity, became exclusively artistic genius and creativity" (*R*, 97, translation modified). It seems, in other words, that in these later self-images Rembrandt's age can no longer be read from the details with which his face is rendered but becomes visible (and tangible) only in the roughness of the artistic material itself. It appears, likewise, that the long years of his life have not so much settled in the folds of his skin as in the crust of the paint. It is now nothing so much as the layers (*Schichte*) of the artworks which allow the history (*Geschichte*) of Rembrandt the painter to manifest itself as a unity.[50]

The Religious A Priori

In Simmel's view, an individualized life is never fully determined by an all-determining law. On account of their bodies, for instance, human beings do participate in life's physiological striving to ceaselessly bring about "more-life," but they also transcend this natural dynamic of mere regeneration. Human beings, according to Simmel, are "creatures that can place themselves beyond life" (*VoL*, 29; *GSG 16*, 250).[51] According to Simmel, Rembrandt captures the genuinely productive and free dimension in a sitter's life. Individuality is thereby understood as a *product* or a "more-*than*-life" that is built up *by way of* and not *despite of* the many relations with elements coming from elsewhere. Even though Rembrandt's sitters are believed to "lack . . . heroic gesture and monumental mightiness," and are "often enough weighed down and crushed by external forces," they "still allow us to a feel a point of freedom [*einen Freiheitspunkt*]" (*R*, 104; *GSG 15*, 444). In Rembrandt's portraits, the "struggle without a chance of victory" of Michelangelo's figures has retreated in favor of an intimate interaction with an outside world that *does* carve out a space for a sense of liberty.[52] Simmel argues that Rembrandt's portraits show a life that is in no way predetermined by any power of Fate. In his view Rembrandt's sitters are visibly affected by all that they have undergone in the course of their existence, but still, and this is what matters most, they retain a distinct form of true autonomy. Their life is taken to be one of genuine sovereignty, despite the fact that it cannot be released from elements that remain beyond their control.

In the short text "The Problem of Fate" (1913) and the "Note on the Concept of Fate" that is included in the essay "Death and Immortality" (1918), Simmel distinguishes the concept of Fate that underlies the experience of the tragic hero from experiences of fatefulness that he sees as part and parcel of a truly human existence. For Simmel, ordinary existence does not include experiences that are to be termed fated in the most "pure" sense of that term (*in einer Reinheit*) (*GSG 12*, 490). In Simmel's view, the concept of Fate (or Destiny) in its most proper significance indicates the ambiguous unity between, on the one hand, a force that is experienced as wholly external to one's self and, on the other, the course of one's own singular life. In this context Simmel develops a theory of tragedy that is very similar to Benjamin's view of the same topic. I will return to Benjamin's philosophy of tragedy in the final chapter of this book, but I would already like to emphasize here the following point: Simmel and Benjamin agree that, in tragedy, events that are deemed wholly objective are nevertheless fully absorbed by the hero since the latter manages to experience Destiny both as an absolute power *and* as something that is aimed directly and solely at him. Therefore, in the tragic experience of Fate, contingency has been entirely annihilated, and it has become one with an experience of necessity. "In the resolution of the uncanniness of coincidence into necessity lies what is 'reconciling' [*das Versöhnende*] through tragedy, which in this regard is always a tragedy of 'Fate.' "[53]

Simmel argues that using the concept of Fate in this "pure" sense to describe an event in daily life testifies to "a grandiloquent abuse of the term."[54] In its stead, one could argue, he develops a theory where Fate (*das Schicksal*) loses its capital and is turned into its plural form, thereby shedding its nature as an ahistorical, overpowering, and all-encompassing force. It is this philosophy of the multiplicity of historical "fates" (*die Schicksale*) that underlies Simmel's book on Rembrandt.[55] For the life of the sitters, it is stated, "does not soar above them as human Fate in general only descending upon the particular [human being]; rather it bursts out of them" (*R*, 102; *GSG 15*, 441, translation modified).[56] Rembrandt has substituted the towering presence of Fate for the steady rhythm of a series of fates because he replaced the purity of ahistorical essences and ideals with the vicissitudes of history. Whereas the atemporal force of Destiny predetermines an existence that for this reason can know nothing but an "expiration" (*Ablauf*), a truly individualized existence is marked by a temporal course (*Verlauf*) of its own. Whereas Michelangelo represents his figures as being wholly determined by Fate "in general," Simmel suggests that Rembrandt's work is capable of doing the opposite, that is, of bringing to the fore that no fate exists independently of a singular self. "Fate," writes Simmel in his essay on this issue, "does determine [*bestimmt*] the life of the individual, but only because the individual has selected those events which have a certain affinity by imparting a meaning to them that allows them to become his 'fate.' "[57] Such fateful moments do not leave us powerless since they highlight, to the contrary, that it is our own capacity to pay heed to them that *makes* them fateful. These moments do not at all take away the freedom that motivates our actions and decisions as they even impart this freedom with a specific weight and relevancy.

In opposition to the absolute power of an ahistorical Fate that is absorbed by the tragic hero, the many fates that color a life lived ordinarily cannot let go of "the uncanny feeling that even the absolute necessity of our life may somehow be coincidental."[58] Simmel, in other words, suggests that when a human being experiences an event as fateful, the contingency of this event is not simply annulled or overcome by the experience of necessity since the former enters into the latter and gives it its sharpness. In such moments, he writes, "we sublate the contingency that stands between [random] events on the one hand and the deeper meaning of our life" and give it "a higher meaning" (*höhere Würde*).[59] This explains why Simmel emphasizes that, rather than an ambiguous and enigmatic unity, a fundamental *disparity* (*Doppelaspekt*, *Doppeleinstellung*) and even "splitting" (*skizzierten*, *gespalten*) (*GSG 12*, 486–87) lies at the heart of every historical event that can be called fateful. Such moments are experienced *simultaneously* as ordinary *and* as out of the ordinary, and neither of these two opposing emotive associations is capable of mitigating the other. "Fate," writes Simmel, "consists in that characteristic relationship between what is peripheral and what is central, what is passive and what is active, what merely occurs and what has purpose and meaning."[60] As a consequence, Simmel emphasizes that a fateful event necessarily "allows for something dark and indissoluble to persist in this world" and that it cannot ever fully separate from the awareness that it is a "mere fact" (*eine bloße Tatsache*).[61] Even an event that is of extraordinary value to an individual can just as well be experienced as a "given" (*gegeben*) with a "content [that] cannot be constructed out of the mind alone."[62] This "heterogeneous core or remainder" (*heterogener Kern oder Rest*) is to be understood as the irreducible "too-much" that blocks the full and therefore tragic identification with a supposedly absolute Destiny, and it indicates something that "is not fully assimilated."[63]

Simmel ultimately connects this issue of individual freedom to the topic of Rembrandt's religiosity. Opposing the concept of the "religious image" to that of the "image of the religious," he maintains that Rembrandt was a proponent of the former (*R*, 132; *GSG 15*, 479).[64] This means for Simmel that Rembrandt's religiosity is unconnected to his beliefs as a "private person" (Simmel expresses serious doubts about the existence of "any evidence . . . for a very positive religiosity" in his life) and that he "as *painter*—functionally [*funktionell*], as the creator of paintings—is religious."[65] The consequence of this is that religiosity becomes visible as a "functional a priori" or an "immanent law" of Rembrandt's work in toto and not as "a living reality in its own right for which the painting is merely a means of expression" (*R*, 134). In sharp contrast to Michelangelo's figures who "must specifically be called impious," Simmel therefore discovers "piety" as a crucial element in some of Rembrandt's works (*R*, 103). For Simmel this piety has nothing to do with the visibility of specific particularities that are supposedly shared by the portrayed people and other religiously inspired people.[66] Neither can the piety of Rembrandt's figures be made dependent on the merely subjective experience of supposedly divine qualities pertaining to the outside world.[67] This is most obvious in the paintings that have a religious subject matter: according to Simmel, "not what a person believes, not the specific content of the religious life, but the specificity of the life in so far as it is religious constitutes [Rembrandt's] problem" (*R*, 121; *GSG 15*, 464).[68] For Simmel, in other words, Rembrandt's work does not just demonstrate that a pious person does not need to necessarily believe in the existence of God, but also that in some cases such a belief can even become downright antithetical to piety.[69] Deducing religiosity or piety from a belief in something external makes what has the power to singularize an individual dependent on the existence of something that has a "super-individual," universal validity.[70] Simmel writes: "For the religious uniqueness of Rembrandt's figures . . . the question of this-life and the beyond does not arise at all because it is exclusively a matter of soulful life that is marked neither by the one nor by the other; in this, the people of these peaceful, familiar paintings do not *have* religion as the objective content of life; rather, they *are* religious" (*R*, 117; *GSG 12*, 489, translation modified).[71] Piety and religiosity do not presuppose the belief in transcendence, but they denote an "immanent moment" (*immanente Moment*) that leaves "the connection to the earthly undisturbed" (*R*, 118; *GSG 15*, 459–60, translation modified).[72] They are, in Simmel's view, neither qualities of a subject nor qualities of a world, but they indicate a specific manner through which the former relates to or connects with the latter. Some people can be said to live a religious life or, put more precisely, to live religiously, not because they do or believe in certain things but because, within all of these actions and thoughts, a religious dimension can be brought to the surface.[73]

For Simmel this becomes palpable in Rembrandt's painting *Christ and the Woman of Samaria* (1659; figure 7). This painting is not to be considered a religious painting *because* it is a depiction of Christ but, one would almost be inclined to say, *in spite of* this. For Simmel, in Rembrandt, "the exterior—yes, the *banality*—of the manifestations is animated in a religious manner" (*R*, 120; *GSG 15*, 463, my emphasis, translation modified).[74] The religiosity that comes out of this painting is not connected to the supposed double nature of Christ as the God-man, and it does not display anything that is irreconcilable with the existence of a mortal human being. Christ is not at all different from the other people in the painting, save for the fact that something essential about the condition *of being human* is brought to expression through him. More visibly human than the other human beings in the painting, Christ displays his very finiteness and the fact that his existence, for that reason, at all times presupposes the support of something that, literally, remains external and inappropriable. Christ is painted "almost as a shadow, without substance in comparison to the powerful woman who is, as it were solidly rooted in

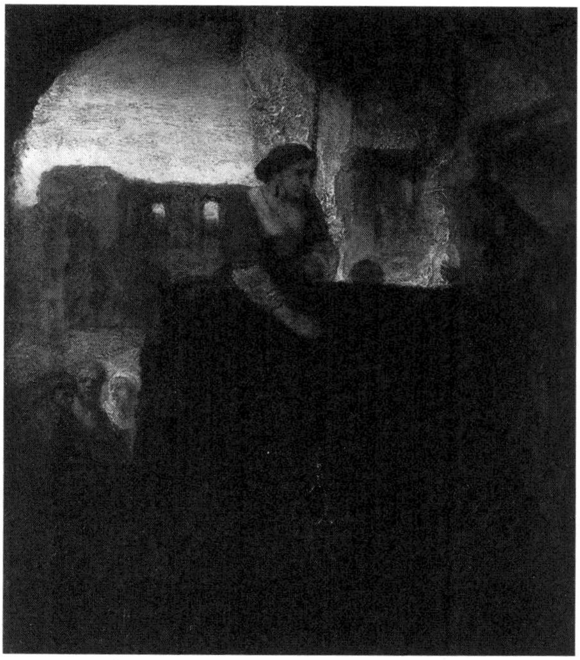

Figure 7. Rembrandt, *Christ and the Woman of Samaria*. 1659. Berlin, Gemäldegallerie.

the earth" but "if one looks only a moment longer" one understands that "this weak as well as swaying being is after all the one really solid thing" (*R*, 125; *GSG 15*, 469, translation modified).[75] In this painting, one could argue, Christ is grasped as an *Über-Mensch* in the *literal* sense of that term, that is, not as a *super*-man but as the *superlative* of a human being. He is here made visible as more-human-than-human and is thereby deprived of the association with anything *super*-human and therefore to an extent *non*-human. No more than the other people he is surrounded by, would he know how to walk on water but, unlike them, he knows how to truly bring to expression the human need to have a solid ground beneath one's feet. Simmel writes: "All the other strong and substantial figures are, in comparison to him, insecure and as though uprooted; as if not they, but only he, had that ground under his feet on which people can really stand" (*R*, 125).

Coda: The *Self-Portrait with Two Circles*

The *Self-Portrait with Two Circles* (1665–69; figure 8) that is now part of the collection of the Kenwood House in London is sometimes considered to be the most brilliant of Rembrandt's late portraits. Better than most other ones,

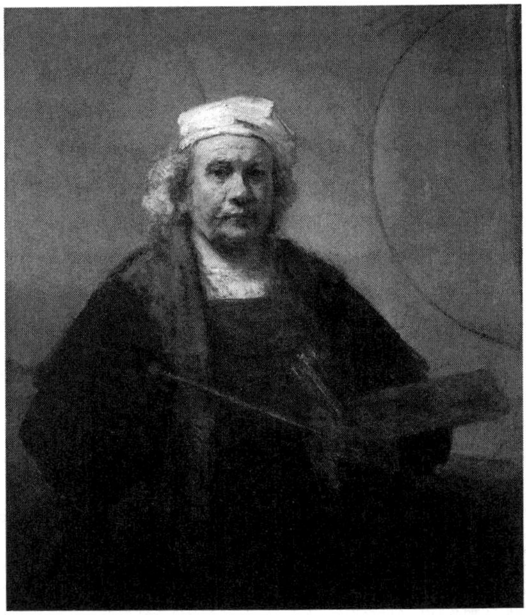

Figure 8. Rembrandt, *Self-Portrait with Two Circles*. 1665–69. London, Kenwood House.

this work exemplifies Simmel's statement that, in his final years, Rembrandt's life and art had blended completely (*R*, 97).

In this portrait, an "immanent quality" of light, the movement of the brushstrokes, and the physicality of the paint bring about a fully individualized picture of the painter. The light in this painting does not work *against* darkness but *with* and *alongside* it or, put more precisely, it is shown as originating from within darkness itself.[76] What results from this late portrait is therefore the complete mirror image of Michelangelo's slave series. Whereas these struggle in an attempt to free themselves, once and for all, from the obscure materiality of the stone, Rembrandt's image is gently pushed in the direction of the beholder by a light that arises, without any genuine contradiction, from the darker parts of the painting themselves. The outcome of this is that the portrait contains a clear "moment of freedom" or "sovereignty" that is not a mere effect of the fact that Rembrandt has depicted himself as a *painter*, that is, as the *creator* of his own image. In opposition to what happens to Michelangelo's slaves, the elderly Rembrandt is not at all depicted as caught up in a tragic "struggle without a chance of victory," for the light has here, in collaboration with the vivacity of the brushwork and the direct visibility of the paint, granted him the necessary confidence and internal balance that make him, on the very brink of death, speak of the "certainty of life's fundament" (*R*, 126).

The *Self-Portrait with Two Circles* completely subverts the impression of always-already-being-completed that marks the works of the Renaissance master. Michelangelo's quest for the eternal is bound to result in the impression that even artworks that were not in fact finished by the artist nevertheless become visible as internally complete. Because the slaves first and foremost embody an a priori–determined type and the universal ideal *of* being a slave, even those specific works that Michelangelo did not finish can fully stand on their own. They are, no less than the ones he *did* finish, individuated as if, in them, *lack itself becomes visible as a structure*. Unlike Michelangelo's slaves, Rembrandt's self-portrait with circles does not hold back from indicating that there is no such thing as an ideal essence that eternally lies in wait for the moment of its ultimate release by an artist's hand. Rembrandt's portrait, to the contrary, is a distinct example of the style that is so aptly called *non-finito*. The movement of the light, the vitality of the brushstrokes, and the visibility of the paint fully release it from the domain of what is eternal and immutable, and they reopen the life of the painter as something that is infinite and has not yet fully run its course. The much-discussed presence of the two half circles that are painted in the background is crucial to make this understandable. These are, first and foremost, witnesses-in-paint of the firmness of Rembrandt's hand and of the ability to still draw a perfect geometrical figure, regardless of the painter's old age. What is more important, however, is that Rembrandt presents himself in a manner that is wholly opposed to the one in which these idealized forms in the background are painted. Whereas these half circles can, on account of their abstract, mathematical nature, easily be *completed* by the beholder, the image of Rembrandt himself retains, on account of the dynamic way in which it is painted, the impression of still somehow being alive and of remaining *open to change*. As such, whereas these mathematical figures are halfway on the road to being closed and can usher forth no other movement but the act of being completed in the beholder's mind, the dynamic rendering of Rembrandt's worn-out traces allows them to nevertheless embody the "potentiality" and the "charged energy" of the future. In this body-become-paint, however worn-out it may look, no circle or cycle is fully closed off, and not even death can be regarded as a necessity since, in the realm of art, it is but a possibility.[77]

Chapter 3

Auguste Rodin

Reexperiencing One's Deepest Life in the Sphere of Art

In the spring of 1902, Simmel travels to Prague and visits the major Rodin exhibition that was organized there by the Mánes Union of Artists. A few months later, he publishes a first article on the French sculptor in the *Berliner Tageblatt* with the title "Rodin's Sculpture and Today's Spiritual Direction." Rodin sends him a letter of thanks and invites Simmel over for a visit.[1] Three years later, in April 1905, Simmel asks Rainer Maria Rilke, Rodin's then secretary and a longtime acquaintance of Simmel, to remind Rodin of his invitation.[2] Although no details have been preserved about this first meeting that will take place a few days later, it is no exaggeration to say that it indicates the start of a "true friendship" between the two men (Pierre Bucher in *GSG 23*, 328). By the end of the year, Rodin sends Simmel two pages of sketches as a "tribute to friendship" and "in honor of the great thinker Georg Simmel" (*GSG 22*, 531). Simmel is extraordinarily moved: "Of all the material property that I possess," he writes back, "these two pages are the most valuable and the most precious to me. To have a human soul is the one thing that exceeds its value" (*GSG 22*, 532). In November 1906 Simmel sends Rodin a copy of his book on Kant and Goethe and adds to this his "veneration for the greatest artist of our time."[3] For the rest of their lives, the two men will stay in relatively close contact, and Simmel will remain interested in Rodin's work, dedicating no less than an additional three texts to it: the essays "The Art of Rodin and the Motif of Movement in Sculpture" (1909), "In Memory of Rodin" (1917), and his main elaboration of his ideas on the topic, "Rodin: With a Preliminary Remark on Meunier" (1911).

In the commemorative essay that he wrote immediately after Rodin's death, Simmel recalls an amusing conversation with the French sculptor in which the two men disagree about the supposed naturalness of Rodin's work. While the sculptor insists that he "merely imitates what he sees," Simmel points at one of the surrounding works and asks whether this might indeed be the kind of head he comes across in nature. Rodin answers: "No, obviously, I have modified things a little bit." Simmel's reply is revelatory: "The little bit, that is Rodin" (*Eh bien, ce peu, c'est Rodin*) (*GSG 13*, 309; see also *GSG 22*, 511). This anecdote, whether it is accurate or not, illuminates an important element of Simmel's interpretation of Rodin's work. From the very first text on, Simmel emphasizes that Rodin should not be regarded as a naturalist since he is not a "copyist" (*Abschreiber*) but a "genuine creator" (*eigentlichen Schöpfer*) (*GSG 7*, 95). In Simmel's account, Rodin's creativity is to be understood as the endeavor to *re*-create nature: by modifying nature, he produces it anew *in* and *as* a work of art. "The lack of independence [*Unselbständigkeit*] of naturalism," writes Simmel, "chains us to the mere givenness of things," whereas Rodin gives shape to "a *formation* of the material . . . through which it gains a purely aesthetic interest" (*GSG 7*, 95, 97, my emphasis).[4] According to Simmel, Rodin thereby succeeds in returning to art the foremost capacity that it had lost after Michelangelo, that is, the ability to express something absolute. "The history of sculpture, which had ended with Michelangelo," writes Simmel on the first page of his first essay on the French sculptor, "begins again with Rodin" and this, he adds at a later stage, because Rodin captures "not the immediately recognizable world, but precisely the true essence that is concealed by it, an ideal that can only be grasped from within" (*GSG 7*, 92 and *GSG 13*, 309).[5] For Simmel, Rodin incarnates "the modern spirit" because, in reopening nature within the context of art, he brings to visibility the one thing that can still be considered absolute: movement and change itself. Simmel's interpretation of the work of Rodin therefore revolves around the paradox that, in modernity, nothing has remained stable and unchanging except instability and change themselves: the nineteenth century discovers variability as the new absolute. "The modern *transmutabilità*," he writes, "[indicates] a continuous gliding [*ein kontinuierliches Gleiten*] without established poles of determination or points of rest . . . less a shifting between yes and no than a simultaneity of yes and no" (*GSG 12*, 33).[6] The most plausible explanation for Simmel's fascination with Rodin's work, hence, is that, however different their means may be, they are engaged with a similar aim: the exploration of the potential for modification and renewal that they deem internal to the principle of life itself.[7]

Dividuals: Surface, Fragment, Gesture

Simmel is particularly taken with Rodin's ability to bring to expression nothing less than the ontological structure of reality. In his view, Rodin's works make visible a dynamic that is shared with the outside world—one that Simmel, quite simply it seems at first sight, identifies with the "dynamic of life" (*Dynamik des Lebens*) or the principle of change that is at work in the universe as such. "Rodin's beings are delivered from within to this [dynamic of life], they are to their very core overpowered by something that one surely cannot call external, little as [one can call] the wind external to the particle of air that is carried by it—since the movement of particles of air is precisely what constitutes 'wind'" (*GSG 14*, 344).[8] However, in this attempt to reconcile the modern condition of mobility and change with the aspiration to express something absolute, one important element is lost: human individuality. As we know from the previous chapter, the expression of a truly individualized life is the one thing that shields Rembrandt's art from the concomitant realization that the realm of history, in which such a truly individualized life is lived out, is cut off from anything essential or absolute. Rembrandt, it seems, brings history pure and proper on stage for the first time, exposing it in all its vicissitudes and contingencies; his portraits, however, remain standing proof of the "soulful life of the sitter." In reaching for the absolute, Rodin's works cannot but shatter this final vestige of the individual's internal unity and coherence. Lifting the veil of the absolute as an ontological dynamic of change, Rodin simultaneously uncovers its *indifference* to the fate of a singular human being. For this reason, the heteronomy of Rodin's works (their being delivered to the flux of life as such) prevents them from expressing anything that can still be described as individualized: "All of Rembrandt's people still . . . [retain] something essentially self-assured, while Rodin's people are overcome [*aufgelöst*]—and this indeed by something more overpowering than a merely personal fate, rather [by] an adversity of existence [*einem Verhängnis des Daseins*] which fills up space as such, and with this [their] own space, [an adversity, which] has thus also become their own" (*GSG 14*, 343; see also *GSG 12*, 35).[9] Rodin's figures, as a consequence, do not make visible a personalized existence built up in dialogue with life's infinities: they are, instead, *overpowered* by these infinities and they have thereby shed everything that can be properly called individualized. Rodin breaks away from an "ideal of individuality" (*Individualitätsideal*), from "a well-circumscribed personality," and from "an established, persistent kernel or contour that has been withdrawn from what is in flux" (*GSG 14*, 344).[10] In this manner, Simmel suggests that Rodin counters the evolution that was noticeable from Michelangelo to Rembrandt, that is, the attempt to express how an individuated (Michelangelo) or individualized (Rembrandt) life arises from an otherwise anonymous and nonhuman realm, be it the materiality of the stone (Michelangelo) or the dark background in a portrait (Rembrandt). Rodin's figures, on the contrary, are neither experienced as always-already-having-freed-themselves from the material out of which they arise (Michelangelo), nor as forever-still-in-the-process-of-freeing-themselves from such an overarching and alien realm (Rembrandt's late portraits), but they are to a certain extent visibly *succumbing* to it and *vanishing* along with it. Simmel emphasizes that Rodin's works appear "incomplete" (*unvollendet*) and that his figures are "still hidden in stone" (*GSG 7*, 99–100) and states the following: "Rodin often leaves the figure partly embraced [by stone] [and] its lifting itself from the stone is the direct materialization of *becoming*, which now makes up the essence of his work. Each figure is caught at a station on an infinite road through which it passes without delay, often at such an early [station] that it protrudes from the block [of stone] with contours that are hardly recognizable as such" (*GSG 14*, 337).[11]

Because Rodin's figures are always to a certain degree lacking in both individuation and individualization, the human body is neither depicted as a particularity (*ein Einzelne*), that is, as deriving its individuation from an internalized, "super-individual lawfulness," nor as a singularity (*ein Einzige*), that is, as deriving its individualization from the relation between an inner-I and the many, external fates it has visibly undergone. For this reason, one could argue that Rodin presents the human body as a "dividual" (*dividuel*). Following up on Brecht's suggestions, the concept of dividuality was coined by Deleuze in the essay "Postscript on the Societies of Control" (1990) and describes human beings as caught up in a continuous stream of modulation and exposed to an unceasing movement of variation and control.[12] In contrast to an *in*dividual, therefore, a dividual can no longer properly be considered as meaningful in its own right. Lacking a unity of its own, a dividual is, to use once again a Deleuzean concept, to be likened to a "plane" in which differential relationships play themselves out. In Simmel's view, likewise, Rodin strives for the "dissolution of the fixed contents in the fleeting element of the soul, from which all substance has been filtered out, and whose forms are nothing but forms of movement" (*GSG 12*, 35).[13] As dividuals, Rodin's works bring together a variety of elements that are seemingly unrelated. They are divisible to the core and invite the spectator's gaze to share in the expressed movement by mentally splitting up different parts that are forever released from an encompassing totality.[14] Embodying movement and change, they prevent his gaze from finding rest in an overarching sense of wholeness and they exemplify an uninterrupted dynamic of becoming-other.

Three concepts are illustrative of the dividual nature of Rodin's works: the surface, the fragment, and the gesture. That Rodin's works manage to make the surface (*Oberflach*) operational is the most telling point in this regard because a surface cannot in actuality be more than a mere interface or "shared space" that connects things that have otherwise nothing in common. A surface, that is, has meaning only by virtue of its capacity to relate various elements to each other and inevitably introduces multiplicity into one's experience. In Rodin's work, however, surfaces *do* stand on their own. In Simmel's view, Rodin's genius consists in turning the surface itself into an artwork, thereby endowing it with a unity it cannot possibly have otherwise and giving it, as an artwork, the status of a monad. Rodin "has introduced a new criterion of movement within the figure" and this by making use of "a new flexibility of the joints, a new autonomy and vibration of surfaces, . . . a new expression of the zones of contact between two bodies or of one body in itself, . . . a new utilization of light [and] a new way of the surfaces to collide with each other, to compete or to flow together." This mobility is

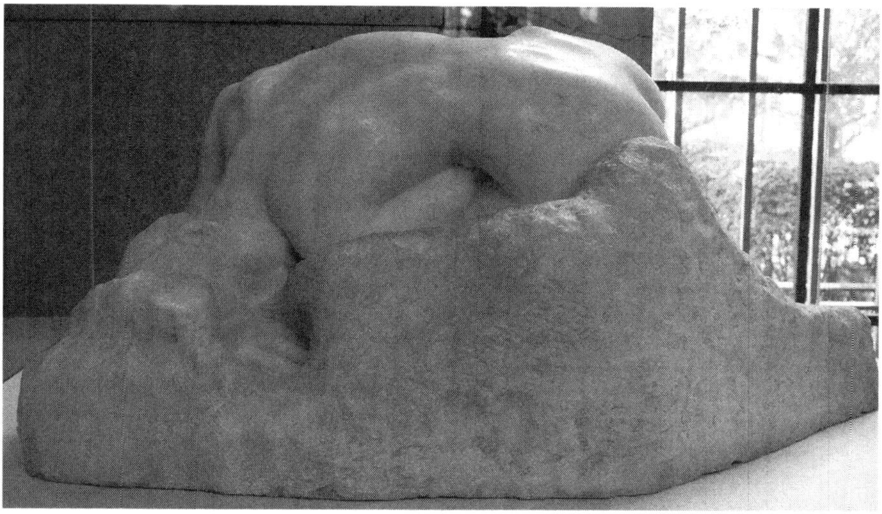

Figure 9. Auguste Rodin, *Danaïd*. Conceived 1886, carved before 1902. Philadelphia, Rodin Museum.

believed to "bring to expression the internal vitality of the human being in its totality, with all feeling, thinking, and experiencing," and this "in a more complete manner than had been possible so far" (*GSG 12*, 31).[15] The surface-become-artwork, as a consequence, ties together multiplicity and change into one indivisible unity.[16] In Rodin's *Danaïd* (1886; figure 9), for instance, the female figure's face does not indeed directly confront the spectator's gaze and partly disappears into the stone, while her back, strangely enough, is stretched in such a manner that it becomes visible as a front. No longer merely referring to the part of a human body that is usually covered up, the figure's back is turned into a screen-like surface that catches the play of shadow and light and, in the smoothness of its swells and curves, almost looks like a dynamic landscape of hills and valleys. Simmel, therefore, argues that Rodin has endowed the entire body with the infinite mobility that is usually only reserved for the human face (*GSG 12*, 35). As we have seen, the face is for Simmel that part of the human body which is most mobile and energetic, holding movement spellbound in a form of individualized and internal unity.[17] In Rodin's works, however, the human face has lost its individual expressivity, whereas entire bodies are being animated with such a restlessness. "The faces of [Rodin's] figures," writes Simmel, "are often little developed and [hardly] individualized, and all soulful mobility, . . . which otherwise found the site of its externalization in the face, will become apparent in the bending and stretching of the body." As such, entire bodies are animated with the uncanny movements of "shivers and shudders that run over . . . surfaces" and "vibrations translat[ing] into . . . curves and jumps" (*GSG 12*, 35).[18]

The fragment (*Teil*) is a second component that forms an integral part of Rodin's artistic vocabulary. Rodin's oeuvre famously contains armless bodies and limbs that have been severed from their bodies. In Simmel's view, Rodin was interested in "the twist or bend of whichever member [of the body]; a certain rotation of the hip, a raised arm, the angle of a joint—and this part alone he accentuates and holds fast in its movement without the rest of the body" (*GSG 14*, 339).[19] The fragment is to be considered a dividual because, like the surface, it cannot in its actual existence be taken for a whole in itself, remaining essentially incomplete as long as it is disconnected from the unity to which it naturally belongs. A body without arms, for instance, is in ordinary experience perceived as *mutilated* and a hand inevitably dies if it is no longer fed by a body. The fragments in Rodin's works, however, are no merely incomplete entities since they have taken on an added and entirely novel layer of meaning precisely *as* fragments. Simmel puts it as follows: "The movement has constructed a body of its own" (*Die Bewegung hat sich ihren Leib gebaut*) (*GSG 12*, 32).[20] While they would be radically incomplete as an actual object, in other words, these fragments *do* stand fully on their own as *artworks*. Rodin's *Walking Man* (1877–78; figure 10), for instance, is marked by the pride of his stride in spite of the fact that he does not even have a head.[21] Moreover, the mobility that is expressed in this mutilated body does not differ in any way from the mobility that is rendered in Rodin's *St. John the Baptist* (1878–80), whose body-cum-head is the complete(d) version of the *Walking Man*. When Rodin presents us with fragments-become-artworks, as Rilke puts it, "nothing necessary is lacking. One stands before them as before something whole. The feeling of incompleteness does not rise from the mere aspect of a thing, but from the assumption of a narrow-minded pedantry, which says that arms are a necessary part of the body and that a body without arms cannot be perfect."[22]

Third, Simmel opposes the concept of bodily gesture (*Geste, Gebar*) and its mobility to the "non-changing form of bodily appearance" (*nicht ändernde Form der Körpererscheinung*) in Renaissance sculpture. From this perspective, gestures are "vague—because they cannot be described with timeless *concepts*." Nevertheless, these same gestures are "completely determined [*bestimmt*] and vivid [*klar*] from the perspective of the feeling that accompanies their flux. Of course, they only show one moment, but this moment is the totality, the totality of fate" (*GSG 14*, 340).[23] Like the surface and the fragment, a gesture is a dividual because it briefly pauses a homogeneous context of meaning and subsequently crystallizes it into a non-anticipatable and highly charged meeting point of seemingly unrelated elements. Rodin's artistic expression of gestures, in fact, is to time what his rendering of the surface is to space. In a gesture, the entirety of a series of clearly distinct moments is monadically contracted and perceived as one inseparable continuity. Rodin

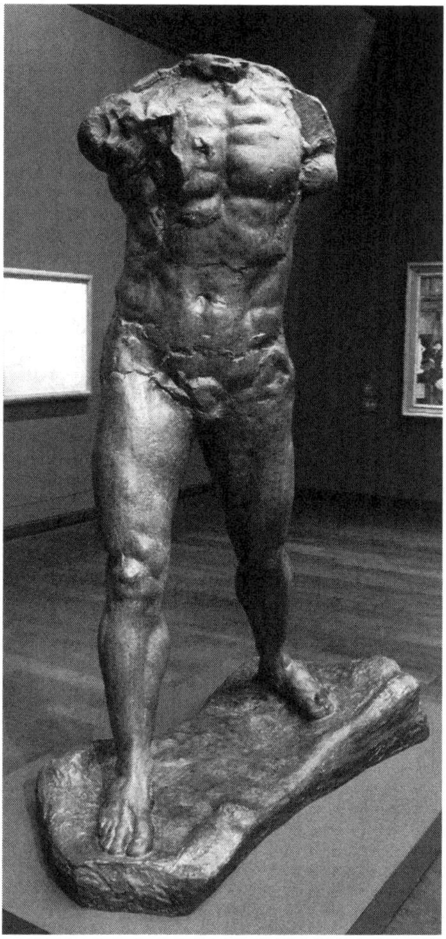

Figure 10. Auguste Rodin, *Walking Man*. 1877–78. Paris, Musée d'Orsay.

knows how "to unconsciously and without hesitation extend a specific gesture" and to "fashion for it the body that belongs to it" (*GSG 12*, 32). Describing the raised arm in Rodin's aptly named *The Man of Primal Times: The Age of Bronze* (1875–77; figure 11), Rilke is helpful in further elucidating Simmel's intuitions. "That gesture which grew and developed to such greatness and power, here bursts forth like a spring that softly ripples over this body. It awakens in the darkness of primal times and in its growth seems to flow through the breadth of this work as though reaching out from bygone centuries to those that are to come."[24] Unlike linguistic signs, gestures bring a material presence into play and they are visibly embodied. In Simmel's and Rilke's view, gesture has the ability to suddenly re-enliven a body that was,

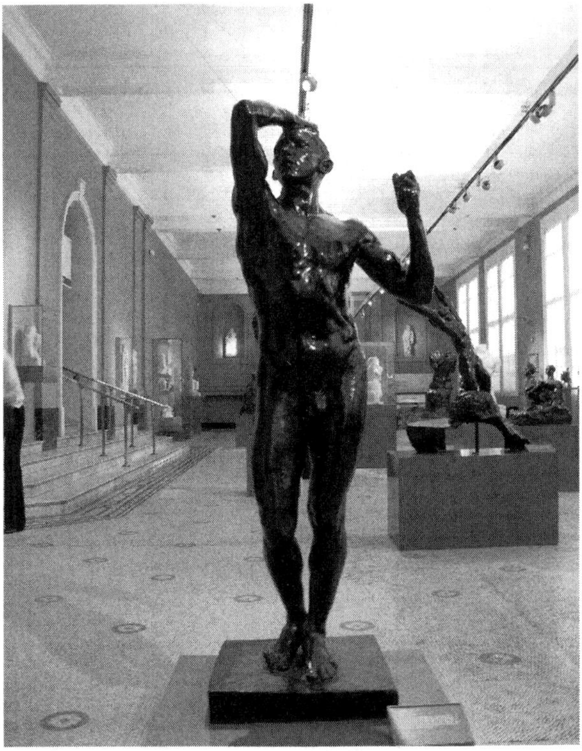

Figure 11. Auguste Rodin, *The Man of Primal Times: The Age of Bronze.* 1875–77. London, Victoria and Albert Museum.

a brief moment before, still experienced as having grown old and weary: it sets the stage for a movement that takes place in spite of a general sense of entropy. Rilke again: "Hesitatingly [gesture] unfolds itself in the lifted arms. These arms are still so heavy that the hand of one rests upon the top of the head. But this hand is roused from its sleep, it concentrates itself quite high on the top of the brain where it lies solitary. It [is] prepared for the work of centuries, a work that has no measure and no end. And the right foot stands expectant with a first step."[25] Simmel emphasizes that the dynamic of the gesture is opposed to that of the "fertile moment" (*fruchtbare Moment*) (*GSG 14*, 340). For while the latter is the apex of a teleological movement that gives meaning to some of the movements that have either built up to it or will follow from it, gesture is here believed to restore the continuous renewal of the All and this through a sudden, short, moment of interruption. Gesture, in this sense, briefly suspends a general movement but not without then restoring its ultimate dynamic of change. It lacks the slow "building up" (*Zuspitzung*) of the fertile moment but expresses the foundational capacity of life to always renew itself. While "in the fertile moment there is always but 'a lot,' in Rodin's gesture, there is 'everything'" (*GSG*, 14, 340).[26]

In Simmel's view, Rodin lets go of the idea that the life of a human being can be glimpsed as one unique and indivisible or soulful unity, but he replaces this ideal with the purpose of capturing the great movement of the All. Picking up the thread that he follows in the Rembrandt book, Simmel repeats in his essay on Rodin that "Rembrandt's people lack what one can call [the] cosmic. On their faces, the stations of this one trajectory of life [*dieses einen Lebensweges*] have been layered [*abgelagert*], from the starting point on, and they are fashioned [*gebildet*] out of this unity of their internal life. But the adversities, the obscurities and joys which encompass a particular soul as the metaphysics of Being as such [*das Metaphysische des Seins überhaupt*], as the ground of things as such [*der Grund der Dinge überhaupt*]—[these] do not resonate from these people" (*GSG 14*, 343).[27] Rodin's work, on the contrary, confronts these "adversities, obscurities and joys" head-on and it does not shrink before these ontological foundations. The "specifically Germanic concept of individuality" may be entirely foreign to him, but what he loses on that end is won on a plane that can only be called "cosmic": "He takes the lifeline of his figures in the direction and to a level that one can call cosmic" (*GSG 14*, 343).[28]

Rodin's most famous work, *The Thinker* (1880; figure 12), is illustrative of Simmel's argument. This work can indeed be interpreted as the expression of a cosmic and metaphysical dimension, albeit not in the merely universalized and idealized manner that is characteristic of the classicist approach of the Renaissance. Rodin's *Thinker* is distinctly *not* the man entirely made of muscle who is seemingly untouched by all that goes on around him. His is not the proud and autonomous existence of Michelangelo's men of action who seem to know at all times how to mold the stuff of the world into the material of their will. *The Thinker*'s life, however, is no less distinct from that of Rembrandt's individuals whose modest existence is all face and gaze and bears witness to the many intimate fates a single human being undergoes throughout his life. Like many of Rodin's other figures, *The Thinker* has seemingly retreated from the world, curling up inside himself and bearing no visible traces of a private life or a unique and personal history. Rodin's *Thinker* lacks both the "closure" (*Geschlossenheit*) of Michelangelo's figures *and* the "non-closure" (*Unabgeschlossenheit*) of Rembrandt's sitters. As a consequence, his manner of existing is presented as neither merely active nor purely *re*active. *The Thinker*, rather, is *un*involved with the space around him, and the seeming immobility of the thinking gesture indicates an interruption of the sensory-motor continuity that would allow for a practical orientation and a normal condition of being-in-the-world. It would be a mistake, however, to consider this thinking stance as mere passivity. For all its apparent immobility, that is, Rodin's *Thinker* is a highly dynamic work, bristling to the highest degree with an energy that is foreign to both the proud voluntarism

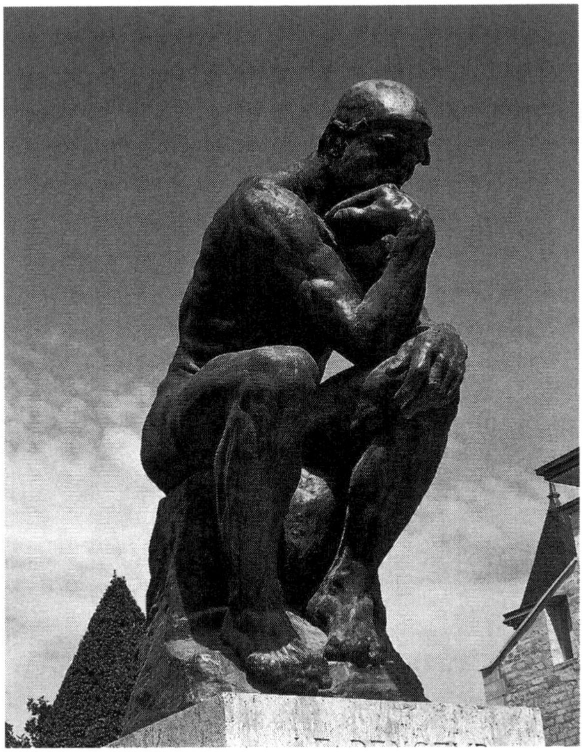

Figure 12. Auguste Rodin, *The Thinker*. 1880. Paris, Musée Rodin.

of Michelangelo's figures and the intimate contemplation of Rembrandt's sitters.[29] For Rodin's *Thinker* is an Atlas of the mind: if he seems disconnected from the world, this is not because it seems insignificant to him but, to the contrary, because it has taken on such urgency that he seeks to conjure the universe *in its entirety*. *The Thinker*, Rodin seems to suggest, has retreated from his immediate surroundings because he wants to re-create the world, *in its totality* and *as a mental object*. The metaphysical or cosmic dimension that Simmel deems crucial to Rodin's work is visible in *The Thinker* to the extent that he is perceived neither as reflecting on anything in particular nor as solipsistically contemplating his own private existence: he appears engaged, rather, in a mental activity that seeks to include nothing less than the unity of the entire world. Therefore, disrupting the action schema that underlies and orients our ordinary being-in-the-world does not in this case indicate a form of disengagement, but rather points to the grandiose attempt to bring the faculty of thinking to its utmost capability. The retreat from the world as a material object has here become the sign that one seeks to create it anew by modifying it into a unified object of thought.

Contingency and Generality

In Simmel's oeuvre at large, most notably in essays like "The Tragedy of Culture," "The Crisis of Culture," and "The Metropolis and Mental Life" and in the book *The Philosophy of Money*, the modern condition is understood as one in which human beings increasingly identify with values that are abstract, anonymous, and apathetic to the individual. Money, for instance, is at once the "equivalent for everything and anything, . . . pull[ing] the highest thing down to the level of the lowest" *and* the main driving force behind the lives of a great many individuals.[30] Likewise, the metropolis is the site of an "indifferen(ce) to all genuine individuality," yet it motivates the individual to consciously reflect on his manner of existence.[31] The same duality between anonymity and individualization underlies Simmel's concept of movement in the essays on Rodin. For Simmel, Rodin's works are modern because they explore mobility and restlessness as fundamental to both life *as such* and to *modern* life pure and proper. Rodin's work is believed to discover movement at once as an indifferent element of reality as such *and* as "the general term [*Generalnenner*] for the human body and soul": "for no other determination of our being [*Bestimmung unseres Seins*] is shared [*gemeinsam*] by body and soul" (*GSG 14*, 337). In going beyond what is unique and irreplaceable to one singular individual, Rodin manages to simultaneously express the flux of life in general and "the modern soul, which is so much more unstable in its moods . . . and thus much more attuned to the 'factor of mobility' [*Bewegungselement*] than the soul of Renaissance people" (*GSG 12*, 31).[32]

A first consequence of this ability is that, for Rodin, the visibility of the Heraclitic and indifferent flux of life itself is not at all antithetical to an expression of the grand themes of human existence. In Simmel's view, Rodin underscores how modern individuals are prone to experiencing even their most intimate emotions as not truly "their own": "In Rodin, it is love *as such*, despair *as such*, contemplation *as such*, which become fateful for the individual as a cosmic dynamic [*kosmische Dynamik*]—not as a universal concept [*Allgemeinbegriff*], as in classicism, which allegorized the figure, but as unmediated life [*unmittelbares Leben*]." Simmel calls "Being" the "carrier" (*Träger*) of this cosmic flux and states that its "heartbeat" (*Pulsschlag*) is also that "of the individual" (*GSG 14*, 343–44, my emphasis).[33] In thus breaking down the barriers of the inner-I, one could therefore argue, Rodin's works have replaced the self-aggrandizing appeal to what is *universal* by a self-diminishing sensibility for what is merely *general*: in contrast to the Renaissance individual, the modern individual does not any longer encounter the awareness that certain characteristics are potentially shared by all human beings as an uplifting experience, since this is difficult to square with his longing for a sense of individual uniqueness and irreplaceability (see also *GSG 7*, 93). In Simmel's view, modern man does not any longer recognize types and essences as individuating forces since they are but reminders of a numbing sense of sameness and overall replaceability. In the metropolis, for instance, the increased identification with types indicates a *lack* of singularity and the *foreclosure* of universal ideals. Here, as Simmel puts it in his essay on metropolitan existence, "life is composed more and more of . . . impersonal contents and offerings which tend to displace the genuine personal colorations and incomparabilities" (*SoC*, 184).

For this very reason, however, Simmel argues that Rodin's works are charged with a sense of openness that can have a redemptive effect.[34] Simmel differentiates Rodin's figures from the ones sculpted by Michelangelo and portrayed by Rembrandt because both of the latter, as we have seen, radiate with a sense of internal necessity. "With regard to the bodies of Michelangelo," writes Simmel, "one does not at all get the idea that they could also move differently; and vice versa, the progress of the soul, so to speak the formula that is spelled out by the movement, cannot have another subject than this [specific] body" (*GSG 14*, 336).[35] Similarly, in Rembrandt "one feels the necessity with which all parts belong together, an organic growth, with an internal determination that excludes all contingency" (*GSG 7*, 94).[36] On account of their "generality" and lack of both individuation and individualization, Rodin's figures remain outside of this space that is "beyond contingency" (*jenseits des Zufalles*) and, rather than expressing a tragic "incapacity of being different" (*Nichtandersseinkönnen*), they make a show of not-yet-having-found-their-definitive-form: "The specific Fate, which is for Michelangelo something definitive [is for Rodin] rather a point of transition for a journey that comes from the indeterminate and continues into the indeterminate." According to Simmel, Rodin "loves roads/methods [*Wege*] without destinations/goals [*Ziele*] and destinations/goals without roads/methods" (*GSG 12*, 34; see also *GSG 7*, 100).[37] The perception that Rodin's works could just as well have turned out completely different casts light on the final phrase of two of Simmel's essays on Rodin. "To the extent that he allows us to experience our most profound life once again in the context of art, he redeems [*erlöst*] us precisely from how we live through it in the context of [actual] existence" (*GSG 12*, 36, and *GSG 14*, 348).[38] Simmel suggests that Rodin's endeavor to re-create the actual world in and as art introduces a fundamental sense of contingency into his work since it puts on display that nothing from what is captured by the artwork can claim a "final" and "definitive" value. In Rodin's work, it appears, the mere fact that something can be repeated as an artwork brings it down to the level of the historical and, as such, exposes it as belonging to a realm in which no meaning can be rendered fully complete. In Simmel's view, Rodin understands that none of the fates that a human being undergoes in his life can be considered all-determining since his existence is played out in a sphere of ongoing change and unceasing modification. Simmel takes this experience of contingency to be a redemptive one because it restores a sense of continuity to what would otherwise remain fragmented: in Rodin's oeuvre even the cut-off hands or armless bodies are animated by a dynamic of renewal that has not yet fully exhausted itself. The act of artistically re-producing a seemingly random part of the actual world safely delivers it back to the flux of life, and this return is believed to recover an irreducible potential for change and internal rejuvenation. In such works, "movement . . . serves the *expression* in the most perfect manner" (*GSG 12*, 31).[39] Rodin "goes along the path toward a novel monumentality—the [monumentality] of becoming, of mobility" and knows how to "give movement a non-temporal significance" (*GSG 14*, 340 and 339).[40]

Coda: *The Burghers of Calais*

Nowhere in his essays does Simmel mention Rodin's monumental group sculpture *The Burghers of Calais* (1886–89; figure 13). Still, his conceptual framework proves most fitting in the context of an interpretation of this group sculpture. The story, as recounted by the medieval chronicler Jean Froissart, is well known. Besieged by the English king Edward III in 1347, and in response to dire circumstances and extreme starvation, the city of Calais is finally forced to negotiate the terms of its surrender to the besieging English troops. Ultimately the English king consents to spare the city's inhabitants on the condition that six of its most notable burghers leave the city and turn themselves in to him bareheaded, dressed in nothing but a shirt, with ropes dangling about their necks and the keys to the city and citadel in their hands. The bells are rung, the citizens assemble in the marketplace, and six of the most important and wealthy men step forward and prepare themselves for the worst. They reach the king's camp and are lined up beside the executioner until, at the very last moment, the king's wife intervenes on their behalf and the decision is made to spare their lives. "The king listened to his wife," writes Froissart, "because she was very pregnant."[41] One of the first things that one notices in Rodin's group of figures is that, in spite of their heroic and tragic character, the citizens of Calais do not share in the absolute ideals of pride and courage that are represented by Michelangelo's figures. Though equally caught up in a "struggle without any chance of victory," these citizens are no supermen and, unlike Michelangelo's heroes, their physical presence in space lacks the autonomy and solidity of bodies that visibly merge with abstract values and principles. To be sure, ideals like decisiveness and defiance are clearly expressed in Rodin's *Burghers of Calais* but, contrary to what can be perceived in, for instance, Michelangelo's slave series, these qualities are in no way the outcome of a fundamental ability to set oneself apart and to retain a sense of invulnerability even in the face of the most severe hardship. Rodin's burghers, rather, carry the instrument of their execution already around their necks and they express their resoluteness only by way of a meaningful tension with something they cannot possibly overpower. There is no doubt in their minds that they are walking to their death and all hope

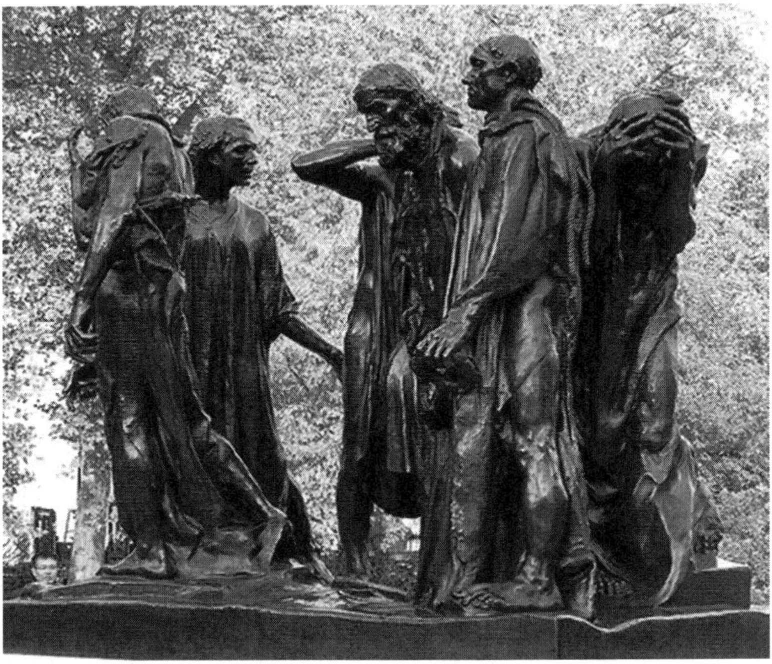

Figure 13. Auguste Rodin, *The Burghers of Calais*. 1886–89. London, Victoria Tower Gardens.

has visibly disappeared from their limbs. As such, insurmountable opposition forms an integral part of the moment of resignation. Their decisiveness and mental strength are felt to be all the more exceptional because it is made visible in the heaviness of their steps, the weight of their dangling arms, and the vulnerability of the exposed veins under their skin. These burghers do not simply bow down in the face of the king's command. Their bodies do manage to extract themselves from a sense of all-encompassing entropy, but they are deprived of all idealization and they are worn out through and through. In a line that Simmel quotes at the end of his essay, something similar is described as follows: "It's Michelangelo with three more centuries of misery" (*C'est Michelange avec trois siècles de misère de plus*) (*GSG 14*, 348).[42]

Compared to Rembrandt's group portraits, Rodin's six burghers of Calais have visibly dispensed with the dynamic of individualization. Rembrandt's large painting *The Nightwatch* (1642; figure 14), for instance, manages to rework a series of individuals with unique personalities of their own into a novel, deeply felt, and internally supported totality: radiating from this work is the decision, freely taken by each of the depicted individuals, to engage in collective action. Aptly called a "group portrait," *The Nightwatch* brings the various men together in the framed space of the painting and thus captures

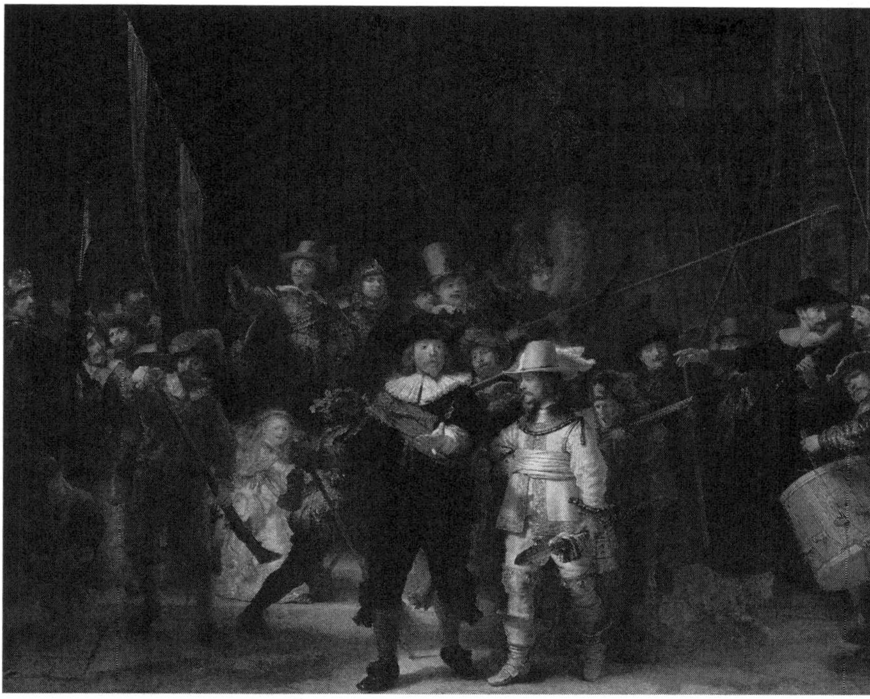

Figure 14. Rembrandt, *The Nightwatch*. 1642. Amsterdam, Rijksmuseum.

both the singular and irreplaceable nature of each of the depicted individuals *and* the newly created community that embodies a shared sense of belonging. In Simmel's view, *The Nightwatch* testifies to "the old Germanic drive toward a unity that . . . can only be realized through the individual bearers" and to a "unity [that is] . . . not to be abstracted from the painting" (*R*, 47 and *R*, 43).[43] In *The Burghers of Calais*, however, none of the men is grasped as an individual with a unique personality of his own, and their teaming up together does not at all embody an internalized sense of communal belonging.[44] As Geoff Dyer notes, "for all its grandeur there is a persistent sense of futility about the whole scene."[45] Making use of the limits of the medium of sculpture in a succinctly expressive manner, Rodin presents six human figures that, despite their making up a group, prevent the construction of a shared and enclosed realm. The outside world will always visibly intrude within the group and a spatial interval cannot but, to a degree, isolate these various figures from each other.[46] The outcome is that *The Burghers of Calais* exposes the most un-Rembrandtian sentiment imaginable: the *in*ability of the men to fully identify with their fate. No choice or decision on their part gives them the power to make their destiny truly their own. Rodin's men, as a consequence, are shown as having been condemned to each other's company against their will. The brutal command of the foreign and conquering king is expressed as an external violence that is wholly antithetical to their sense of selfhood.

The Burghers of Calais introduces a puzzling sense of openness into a realm that is nevertheless experienced as fully determined in both space and time. It presents a historical fact as something that has, however strange it may sound, not entirely run its course, for the disjointed gestures and the awkward movements embody a dynamic of meaning that is radically unfulfilled. These figures neither represent ideals that are always already complete on their own, nor do they express irreplaceable and unique lives that will forever remain internally unified, but, on the contrary, they expose a fundamental inability to find closure. In Dyer's words, "what Rodin depicted in the Burghers was the birth of a specifically modern *form* of despair: . . . the knowledge that one's life might not be capable of generating its own capacity for redemption."[47] It is on this level that we can understand Simmel's suggestion that the power of redemption entails the capacity to "relive," in and through *art*, what has, in and as actual reality, irredeemably occurred. The artwork is redemptive as the materialization of a "yet again" (*noch einmal*) and to the extent that it manages to save a unique moment of the past from its inevitably having already passed. It repeats what cannot in fact be repeated, and the artwork thus actively restores a force of duration and continuity that the simply actual cannot in any way bring about on its own. As such, laying bare the inability of what is a mere given to find fulfillment on its own, it simultaneously testifies to the power of what can only be constructed: nowhere but in the immobility of the artwork, the course of time is kept open and, though no faith in any super-individual ideal or internally completed life survives this re-production, it does firmly restore the belief that the closure of the past can be won over by an act of human thought, imagination, and creation. In Simmel's view, Rodin "has in principle discovered the *artistic* timelessness of pure movement" (*die künstlerische Zeitlosigkeit der reinen Bewegung*) and his work is marked by what "conceptually speaking" is a "paradox": he "seeks the impression of the supra-momentary [*die Impression des Übermomentanen*], the timeless impression" (*GSG 14*, 339 and 340, my emphasis). Rodin shows the moment in which six men set off to march toward their death but it seems that, in holding this moment spellbound, the work of art arrests their movements and prevents them from acquiring completion. In a manner that is not simply derived from the awareness that, in the final moment, the king reconsidered and allowed these men to live, Rodin's reworking of Froissart's historical account introduces a principle of indetermination to enter into the men's resignation. It is, one could say, one thing to say that these men are represented as leaving the city, but an altogether different one to say that they are expressed as having ever really arrived at the place of their execution. Even though they represent first and foremost the necessity that forces these men on their way, the constitutive openness of these works allows them to simultaneously express the possibility that, in spite of all the indications to the contrary, their deaths might ultimately have been averted.

Finally, the title of Rodin's group sculpture is very relevant and accurate in this regard. For the concepts "burgher" (*bourgeois*) and "citizen" belong to the sphere of culture and not to that of nature. They belong to a category that needs to be created again and again and that can never be simply considered as a given. As noted by many political thinkers, one is never *born* as a citizen and can only *become* one by way of a set of criteria and conditions that form an integral part of a historically and socially determined, political negotiation.[48] The six men in Rodin's sculpture do indeed suffer as members of a community that can never be considered as an internally completed and enclosed unity. Rodin's men act neither as individuals nor in the name of the overarching and naturalized class of "humanity as such." As Rilke puts it, Rodin "concentrated . . . a hundred [men] into six."[49] As a consequence, these six lives are, as it were, stuck in the realm of the merely general, that is, isolated from both the level of the singular and the universal. As such they are never reducible to a handful of historical individuals, nor do they exemplify the power of "mankind at large." It is only in this manner that Rodin's work touches upon what seems to be its most "metaphysical" and "cosmic" layer of meaning. *The Burghers of Calais* expresses not just despair and resignation, exhaustion and resolution but, first and foremost, human dignity. Moreover, human dignity is here expressed as inseparable from a fundamental openness. It is neither a mere given belonging to the individual as individual nor an inalienable quality of the person as a member of the human species. In expressing the redemptive openness of a "yet again," *The Burghers of Calais* manages to capture human dignity not as a quality that always already belongs to human beings, but as something that is forever to be constructed. Rather than something that one always already possesses, Rodin seems to suggest, human dignity is something that one forever needs to receive.

Part II

✦

Walter Benjamin

Introduction

✦

Walter Benjamin and Georg Simmel

"A Duel That Is the Creative Process Itself"

In a letter to Theodor Adorno that is sent from Paris in February 1939, Benjamin states that it is "time [Simmel] got some respect as one of the ancestors of 'cultural Bolshevism' " (*SW* 4, 209). In the same manner that Rembrandt's religiosity can be regarded as a "*functional* a priori" that does not directly follow from any of his personal beliefs, the writings of both Simmel and Benjamin do indeed embody a Bolshevism that is not simply deducible from their political convictions.[1] Both are what one could call "masters of the minutiae."[2] Together with like-minded friends and disciples such as Ernst Bloch and Siegfried Kracauer, Simmel and Benjamin have established the novel way of looking at historical material that today receives the fairly accurate label of "microhistory." Based on the feeling that, as Benjamin puts it, "nothing that has ever happened should be regarded as lost to history," Simmel and Benjamin recast philosophical writing into a challenge and a promise at once (*SW* 4, 390). Aiming both to reveal *and* redeem some of reality's shortcomings, Simmel and Benjamin practice philosophy, as it were, *against the grain*, injecting the master narrative of victors and legislators with the "minor literature" (Deleuze and Guattari) that talks about what has seemingly been forgotten or, in some cases, deliberately been left out. "In the superficial and transient," Simmel therefore writes in 1896, "the essence and significance of things [*das Wesen und die Bedeutung der Dinge*] come to the front" (*GSG* 5, 198). "In any case," Benjamin adds forty years later, "the eternal is far more the ruffle on a dress than some idea" (*AP*, 463).[3] However, in spite of all the talk about the *modernist* predecessors of *post*modernist thought, it is important to differentiate Simmel and Benjamin's project from the ambition to dispel with the need for overarching political and social ideals and to deconstruct concepts like truth and reality. Simmel and Benjamin both emphasize that the interest in the accidental and the inessential indicates a wish to retrieve a kernel of the absolute and not at all a drive to dismiss the longing for an experience of truth altogether. In this regard, Simmel's short pieces for the journal *Jugend* should be read alongside, for instance,

Benjamin's stories for the radio. Likewise, Benjamin's views on the interior, children's toys, or the ragpicker are the successors of Simmel's remarks about the façade, the handle, or the prostitute. Both are convinced that "the essential task of philosophy [is] to lower a plumb line through the immediate singular" (Simmel, *R*, 3) and that, for this reason, a "resolute refusal of the concept of 'timeless truth' is in order" (Benjamin, *AP*, 463). Both share an affinity for the restlessness of modern life and the contemporary infatuation with novelty. Both are avid collectors. Both are fascinated by fashion and, as we will see in a moment, metropolitan existence.[4] And finally, both are inspired by the capacities of philosophical thinking to construct *Momentbilder* (snapshots, Simmel) or *Denkbilder* (thought-images, Benjamin) that salvage truth from within what has seemingly shed all importance. As Simmel puts it, "in the most irrelevant [*das Gleichgiltigste*], in what is in its isolated appearance banal or repulsive to us, nothing more than a deep and loving concentration is required to encounter this too as the beam and word of the ultimate unity of all things" (*GSG 5*, 198).

This persistent interest in the precarious and seemingly insignificant will largely spare Simmel from the sad fate that awaits some of the other philosophers of life. The ideas of not a few among the thinkers who emphasize the continuity and flux of life will be used, with or without their consent, to legitimize the inflated metaphysics behind fascist ideology and rhetoric.[5] The work of Simmel's contemporary Ludwig Klages (1872–1956), to give but one example, builds on the reactionary view that one is to translate nature's supposed capacity for immanent renewal directly into cultural forms. In his view, natural movement or rhythm (*Rhythmus*) is deeply significant in that it brings about change in an entirely spontaneous manner. As a consequence, it should be the aim of art (and politics) to recuperate this pure but irrational dynamic of nature since this is believed to align human life with the great movement of the All.[6] Simmel's foundational distinction between the "physiological" regeneration of nature ("more life") on the one hand and the constructs and forms of culture ("more-*than*-life") on the other depletes nature and natural movement of such a supposed purity. While marking life as such with an infinite capacity for variation, Simmel nevertheless argues that the creation of meaning is not indicative of a "primal phenomenon" (*Urphänomen*) since it requires a prior moment in which nature is *modified* (*umgebaut*) by man.[7] Simmel thereby charges culture with an openness that is at odds with the inner necessity of natural laws. For him, meaning is never simply "found" but is forever to be *constructed*. His ideas, therefore, run counter to the reactionary naturalization or essentialization of cultural, historical, and, for that matter, political formations. In Simmel's view, cultural forms, constructs, and images are expressions of "human freedom" for the very reason that they could always also have been different (*VoL*, 60). They will never fully share in the supposed purity of what is a mere given and cannot recover the ultimate harmony of the natural. Moreover, as we have seen,

Simmel considers life to be a nonstop force of change that will inevitably bring down the very cultural artifacts that make life meaningful in the first place. For this reason as well, a "tragedy," "conflict," or "crisis" of culture is in his view inherent in the very concept of culture and makes it unfit to carry lofty associations with eternal values or fated meanings.

In spite of such philosophical nuances and subtleties, none of his best-known students will manage to digest the ontological foundation that underlies Simmel's *Lebensphilosophie*. The list of authors who have expressed an intellectual debt to Simmel reads as the compiled canon of Weimar philosophy. Ernst Bloch, Georg Lukács, Karl Mannheim, Max Horkheimer, Siegfried Kracauer, Theodor Adorno, and Walter Benjamin are but a handful of the prominent authors who have absorbed some of Simmel's insights on culture and life. However, without a single exception, all of these authors take issue with Simmel's self-professed "attempt . . . to construct a new storey beneath historical materialism" by diving head first into its "metaphysical preconditions" (*PhoM*, 54). Bloch, for instance, writes that "Simmel has the finest mind of all contemporaries. But beyond this, he is wholly empty and aimless, desiring everything except the truth."[8] In a similar vein, in spite of being influenced by Simmel's *Philosophy of Money* from an early stage on, Lukács criticizes him for failing to include a genuinely *historical* perspective in his analysis of capitalism. In Lukács's opinion, Simmel's interest in the capacity of life to continuously renew itself results in an inability to distinguish the pernicious manifestations of capitalism from "the timeless model of human relations in general."[9] Likewise, Mannheim highlights Simmel's "impressionism" and "aestheticism," noting the absence of "a constructive view of the whole of society," while Horkheimer points out that Simmel's "concept of life itself is cut off from history [*ein der Historie enthobener Begriff*] . . . [and] does not have a history but only creates it."[10] Even Siegfried Kracauer, the only member of Simmel's salon to have written a substantial study on his work, mentions that his "venture into the realm of the absolute met with failure" and takes him to task for crafting a philosophical framework that "gets lost in the infinite."[11]

Adorno joins the league of those who claim that Simmel conflates a genuinely *historical* analysis of societal and cultural elements with a *metaphysical* interest in life as such. In an essay from 1965, "The Handle, the Pot, and Early Experience," he will fill in the blanks of this widely shared criticism. In the text that Adorno focuses on, "The Handle," Simmel displays his talents as a miniaturist of things that are usually not deemed worthy of philosophical attention. Simmel zooms in on the fact that vases and vessels are both aesthetic entities *and* objects of use. In Simmel's mind, the vessel "stands in two worlds at one and the same time: whereas reality is completely irrelevant to the 'pure' work of art and, as it were, is consumed in it, reality does make claims upon the vase as an object that is handled, filled and emptied, proffered, and set down here and there."[12] In Simmel's mind, this dual nature sets apart both the handle and the spout of any given vessel. The handle and the spout of a vessel visibly determine its practical use, but they simultaneously play an important role in making it look beautiful. According to Simmel, it is vital that these two very different tasks are balanced out in such a manner that practical use and aesthetic value join in one dynamic unity. "When, in the appearance of the handle, one of its two functions is completely neglected in favor of the other," Simmel writes, "the impression made strikes a discordant note."[13] This balanced unity between practical and aesthetic qualities brings Simmel to the conclusion that a seemingly insignificant object like a vessel can in fact bring to expression the "unanalyzable secret of life."[14] The reconciliation of practical use and aesthetic value in a single vessel is to be understood as evidence of life's capacity to ceaselessly build up novel totalities from within otherwise distinct elements. While practical issues are seemingly unrelated to aesthetic ones, the subtlety and charm with which an ordinary object can nevertheless resolve this distinction provides proof of the existence of an underlying continuity of life. In Simmel's opinion, therefore, a simple vessel can establish what, in the essay on Rembrandt, was called the "openness" that marks a truly individualized or soulful existence: "While of course [the handle and spout of a vessel] serve as the enclosing boundaries of the vessel, they still connect it with the practical world. . . . It is like the relation of man as soul to existence outside him."[15] Far from being a mere object at hand, a beautiful vessel needs to be regarded as a soulful entity in its own right, animated by a more fundamental dynamic of unity and continuity. In Simmel's view, therefore, a vessel can restore a cherished contact between an individual and his surroundings, thereby allowing an unsuspected glimpse of the totality of life from within an otherwise unremarkable part. "With the handle the world approaches the vessel," writes Simmel, "with the spout the vessel reaches out into the world."[16]

The argument that underlies Adorno's criticism of Simmel's essay on the remarkable significance of a simple handle is vintage Adorno: Simmel is found guilty of a lack of mediation in that he "neutralize[s] [works of art] from the outset" and turns them into "objects of contemplative enjoyment."[17] What disappears from sight in such an analysis are, of course, the "moments of empirical reality" that "survive" in works of art or, translated into layman terms, the social and political world in which works of art are produced, reproduced, and consumed.[18] For this reason, Adorno reproaches Simmel for "platitudes" and "academic pedantry" and accuses him of presenting a thesis that is "undialectical," which to him is just about the most serious offense a thinker can possibly commit.[19] In focusing on abstract values like "use" and "beauty," Simmel's thought either "surround[s] . . . posh objects with simple categories or supplement[s] them with general reflections, without ever losing itself unreservedly in the material itself, as is required if knowledge is to be more than a self-satisfied spinning of the wheels of its preestablished apparatus."[20] Like Bloch, Lukács, Mannheim, Horkheimer, and Kracauer, Adorno thus attacks Simmel's "impoverished scaffolding of invariant fundamental concepts . . . such as form and life" and detects a "blindness to the aspects of the phenomenon that philosophy ought to redeem."[21] In Adorno's opinion, the recourse to concepts like "form" and "life" to describe the ultimate value of a given object is bound to fail because neither of them can be considered a simple given. As such, both remain cut off from what matters the most from Adorno's point of view: the discovery of hitherto undiscovered possibilities within the concrete material of reality. Simmel's descriptions of the balanced unity of practical and aesthetic issues, to the contrary, install a preference for what is harmonious, symmetrical, and always already adapted for easy use. Adorno seeks to replace a passive stance toward what is preestablished with an active quest for change. For this reason, he argues for an "immersion in the incommensurable aspects of the object" and the importance of discovering "anything about the human being that might be hidden from him, or anything he might not already know about the object."[22]

Any comparison between Simmel's and Benjamin's essays on the metropolis should include the recovery of a similarly critical stance against the obfuscation of societal issues by metaphysical ones. To be sure, the explicit reference to Simmel's ideas about big-city life in Benjamin's writings marks the locus classicus of the analysis of the relationship between both thinkers, and Benjamin has clearly absorbed some of Simmel's views. Nevertheless, while almost all commentators emphasize Benjamin's intellectual debt to Simmel, it is important to also bring out that both Benjamin's overall interest in the modern metropolis *and* the philosophical foundations of his views come from an altogether different place.[23]

The first line in Simmel's text sets the tone for the remainder of his analysis of metropolitan existence: "The deepest problems of modern life derive from the claim of the individual to preserve the autonomy and individuality of his existence in the face of overwhelming social forces, of historical heritage, of external culture, and of the technique of life" (*SoC*, 175). As is indicated in the title of his text, "The Metropolis and Mental/Spiritual Life [*Geistesleben*]," Simmel's understanding of metropolitan existence does not so much focus on the built environment of the city itself as on the life of its inhabitants. Simmel starts from the idea that human beings are "discriminating creature[s]" in that their perceptual and cognitive faculties are most intensely stimulated by experiences that are somehow different from what they had expected. However, metropolitan existence is marked by an enormous and potentially harmful amount of such experiences because it confronts individuals with an "*intensification of nervous stimulation*" (*SoC*, 175). For this reason, big-city life differs drastically from an existence in villages or smaller towns. "The metropolis," Simmel writes, "exacts from man as a discriminating creature a different amount of consciousness than does rural life" (*SoC*, 175). At this stage of the discussion, Simmel introduces the concept that will become the centerpiece of his intellectual heritage in modern sociology: the "protective organ" (*Schutzorgan*) which serves metropolitan man as a shield against "the threatening currents and discrepancies of his external environment which would uproot him" (*SoC*, 176). Because man is so easily prone to respond to stimuli, that is to say, it is vital that he learns to somehow cope with the metropolitan condition of *excess* stimulation.

Simmel describes three different attitudes that testify to this need to "preserve subjective life against the overwhelming power of metropolitan life" (*SoC*, 176).[24] The first one refers to the increased importance of the individual's intellectual capacities in the metropolis. In opposition to the "felt and emotional relationships" that easily survive in communities of a smaller scale, big-city life invites the distancing approach of the intellect because the intellect is "least sensitive and quite remote from the depth of the personality" (*SoC*, 175–76). For Simmel, an intellectual attitude allows for an easier assimilation of one's impressions because it brings out the common traits in experiences that might otherwise be puzzling and disorienting. Such a cerebral position illuminates the intimate connection between the modern metropolis and the money economy and serves to explain why so many relations in big cities are marked by a businesslike "anonymity" and even an "unmerciful matter-of-factness." "Money economy and the dominance of the intellect," writes Simmel, "are intrinsically connected. They share a matter-of-fact attitude in dealing with men and things; and, in this attitude, a formal justice is often coupled with inconsiderable hardness" (*SoC*, 176). A second, and related characteristic of metropolitan existence is the blasé attitude (*Blasiertheit*). The blasé attitude indicates an incapability on the part of the individual to respond at once to the many impressions and changes that give color to modern existence, resulting in an overall absence of stimulation. Simmel describes the blasé attitude as a form of mental survival in cases of overexcitation: "Through the rapidity and contradictoriness of the changes [in an individual's nerves], more harmless impressions force such violent responses, tearing the nerves so brutally hither and thither that their last reserves of strength are spent; and if one remains in the same milieu they have no time to gather new strength" (*SoC*, 178). Unlike the intellectual attitude, however, Simmel notes that the blasé attitude does not indicate "a structure of the highest impersonality" but "a highly personal subjectivity" (*SoC*, 178). The blasé attitude, that is to say, refers to a specific experience of the outside world and not at all to an overall *absence* of experience. "The essence of the blasé experience," he writes "consists in the blunting of discrimination. This does not mean that the objects are not perceived, as is the case with the half-wit, but rather that the meaning and differing values of things, and thereby the things themselves, are experienced as insubstantial" (*SoC*, 178). While Simmel uses the term "blasé attitude" to describe an attitude to objects, the equally important attitude of reserve (*Reserviertheit*) can be understood as its *social* variant. Such an attitude of mental distancing indicates for Simmel "one of [the] elemental forms of socialization" and merely "*appears* . . . as dissociation" (*SoC*, 180, my emphasis). In Simmel's view, that is to say, even the seeming indifference of a human being toward things or other human beings marks in truth a whole plethora of "unconscious, fluid and changing" impressions that, while not readily available to the individual himself, do make up an important part of his mental life. "If I do not deceive myself," Simmel writes, "the inner aspect of this outer reserve is not only indifference but, more often than we are aware, it is a slight aversion, a mutual strangeness and repulsion, which will break into hatred and fight at the moment of a close contact, however caused. . . . The sphere of indifference in this hierarchy is not as large as might appear on the surface" (*SoC*, 179).

The third element that helps Simmel to understand how metropolitan existence testifies to capacities of mental distancing revolves around what he calls "the difficulty of asserting [one's] own personality within the dimensions of metropolitan existence" (*SoC*, 183). Exposure to an enormous variety of different lifestyles, looks, and personalities often triggers the melancholy experience that one's own identity does not just come about in a spontaneous manner. For this reason, the third "protective" strategy of metropolitan man is to set himself apart from other individuals in a final attempt to assert his being "different." "Man is tempted to adopt the most tendentious peculiarities, that is, the specifically metropolitan extravagances of mannerism, caprice and preciousness. Now, the meaning of these extravagances does not at all lie in the contents of such behavior, but rather in its form of 'being different,' of standing out in a striking manner and thereby attracting attention" (*SoC*, 183). In such instances, in short, metropolitan existence seems to replace the intimate feeling that one is a self with the sharply felt need to become nothing but "other."

In certain passages of his text Simmel hints at a new type of freedom (see *SoC*, 181, 183, 184) because metropolitan existence can invite the individual to surpass the "pettiness and prejudices which hem in the small-town man" (*SoC*, 181). Still, a pessimistic undertone is resonant in most of the material: "Indeed, at some points we notice a retrogression in the culture of the individual with reference to spirituality, delicacy, and idealism. . . . Life is composed more and more of . . . impersonal contents and offerings which tend to displace the genuine personal colorations and incomparabilities" (*SoC*, 183–84). Simmel's essay on metropolitan existence, in fact, revolves around a deep ambiguity. In this text, a tension that was already at play in the second and third chapters of the first part of this book acquires more sharpness. From the comparison between the metaphysics of the self in the discussion about Rembrandt and the insights on the aesthetics of fragmentation in Rodin, it has already been clear that Simmel seeks to reconcile philosophical ideas about a genuinely individualized existence with a philosophy of modernity that goes in very different directions. The same tension marks his text on the metropolis: Simmel clings to the idea that human identity indicates a spontaneously evolving and unique, continuous unity while he nevertheless pinpoints the modern discovery that the self's singularity and continuity might be illusions after all. While sharply describing modern phenomena of mental and social fragmentation, the essay on metropolitan existence nevertheless presupposes, from the very first sentence on, that what matters the most to the individual is "to preserve the autonomy and individuality of his existence" (*SoC*, 174). As such, Simmel's focus on the *mental/spiritual life* in the metropolis results in a fusion between a succinct analysis of modern phenomena and a metaphysical framework that is strangely at odds with it. It is most likely for this reason that Adorno points out that "if [his generation] reacted so strongly against Simmel at one time, it was only because he withheld from [them] the very thing with which he enticed [them]."[25] Simmel's presuppositions on the level of his metaphysics of life do indeed prevent him from embracing the modern condition that he describes so well. Simmel does explore how, in modern existence, "life is made infinitely easy for the personality in that stimulations, interests, uses of time and consciousness are offered to it from all sides" and understands the need for a new model to comprehend how human beings come to self-understanding (*SoC*, 184). Yet, at the same time, he is unable to take on this challenge and overcome his own metaphysical concept of a unique and unified self. Even in his final text, written fifteen years after the essay on the metropolis, Simmel clings to the idea that human identity indicates a unified, continuous stream of life: "Th[e] inner knowledge of the identity of the individual amid full variability evidently extending into the deepest level is a fundamental fact in the face of which, for the present, all analytic conceptualizations fail" (*VoL*, 139). In spite of Simmel's own claim, in the final line of the essay, that "it is not our task either to accuse or to pardon, but only to understand," the ultimate ambition of his essay on the metropolis is therefore to understand how modern man can still recover such a rooted type of identity or what he, in his essay on Rembrandt, describes as a "soulful life" (*SoC*, 185). Even the descriptions of mental isolation are welded on a framework that clings to the idea that human beings are, first and foremost, *individuals* who build up a singular existence through an irreducible openness to their surroundings. By claiming that even symptoms of mental isolation (an overly intellectual attitude, the sentiments of blasé and reserve, and the need to be merely "different") are in fact not forms of *dis*sociation but "elemental forms of socialization," Simmel presupposes, yet again, an overarching and unifying dynamic of life that is capable of overcoming the differences and even oppositions of ordinary existence. The stakes behind Simmel's concept of "protective organs" are not merely descriptive but also prescriptive: if, in a modern society and metropolitan environment, the irreducible openness of an individual to his surroundings is not to result in a dangerous loss of self-esteem, it is vital that he somehow teaches himself to "effect the distances and aversions without which this mode of life could not at all be led" (*SoC*, 180).

As is well known, Benjamin makes explicit mention of Simmel's theories of the metropolis in some of his own texts on the same topic, that is, in his essays on Baudelaire. Benjamin refers to Simmel's (and Freud's) insights about the "protective functions" that are at work in the city dweller and calls this "obvious" (*SW* 4, 341). Still, in spite of the shared language in describing processes of mental protection, it is important to note that Benjamin is ultimately most interested in what happens when this mechanism *fails*. Benjamin coins the concept "shock experience" (*Chockerlebnis*) to denote what manages to penetrate through the "protective shield" of an individual (*SW* 4, 317). As was already mentioned in the introduction, Benjamin remains at all times fascinated with the possibility that "depersonalization" can be "set in an incomparably productive context" (*O*, 140). This same interest returns in Benjamin's essays on Baudelaire. "The failure of the shock defense," it is mentioned there, lies "at the very center of [Baudelaire's] art" and constitutes a "duel" that indicates "the creative process itself" (*SW* 4, 319).

Such analyses of creative shock and self-estrangement are at play in the majority of Benjamin's descriptions of modern existence. Therefore, Benjamin's essays on Baudelaire do include discussions of the same three phenomena that were important in Simmel's analysis, that is, intelligence, blasé or reserve, and the urge to be "different," but his dealings with them are remarkably different from Simmel's. Benjamin, for instance, adopts Simmel's idea that "consciousness" serves as a "protection against stimuli," and describes the function of intelligence to ward off impressions that are potentially harmful to the self: "The more readily consciousness registers these shocks, the less likely they are to have a traumatic effect" (*SW* 4, 317). In Benjamin's view, as well, the successful "screening" of stimuli results in "lived experiences" (*Elebnisse*) that mainly register "sameness" and do not leave a memory trace (*SW* 4, 319, translation modified). However, Benjamin's views on modern existence are steeped in the awareness that the modern gaze is mostly drawn to elements that are *not* readily accessible to the intellect and, *precisely for this reason*, resonate with a specific sense of importance. The attitude of the detective (in Poe, Baudelaire, or Dumas), to give but one example, is quintessentially modern because, for all the mental strength and the intelligence that detective work requires, it is ultimately rooted in an immersive experience of one's surroundings. The detective, moreover, is on the lookout for traces that render a given situation *different* from other ones. Benjamin considers even the flâneur to be a detective of sorts and writes that "regardless of its sober calculations, [the detective story] also participates in the phantasmagoria of Parisian life" (*SW* 4, 22). Similarly, Benjamin is fascinated by experiences of blasé or mental reserve but, unlike Simmel, his aim is not to describe the "blunting of discrimination" or the experience that "the things themselves, are . . . insubstantial" (*SoC*, 178). His interpretation of Proust, for instance, focuses on the evocative experience of the *souvenir involontaire* (involuntary memory) as an instance of sudden rejuvenation and a momentary *dissipation* of the blasé-sentiment. The *souvenir involontaire* "has not been experienced explicitly and consciously [and] has not happened to the subject as a lived experience" (*SW 4*, 317, translation modified). For this very reason, the *souvenir involontaire* is capable of briefly dislodging an overall sentiment of detachment and of reanimating a fleeting moment of remarkable expressivity. "Proust," writes Benjamin, "complain[ed] of the barrenness and lack of depth in the images of Venice that his mémoire volontaire presented to him [but] note[d] that the very word 'Venice' made those images seem to him as vapid as an exhibition of photographs" (*SW 4*, 338). Finally, Benjamin's essay on Baudelaire includes an analysis of the importance of crowds in modern literature. This analysis revolves around the idea that Baudelaire's poetry shows that "far from experiencing the crowd as an opposing, antagonistic element, the city dweller discovers in the crowd what fascinates him" (*SW 4*, 324). Unlike Simmel, who suggests that masses are most often a disenchanting sight because they invite an insatiable desire to assert nothing but one's being "different," Benjamin gives the masses a central position in modern literature. Baudelaire's famous poem "To a Passerby," ("À une passante") for instance, describes in Benjamin's account how an otherwise anonymous and unknown woman in the crowd suddenly stands out from the rest but, in thus asserting a surprising "uniqueness," becomes an unsuspected object of infatuation rather than a figure of mere "mannerism, caprice or preciousness": "The delight of the urban poet is love—not at first sight, but at last sight" (*SoC*, 183; *SW 4*, 324).

Benjamin's interest in the modern shock experience is the outcome of philosophical presuppositions that are at odds with Simmel's own metaphysical groundwork. While Simmel maintains that even the modern phenomena of seeming dissociation are in fact indicative of a more fundamental socialization, Benjamin's analyses are rooted in the opposite point of view: the mental isolation of the modern individual cannot in his view be understood as indicative of a primary social connection. The essays on Baudelaire seek to understand why the modern mind becomes increasingly detached from what Benjamin calls "long experience" (*Erfahrung*). With this concept, Benjamin describes experiences that do manage to reach the most intimate layers of the individual psyche and thereby establish a deeply felt sense of belonging. "Where there is experience in the strict sense of the word, certain elements of the individual past combine in the memory with material from the collective past. Rituals, with their ceremonies and their festivals (probably nowhere recalled in Proust's work), kept producing the amalgamation of these two elements of memory over and over again" (*SW 4*, 316). The ambition of Benjamin's theory of modernity is to come to term with the downright *absence* of such a form of memory and the concomitant *lack* of communal belonging. This project is picked up in other essays as well, where the same topic of a "poverty of experience" or a "new kind of barbarism" is often linked to the context of the First World War, but references to a deeply felt "sickening of tradition" are a key to Benjamin's views on modernity in general (*SW* 2, 732; *SW* 3, 326).

For this reason, neither the attitude of the detective or the flâneur, nor the experiences recounted by Proust or Baudelaire testify to an almost organic and spontaneous connectedness that had seemingly survived all along. What interests Benjamin the most in the experiences of the "trace," the *souvenir involontaire*, or the crowd, rather, is a wholly unanticipated and brief *interruption* of mental isolation and not at all the recovery of a more fundamental connectedness with one's surroundings. The modern universe remains in Benjamin's view essentially a deserted, indifferent, and even "hellish" place. This sentiment is briefly dislodged when the modern author does manage to "wrest poetic booty" from this universe, but a profound sense of isolation cannot be overcome (*SW* 4, 321). After all, "no matter what trace the flâneur may follow, every one of them will lead him to a crime," and both Proust and Baudelaire can be said to "impart a sense of boundless desolation" even when they capture the evocative power of recollection or the poetry of the crowd (*SW* 4, 22, 335).

While the presence of Simmel will only be implicit in the second part of this book, our discussion of Benjamin sets up a critical dialogue with some of the ideas that were laid out in the first three chapters. The underlying argument of the final two chapters will be that Benjamin *does* take up the challenge that Simmel formulates but ultimately leaves behind. As I have laid out in the introduction to this book, Benjamin rejects Simmel's view of life as a continuous unity of infinite and meaningful renewal. For this reason, his writings do manage to embrace the modern condition of mental detachment and prepare the path for a genuine philosophy of fragmentation. His overall emphasis on the possibility of a "highly productive use of the human being's self-alienation [*Selbstentfremdung*]" (*SW* 3, 113; *GS VII*, 369) gets rid of all assumptions about an underlying unity that gives meaning to elements that are seemingly distinct.

In the fourth chapter, I will therefore zoom in on experiences of "inconspicuousness" that do not at all derive their significance from an overarching context of meaning but, to the contrary, function as forces of *interruption*. Benjamin's views on melancholy, his philosophy of history, his interpretation of Proust, and his theory of photography share in the awareness that a seemingly unimportant and incomplete part can *disrupt* the totality to which it belongs and thereby animate it with an unsuspected importance. Rather than as an ontological given that ceaselessly creates change and variation, therefore, the homogeneity of life is in Benjamin's mind indicative of a meaningless repetition that needs to be *arrested*. In such moments of momentary interruption, the alienation and isolation of the individual are never overcome but, to borrow a term that was of key importance to both Brecht and Benjamin, they are "functionally transformed" (*umfunktioniert*) into an unanticipated truth-experience.

The final chapter of the book focuses on Benjamin's views on Charlie Chaplin and illuminates why the category of the individual, of such importance to Simmel, is no longer of primary importance to Benjamin. In Benjamin's view, Charlie Chaplin's Tramp is *not* an individual in the way Simmel understands that term: his life is not a "singular" one, and it does not at all refer to a unique and irreplaceable, continuous unity. The Tramp, on the contrary, remains on the surface of things and does not have a mental life to speak of, let alone a deeply rooted and intimate sense of selfhood. Chaplin's self-portrayal as a Tramp therefore requires a frame of analysis that is altogether different from the discussion of Rembrandt's portrait of the beggar as a self in the second chapter of this book. The constitutive elements that give the Tramp such easily recognizable features (the mustache, the bowler hat, the walking cane, his suit) cannot shake off a sense of anonymity. What is more, unlike the nose and eyes that constitute the internal and aesthetic unity of Rembrandt's face, the elements that determine the looks of the Tramp are detachable and, of crucial importance to Benjamin, they always and necessarily refer to an outside world with very specific political and social components. As a consequence, the "openness" that marks the Tramp's existence is very different from the "openness" in Rembrandt's portraits. First of all, it does not only refer to the face but plays itself out in Chaplin's entire body. Second, the Tramp's ongoing responsiveness to the outside world cannot be considered a given but needs to be *created* again and again and, for this very reason, infuses the belief in human intervention as a force of potential change. To indicate such a non-individualized life that nevertheless comes together with a dimension of hope, Benjamin uses the term "character." Rather than building up a continuous and unified identity through a spontaneous connection with the outside world, the Tramp is a character in that it is he himself who becomes a draw to other things. In this sense, the Tramp's closest ally is not a beggar but a Prince, that is, Prince Myshkin (Dostoevsky's *The Idiot*), of whom Benjamin writes that he is "completely unapproachable" and "emanates an order at whose center we find a solitude that is almost absolute." Yet, it is precisely from this state of isolation and detachment that we can "observe . . . a quite remarkable fact: every event, however remote from him it appears to be, seems to gravitate toward him" (*SW 1*, 79).

Chapter 4

Unscheinbarkeit

"Depersonalization Set in an Incomparably Productive Context"

The following, often commented-upon passage on beautiful semblance in Benjamin's essay on Goethe's *Elective Affinities* is surely one of the most enigmatic in Benjamin's entire oeuvre: "Even if everywhere else semblance is deception, the beautiful semblance is the veil thrown over that which is necessarily most veiled. For the beautiful is neither the veil nor the veiled object but rather the object in its veil. Unveiled, however, it would prove to be infinitely inconspicuous [*unscheinbar*]" (*SW 1*, 351). In part a preparation of the discussion of Charlie Chaplin in the next chapter, this chapter zooms in on the notion of *Unscheinbarkeit* (inconspicuousness). The most common English translation of *unscheinbar* as "inconspicuous" is misleading if it would presuppose that this term denotes the mere privation of the quality *scheinbar*. For, based on the references to the word *unscheinbar* in his work and on the many, detailed descriptions of such people, objects, and phenomena, Benjamin deems experiences in which someone or something is encountered as meaningful in an unsuspected or improbable manner more profound and noteworthy than experiences in which someone or something is immediately and from the start already encountered as significant. The descriptions of such instances of meaningful interruption or momentary arrest reveal most clearly that Benjamin, in contrast to Simmel, presupposes that the creation of meaning is not a process that arises from life as such and that life can at most be *made* meaningful. *Unscheinbar* is the term with which Benjamin describes a force of *dis*continuity that briefly suspends the homogeneity of life itself. On account of an "excess" vis-à-vis life as such, *Unscheinbarkeit* refers to a capacity to *shape* meaning and *bring about* a potential of genuine rejuvenation and renewal. In order to understand this dynamic of meaningful interruption, it will be crucial to pay careful attention to all the different stages of Benjamin's work and to the many philosophical perspectives that resonate throughout it.[1]

"Goethe's Elective Affinities" and the "Epistemo-Critical Prologue" (Semblance)

The enigmatic passage about beauty and semblance in Benjamin's Goethe essay, "Goethes Wahlverwandtschaften" (Goethe's "Elective Affinities"), can only be understood when placed in the context of his discussion of the relationship between truth and beauty that is not only dealt with in the Goethe essay but most notably in the "Epistemo-Critical Prologue" to his *Origin of German Tragic Drama*. In that important text Benjamin aligns himself with a fundamental viewpoint put forward in Plato's *Symposium*, that is, the idea that "truth is the content of beauty" and moreover that "truth is beautiful" for "whomsoever seeks it" (*O*, 31). In line with the ideas presented in the Goethe essay (truth "as that which is necessarily most veiled"), Benjamin declares that "truth is not a process of exposure which destroys the secret, but a revelation which does justice to it" (*O*, 31) and thereby connects the revelation of truth to a specific dynamic of mysterious and inaccessible beauty and an ambiguity of meaning. This nexus between truth and beautiful semblance is important for Benjamin's differentiation between genuine, that is, divine and absolute truth on the one hand, and the object of human knowledge on the other: the quest for knowledge, that is to say, is for him to be understood as an attempt on the part of human beings to expose and unveil an object in unambiguous clarity, whereas genuine truth, on the contrary, is marked by the "representational impulse" of an "essence" or "unity" (*O*, 30–31), that is, by an ability of something absolute to "represent *itself*," which thereby precludes it from "being projected . . . into the realm of knowledge" (*O*, 29, my emphasis).[2] It thus seems to be Benjamin's aim to distinguish a semblance that is "deception" (*mere* semblance) from a semblance that does partake in the dynamic of truth presentation (*beautiful* semblance).[3] That the concept of *unscheinbar* seems at first glimpse to indicate a privation and to mark an overall absence of significance has to do with this emphasis on the importance of such a latter form of (positive) semblance. Benjamin writes that "the semblance [in beauty] is just this: not the superfluous veiling of things in themselves but rather the necessary veiling of things for us" and goes on to describe how "unveiled at the wrong time, what is inconspicuous [*unscheinbar*] evaporates into nothing" (*SW 1*, 351; *GS I-1*, 195). It seems, in other words, that Benjamin sets up a clear and simple opposition between, on the one hand, an absolute truth that is endowed with a sense of unity, autonomy, and ambiguity, thereby radiating beauty, mystery, and distance and, on the other, the all too human and all too brutal attempt to approach, expose, unveil, capture, and comprehend a specific object as distinct from other ones. This opposition, it seems, is then used to back up a (Heideggerian) claim that the human quest for knowledge is to be understood as an inability to relate to a fundamental sense of alterity or otherness that pertains to the essence of truth revelation and that it has therefore come at the cost of a certain *Seinsvergessenheit* (forgetting of being).[4] It seems, in other words, that Benjamin is saying that the brutal disruption of all semblance precludes truth from becoming manifest and that this process cannot but leave human beings empty-handed in their longing for truth ("Unveiled at the wrong time, what is inconspicuous evaporates into nothing"). From there on, it appears but a small step to Benjamin's often talked-about ideas on melancholy and mournfulness and his views on an unredeemed and, it seems, unredeemable universe.[5]

In these views on the connection between truth and beautiful semblance and, following from this connection, on the difference between truth and knowledge, two distinct layers of Benjamin's thought are overlaid with each other; that is, the theologically inspired ideas that are the primary mark of his earlier writings and the views on modernity that characterize a large part of his work from the late 1920s on. The quest for knowledge which seems to have disrupted a more natural connection with absolute truth is, according to Benjamin, to be understood first and foremost from a theological perspective, that is, as the event that has both initiated the Fall from Paradise and continues to govern the post-paradisiacal universe.[6] In his important essay on language, Benjamin describes the human quest for knowledge as the primal event (or, rather, primal crime) that instigated history proper because it substituted an immediate language of names, that is, a language of divine essences that "communicates itself absolutely" and "expresses itself purely" to man (*SW 1*, 65), for the multiplicity of fallen, human languages through which human beings seek to possess knowledge of outside objects (language as means to an end). According to Benjamin's reading of the book of Genesis, man was given the task to fulfill creation by opening himself up to what, in objects, is "communicable per se" (*eine Mitteilbarkeit schlechthin*) (*SW 1*, 66; *GS II-1*, 145–46) and by translating this mute communicability into language.[7] In the active quest for knowledge, however, human beings "step outside the purer language of names" and "make language a means" (*SW 1*, 71), thereby using language as an instrument for judgment and abstraction. From that moment on, Benjamin contends, objects are considered to be known only when they are identified as belonging to a super-individual, universal category or totality and the natural connection between language and truth or singular essence is disrupted and substituted for a language of "mere" signs (*SW 1*, 71).[8] Henceforth, writes Benjamin, "the word must communicate *something* (other than itself). In that fact lies the true Fall of the spirit of language. The word as something externally communicating, as it were a parody—by the expressly mediate word—of the expressly immediate, creative word of God, and the decay of the blissful Adamite spirit of language that stands between them" (*SW 1*, 71).

As I have suggested earlier, from the late 1920s on, Benjamin overwrites this story of the (first) Fall with a theory of modernity that, zooming in on phenomena like fragmentation, alienation, and poverty of experience, can be considered a description of a second Fall that is no less disturbing and uprooting than the first. It is striking that in setting up the conceptual framework to understand this modern universe, Benjamin takes recourse to metaphors that are either identical to or only slightly different from the ones that were introduced in the earlier paragraphs on the difference between truth and knowledge and uses concepts that are unmistakably dependent on this earlier framework.[9] The autonomous unity that retains a distance and presents itself to the subject, radiating truth, beautiful semblance, ambiguity, and mystery, has now been famously termed "aura," the destructive quest for possession and knowledge is now described as "the urge to get hold of an object at close range" (*SW 4*, 255), and the object of knowledge that has been divested of all sense of mystery and ambiguity has now taken on the guise of the ascertainable fact and of "information [that] lays claim to prompt verifiability" (*SW 3*, 147). In 1918 already, Benjamin had found fault with Kant's attempt to "take the principles of experience from the sciences—in particular mathematical physics" (*SW 1*, 101) and to thereby reduce the faculty of knowledge to abstract reason and, in general, he marks off the start of modernity with the advent of the allegorical gaze that "recognizes many enigmas, but knows no mystery" (*AP*, 365). For Benjamin, not unlike the German *Trauerspiele* of the same period, the paintings of the baroque reveal that modernity is oblivious to distance and secrets and that it has "nothing at all to do with [a] veil [*Schleier*]" (*AP*, 365; *GS V-1*, 461). Moreover, modernity "ostentatiously rends [*reißt*] [it] and . . . brings even the distance of the skies into a nearness [*rückt . . . in eine Nähe*]" (*AP*, 365, *GS V-1*, 461). The overall verdict on modernity is therefore well known: the second Fall has left us empty-handed twice over in our longing for genuine truth since "the stripping of the veil from the object, the destruction of the aura, is the signature of a perception whose 'sense for sameness in the world' has so increased that, by means of reproduction, it extracts sameness even from what is unique" (*SW 4*, 255–56). From there on, it is for some commentators but a small step toward that side of Benjamin's thinking that is nostalgic about the aura and mournful about a universe that has done away with the power of tradition to build up a continuity between generations and the ability of stories to set up a shared sense of existence.[10]

"Commentary on Poems by Brecht" (Friendliness)

The concept of *unscheinbar* appears in numerous places in Benjamin's work that inevitably refine the interpretations that I have just sketched out, and some of these references even contradict the assumptions that were made. It is worthwhile to go into detail regarding at least four of these places where Benjamin uses the term, and this for two different reasons. The first one is that, beyond clarifying some of Benjamin's most subtle philosophical intuitions, these places will help us to understand why it is that a moment in history, object, or image can strike us as meaningful or truthful without, however, directly referring to something that can be deemed significant. Benjamin, to be precise, uses the term *unscheinbar* to denote, not the *im*possibility that a moment in history, object, or image can become manifest as meaningful or truthful, but precisely the *possibility* that something that seems unremarkable on its own account *does* present a surprising, unanticipated, and even improbable (the second meaning of the word *unscheinbar*) layer of significance. In order to understand this, we must take into account that Benjamin connects the term *Schein* with the "false, errant totality—the absolute totality" of mere life (*SW 1*, 340). The main claim is that *unscheinbarkeit* does not at all refer to an *in*ability but to what one could call a *negative ability*, that is, not to the *in*ability of a phenomenon to "shine" but to its *ability* to *not*-"shine" or, put differently, to its capacity to keep itself untouched by the sense of illusory unity or false totality that endangers all forms of *Schein*.[11] Such a negative ability (the ability to *not* do something) is no less real than a positive one (the ability to do something), and it will reveal how *Unscheinbarkeit* partakes in a dynamic of truth revelation that is fully its own. It is therefore to be regarded as belonging to that list of "*-barkeiten*" or "-abilities" (knowability, criticizability, translatability, reproducibility, recognizability, legibility, etc.) that have been analyzed by Samuel Weber in his important book *Benjamin's -abilities* and that are "inseparable from time insofar as [they] involve an ongoing, ever-unfinished, and unpredictable process."[12] *Unscheinbarkeit* refers to a "virtual condition" of meaningfulness, that is, to a promise of significance that manifests itself in something that seems utterly devoid of life and insignificant (e.g., junk, ruins, detritus, dust, rags, etc.) and which for that reason can only be awakened through the connection with something that is foreign to it. The significance of what is *unscheinbar* is thus dependent on its finding an unpredictable and even improbable extension or actualization (*Nach-* or *Fortleben*, *Nachgeschichte*) in something that it has no immediate connection with or in a future moment that it could not in any way have anticipated.[13]

The second reason why this notion is worthy of attention is that by bringing together the scattered references to *Unscheinbarkeit* in Benjamin's work, we will be able to read his theologically inspired ideas alongside his views on modernity and discover them as complementary, rather than as irreconcilable with each other.[14] Moreover, this will allow us to further explore and deepen that side of Benjamin's thinking that is not to be reduced to melancholy and mournfulness and to even discover, within the very heart of the second Fall that is the modern condition, a succinct and historically novel potential for experiences of change and renewed significance.

One of the most revealing references to the concept *unscheinbar* can be found in the final paragraph of the essay "Commentary on Poems by Brecht" written and partially published by Benjamin in 1939. The last pages of this essay contain a discussion of a poem by Brecht that describes an old teacher (Lao-tzu) who is traveling on foot in search of rest and encounters a customs man who, in return for a meal at his home, asks the sage to write down his teachings before he sets out on his way again. Benjamin bases his discussion on the last two verses of the poem. These praise not only the sage but also the customs man, since it is only thanks to him that the wisdom of the old teacher was written down on paper and thus passed on to other people and future generations. In this analysis, Benjamin zooms in on a concept that seems quite alien to the rest of his oeuvre but which nevertheless brings together some of the richest elements in his entire philosophy: the attitude of friendliness or kindness. The mere fact that Benjamin emphasizes the importance of this notion indicates from the outset how, for him, gentleness, softness of heart, and even passivity are to be regarded as powers or abilities in their own right. This, as we will see, ties this interpretation of Brecht together with the philosophical stakes that will mark, one year later, his philosophy of history and the notion of a *weak* (messianic) *power* that is introduced there as a redemptive force. Benjamin, that is to say, considers the importance of the kindness shown by the customs man to the sage in Brecht's poem to lie in its ability to grant continuity and a prolonged existence to a form of wisdom that is experienced as not readily accessible.[15] He takes the concept of friendliness to exemplify a responsiveness to a truth that comes from outside and that cannot ever be fully appropriated or possessed. Friendliness thus denotes an openness to a wisdom that clearly originates from someone or somewhere else but that is at risk of being irretrievably lost, and it testifies to the subsequent willingness to serve as a mere means to pass it on to others.[16]

Benjamin deems three qualities fundamental to the nature of friendliness: that it is shown only after careful consideration and thinking ("It is not dispensed without due reflection" [*SW* 4, 247]), that it combines a light-hearted attitude with the accomplishment of a great deed ("Friendliness consists not in performing an incidental and trivial service, but in rendering a service as if it were trivial" [*SW* 4, 248]), and that it succeeds in rendering the very distance between human beings productive ("It does not abolish the distance between people, but brings it to life" [*SW* 4, 248]). Because it thus illustrates the importance of remaining kind and gentle when faced with hardship, Benjamin states that Brecht's poem comes together with "a promise nothing short of messianic" (*SW* 4, 248) and is both a lesson for their own troubled times (the essay was, after all, written in 1939) and a universal moral: "Anyone who wishes to see hardness yield should not let slip any opportunity for displaying friendliness" (*SW* 4, 249). The most prominent place in the poem is, however, the saying of the old teacher that made the customs man so eager to learn more of his wisdom in the first place, that is, the statement "that the soft water, as it moves [*das weiche Wasser in Bewegung*] / vanquishes in time the mighty stone [*mit der Zeit den mächtigen Stein besiegt*]. / You understand—what is hard must yield" (*SW* 4, 246; *GS II-2*, 568). It is in the context of his analysis of this specific line that Benjamin takes recourse to the concept *Unscheinbarkeit*, writing that the old man's saying "teaches us that we should not lose sight of the inconstant, mutable aspect of things [*das Unstete und Wandelbare der Dinge*], and that we should take common cause with whatever is unobtrusive and plain but relentless, like water [*mit dem zu halten, was unscheinbar und nüchtern, auch unversieglich ist wie das Wasser*]" (*SW* 4, 248; *GS II-2*, 572). What is extraordinary about Benjamin's phrase is that it brings the concept *unscheinbar* together with the "*unversiegliche*" aspect of water. In this manner, he connects *unscheinbar* to three different characteristics that each play, as we will see, an important role in the three other prominent places where Benjamin mentions the term but which seem nevertheless to be completely at odds with his earlier referred-to (privative) use of the same word in the Goethe essay. In the essay on Brecht's poem, that is to say, "tak[ing] common cause with whatever is *unscheinbar*" denotes, first of all, the ability to share in a power that cannot ever be fully vanquished or annihilated (*unversieglich* has the root *sieg* or "victory," "conquest" in it). In the second place, as suggested by the English translator in his footnote to the essay, it refers to a confrontation with a form of inexhaustibility (the second, literal meaning of *unversieglich*).[17] Third, it indicates the experience of a force of transition, dislocation, and differentiation (the third, literal meaning of *unversieglich* is "ever-changing").

"On the Concept of History" (Recollection)

The place in Benjamin's writings where the term *unscheinbar* is most directly connected with the first of these three meanings, that is, with invincibility, is the essay "On the Concept of History," where it is used to describe the sudden and even improbable significance that specific moments from the past can acquire through their relation with the present. In this essay, Benjamin makes a plea for a kind of historical truth that differs from a set of historical facts since the positivist hunt for the latter brackets the present in order to visit a supposedly immutable and uncontaminated past ("the past *wie es gewesen ist*" [*SW* 4, 391], the "eternal" image of the past [*SW* 4, 396]). Such a historicist ideal inevitably mystifies history into a homogenous force with iron laws that would deliver us on its own account to a certain future of progress. The historical materialist, on the contrary, is to remain attentive to and to *construct* a "unique experience *with* the past" in which it is brought back to the present as a heterogeneous force that "arrests" the movement of our thoughts and therefore contains a "revolutionary chance" in the fight for the oppressed (*SW* 4, 396, my emphasis).[18] The "material" that such historians work with is time in its most dislocated or dislodged state, that is, *Jetztzeiten* (now-time), or dialectical images that allow a hitherto insufficiently acknowledged suffering from the past to "flash up in a moment of danger" (*SW* 4, 391) and, at the same time, to be "shot through with splinters of messianic time" (*SW* 4, 397). It is in this context that Benjamin writes that the "historical materialist must be aware of [the] most inconspicuous of all transformations [*unscheinbarste von allen Veränderungen*]" (*SW* 4, 390; *GS I*-2, 695). Similar to the essay on Brecht's poem, Benjamin addresses the idea that a given softness of heart or kindness can constitute an ability or power in its own right: the "*weak* [*schwache*] messianic power" that the present "has been endowed with" denotes its capacity to "redeem" or "rescue" a moment of the past which was, moreover, itself marked by an equally irreducible weakness (*SW* 4, 390; *GS I*-2, 694, Benjamin's emphasis). That is to say, the past that is to be redeemed is likened to "a breath of the air that pervaded earlier days [and] caresses us" (*SW* 4, 390). Messianic power testifies to a present which makes "legible" a (virtual) truth from the past that lacks the ability to lift *itself* up to the level of meaningfulness: the past is "recognized" (*AP*, 473) and, Benjamin adds, even "actualized" *for the first time* in the present (*AP*, 460). The power to redeem or rescue what is *unscheinbar* is thus, in line with the ideas presented in the essay on Brecht, to be understood as a form of kindness toward the past and it likewise ties a great, important task to an attitude of lightheartedness. Benjamin emphasizes that "the claim (of the past on the present) cannot be settled cheaply" (*SW* 4, 390) but adds to this the statement that "the idea of happiness is indissolubly bound up with the idea of redemption" (*SW* 4, 389). Similar to the Brecht essay, therefore, what is at stake in "On the Concept of History" is the intuition that a heightened form of reflection ("presence of mind," "mindfulness") is not merely passive but actualizes an unanticipated, even improbable, change. That the present is deemed capable of rendering service to a past that, on account of its oppressed state, was deprived of the capacity to preserve, understand, or express itself is, for Benjamin, tantamount to claiming that singular moments in the present are "intended" by singular moments of the past and that they can, *post factum* as it were, transform those moments. In this manner, the present actively rethinks a vanquished past and "call[s] into question every victory . . . of the rulers" (*jeden Sieg, der den Herrschenden jemals zugefallen ist*) (*SW* 4, 390; *GS I*-2, 694). Benjamin's claim is that "recollection" (*Eingedenken*) thereby grows capable of "*modify[ing]*" what science had "determined" and of making "the complete (suffering) . . . into something incomplete again" (*AP*, 471, translation modified).

Crucial in this dynamics of recollection is the emphasis that suffering be testified to *as* suffering and that the oppressed be commemorated *as* oppressed. "The interest which the materialist historian takes in the past," writes Benjamin, "is always, in part, a vital interest in its *being* past—in its having ceased to exist, its being essentially dead" (*AP*, 363, Benjamin's emphasis), and this renewed connection between past and present remains at all times a "tradition of the *oppressed*" (*SW* 4, 392, my emphasis). Similar to the Brecht essay, distance plays an important role in Benjamin's philosophy of history and recollection and, there as well, what matters is that it is not "abolish[ed]" but "br[ought] to life" (*SW 4*, 248). The claim that recollection *transforms* a distinct moment of suffering is therefore not at all to be understood as a claim that a past injustice is simply annihilated or canceled out in and by the present. Stating that an oppressed party can be recollected *as* oppressed does not at all mean that it can become visible as a force of posthumous victory or as a ruling power in its own right. Considering historical redemption or rescue as the ability to "extract, to cite, what has remained inconspicuously buried beneath [*was unscheinbar unter ihm begraben blieb*]—being, as it was, of so little help to the powerful" (*AP*, 364; *GS V-1*, 460) does entail the view that it releases victims of past suffering from "the triumphal procession in which the present rulers step over those who are lying prostrate" (*SW 4*, 391). Still, it neither overcomes the negativity of the initial event nor restores a status quo.[19]

The Origin of German Tragic Drama (Melancholy)

A second prominent passage in Benjamin's oeuvre where the notion of *unscheinbar* is introduced revolves around the second element put forward in the Brecht essay, that is, the idea that it denotes the experience of an inexhaustibility of meaning present within an otherwise unremarkable object. In his discussion of melancholy and mournfulness in the book on the German *Trauerspiel*, Benjamin describes how the Lutheran beliefs of the most important dramatists allow us to understand some of the most revealing characteristics of their work. Lutheranism, that is to say, is marked by an excessively antinomic relationship with the everyday and builds its religious values on a clear-cut opposition between human existence and the world in which it is lived on the one hand and the divine or absolute on the other. Benjamin claims that Lutheranism for this reason results in a double form of disenchantment: both the unity of the outside world and the unity of the empirical self are shattered, since neither of the two can be regarded as meaningful in their own right.[20] The world that is brought on display by the *Trauerspiele*, claims Benjamin, is therefore marked by either an ongoing and never-ending repetition of the same (eternal transience) or a state of deep fragmentation. Moreover, melancholy comes into the picture as the *Grundgefühl* (foundational affect) of the *Trauerspiel* since human beings, for their part, are shown in a state of decomposition or "depersonalization" (*O*, 140). Meaning, that is to say, can be derived neither from practical concerns for the outside world ("the assault on 'good works'" [*O*, 138]) nor from a rational interest in objects or events ("an element of German paganism" [*O*, 138]), nor from an emotional attachment to external circumstances ("it is only one step from stoic apatheia to mourning" [*O*, 140]).[21] It is, however, inevitable that "life itself protested against this" and refuses to "be devalued by faith"

(O, 139), and it is precisely this conflict which characterizes the artistic universe of the German *Trauerspiel* authors most of all. Steeped in the Lutheran awareness that no normal psychic investment in the outside world can be regarded as meaningful or valuable, they developed a penchant for everything that brings itself unambiguously on display as *non*-real, for example, forms of theatricality, play, or disengaged study.[22] It is only by keeping this "protest" of a transformed life against faith in mind that the reference to *unscheinbar* makes any sense. Benjamin describes the attitude of mournfulness as "the pathological state, in which the most simple object [*jedes unscheinbarste Ding*] appears to be a symbol of some enigmatic wisdom because it lacks any natural, creative relationship to us" and adds to it that "depersonalization" was "set in an incomparably productive context" (O, 140; *GS I-1*, 319). In other words, mournfulness—and by extension melancholy pensiveness and contemplation—denote not so much an *in*ability to explore things as intrinsically meaningful as an *ability* to discover them as other-to-themselves and, by that very token, as *potentially* meaningful. Mournfulness is described as "determined by an astounding tenacity of intention" and as "capable of a special intensification, a progressive deepening of its intention" (O, 139), and it exemplifies a form of attentiveness that is directed toward an object, not on account of what it is immediately recognized to be, but on account of its being experienced as a reference to *something other*.[23] Benjamin refers to Albrecht Dürer's engraving *Melencolia I* in which "the utensils of active life are lying around unused on the floor, as objects of contemplation" (O, 140) to reveal how it is from within this very dislocation that the possibility of a renewed sense of meaning arises. In other words, it is only when all normal and expected meaning has been evacuated from an object and when the possessive quest for knowledge is exhausted that an unanticipated significance can be encountered. This latter sense of meaning is, in the process, experienced as a *remains*, an *excess* or a *residue* of meaning that, obviously originating in an "elsewhere," has so to speak transposed its significance onto the initial object in an utterly surprising and even improbable way.[24] In line with insights borrowed from Aby Warburg, Benjamin thus emphasizes that melancholy succeeds in making depersonalization *productive* or *creative* and that distance is, as he put it in the Brecht essay, not "abolished" but "brought to life."[25]

However, objects that are released from our normal attachment and thereby allow for an unexpected manifestation of significance are not themselves experienced as meaningful. What marks the specific dynamics of mournful pensiveness is that an object, in referring to a meaning that comes from without, always and necessarily also draws attention to its own existence and thereby inevitably highlights its own *lack* of significance.[26] In melancholy contemplation, that is to say, an object can refer to something that lies outside of it but never without also and immediately referring to *itself* and thus making visible a profound *absence* of meaning. Such objects, in other words, are experienced as *signs* (they partake in a process of signification) but never as *merely* signs since they, at all times, remain visible as physical entities that fully share in the contingencies of normal life. In productive melancholy, the insignificance of the object itself, the contingency of its location, and the arbitrariness of the moment of the sudden discovery of meaning enter wholly into the experience of meaning or significance itself: the confrontation with significance does not *abolish* or *overcome* the initial impression of contingency but rather *thrives* on it, and it is only the latter which gives the former its proper weight.

This possibility of a creative use of melancholy is the basis of Benjamin's interest in the literary mode of allegory where concrete experiences, objects, or images are used as elements to narrate a story or to develop an argument, but not without at the same time making manifest that they are in themselves *in*capable of awakening our interest.[27] An allegorical way of looking at the world, therefore, "immerses itself into the depths which separate visual being from meaning" (O, 165) and in its excesses it even destroys our normal confidence in life, confronting "the observer with the facies hippocratica of history as a petrified, primordial landscape" (O, 166).[28]

This tension between meaning and the *absence* of meaning explains why experiences of meaningfulness are in Benjamin's view always connected to a force of momentary interruption. This interruptive quality makes up the paradoxical structure of an experience that was very close to Benjamin's heart, that is, the Proustian *souvenir involontaire*.[29] In the famous scene in the *Recherche* where the narrator bends over to undo the buttons of his shoe and is suddenly overcome by the memory of his recently deceased grandmother, the utterly banal character of the activity of taking off a shoe is not *abolished* but *preserved* in the experience.[30] Undoing the buttons of one's shoe remains a perfect example of losing one's time, even if it brings back a moment of the past in an unexpected manner: the activity itself is a highly improbable candidate for any discovery of meaning whatsoever, and it is clearly felt that there is no *necessary* connection between the activity in question and the revelatory powers it suddenly comes together with. Similarly, the taste of the madeleine cake which Proust describes as the medium through which the narrator's childhood experiences "spring into being" is obviously endowed with significance for the experiencing subject, but it derives its overwhelming effect in part from the accompanying feeling that these childhood experiences seem to have attached themselves to the thoroughly known taste of an ordinary biscuit. For this reason, Benjamin deems "boredom" an element of the *souvenir involontaire* and uses a by now familiar term to denote what suddenly opens onto an unsuspected dream world: "inconspicuous gates" (*unscheinbare Pforten*) (*SW* 2, 239; *GS II-1*, 313). A *souvenir involontaire* is indeed marked by the tension that characterizes all things *unscheinbar*: the inconspicuous nature of the experience enters wholly into the feeling that there is nevertheless something meaningful going on.[31] The taste of the madeleine cake is, as

Deleuze puts it, a "sensuous sign," but one that can only refer to something other (the moment of the past that it returns) by drawing attention to itself and to its own insignificance.[32] The *souvenir involontaire* thus highlights that there is no relation of *identity* between the two experiences, but that they are connected by what Benjamin will call a "nonsensuous similarity" (*übersinnliche Ähnlichkeit*): even though the object or activity that brings back the past cannot be released from a specific sensuous experience (the taste, smell, or touch of something), the *relation* between the two cannot itself be considered a sensuous one. The object or activity in the present, that is to say, is no *imitation* or *mere repetition* of the past, and the connection between the two remains utterly *contingent*.[33]

It is only on account of this non-necessary or even contingent connection that it can be understood why Marcel's attempts to repeat the *souvenir involontaire* inevitably remain fruitless.[34] The connection between a present moment and a past experience in the *souvenir involontaire* is in fact both non-sensuous (it is not itself *given* in the senses) and properly speaking nonsensical (it *has* no sense), since the return of the childhood experiences is perceived as an utterly surprising event and does not at all logically follow from the object or activity that conjured it. For this reason, the interruptive force of the *souvenir involontaire* cannot recover any form of continuity and it designates a heterogeneity with regard to the overall flow of life as such. As Deleuze puts it in his book *Logic of Sense*, what "is saying its own sense can only be *nonsense*" since activities and objects that are felt to be genuinely meaningful to an experiencing subject come together with a dynamic that seems to defy mental anticipation or emotional intention.[35] There is thus even "an original type of intrinsic relation" or "a mode of co-presence" between sense and non-sense because the process through which a given object or activity *becomes* truly meaningful and *brings about* sense presents itself as not dependent on any qualities internal to that object or activity.[36] It is for this reason that Deleuze describes non-sense not as the opposite of sense, but as the opposite of the "absence of sense."[37] The process of *becoming*-significant and *producing*-meaning is to be called "*non*-sensical" because the object or activity in question cannot properly be said to "have" sense: it rather *creates* sense, and it can only deliver something truly meaningful if it at the same time lays bare the external nature of meaning as such.

But there is more to it than this. The past that returns in the form of a *souvenir involontaire* is, itself, not experienced as more significant than the object or activity that brings it back. *Souvenirs involontaires* do not at all give us any new information about the past, and they usually revolve around experiences or sensations that are hardly worthy of being remembered: it is not as if the narrator only *learns* about the death of his grandmother through his childhood recollection and, similarly, the past that is brought back by the madeleine cake does not draw the narrator's attention in its own right, since it is already profoundly familiar to him. What is significant is therefore not the *content* of the past but the mere possibility that it can seemingly come back to the present and, moreover, the feeling that this apparent ability for return is not a quality of the past or the former self that accompanies it: neither of the two is endowed with a natural power or a spontaneous strength to keep itself "alive" and to return to the present *wie es gewesen ist*.[38] The *souvenir involontaire* entails an unexpected visit of a past and it denotes the seeming reappearance of a former self, but these retain a constitutive weakness, and they are not made accessible or recovered in the process. In other words, Proust rejects Simmel's view of the past as something that is "collected" (*gesammelt*) in or "narrated" (*erzählt*) by the present, and he replaces Simmel's view of the self as a "continuous stream of becoming" with a multiplicity of *dis*continuous *selves* that have *expired*. The *souvenir involontaire* is overwhelming precisely because it allows one to relive the past *as* past, and it does *not* encounter it as something that has somehow remained a presence all along.[39] In the two earlier mentioned examples, the *souvenir involontaire* authenticates precisely the *death* of the grandmother and the *being-past* of the past. The seeming return of the past and the apparent reappearance of a former self in the *souvenir involontaire* are therefore to be considered as sudden and non-extendable interruptions of an otherwise overall and all-determining rhythm of transience. "Actualizing" or "realizing" the past through a *souvenir involontaire* does not at all entail the restoration of an initial presence or the discovery that it has subsisted all along but, on the contrary, as I will emphasize again in the conclusion to this book, a confrontation with forgetfulness. The *souvenir involontaire* is neither dependent on memories that have survived nor on a "deep" self or inner-I that has endured but, instead, it highlights that the recollected moment, like everything else, has vanished immediately after its first occurrence. "Proust," writes Benjamin, "described not a life as it actually was [*wie es gewesen ist*] but a life as it was remembered by the one who had lived it. . . . The important thing to the remembering author is not what he experienced [*erlebt hat*], but the weaving of his memory [*Erinnerung*], the Penelope work of recollection [*Eingedenken*]. Or should one call it, rather, a Penelope work of forgetting? Is not the involuntary recollection, Proust's *mémoire involontaire*, much closer to forgetting than what is usually called memory?" (*SW 2*, 237–38; *GS II-1*, 311).

At stake in Benjamin's analysis of both melancholic contemplation and the *souvenir involontaire* is the attempt to understand why a double loss of unity (fragmentation of the world and depersonalization of the self) is not always antithetical to a meaningful experience. This can only be explained by describing melancholic contemplation and the *souvenir involontaire* as examples of a highly unusual experience of the relation between part and totality or between fragment and totality.[40] In our attempts to orient ourselves in the surrounding world and to understand it rationally, that is to say, it is vital that we experience little difficulty in grasping to which totality a given part belongs, and it is crucial that we learn to easily derive the meaning of a certain fragment from the corresponding unity to which it belongs. Recognizing the circumstances in which we live for what they are and learning how to act upon them thus entails grasping the objects that surround us and the experiences that we have as naturally connected to a continuous whole. As analyzed by Henri Bergson in a book that Benjamin deemed "monumental" (*SW 4*, 314), it is important for our mental and bodily orientation that we see specific objects as instantiations of categories that we already know and that we comprehend them as being identical to other, already familiar, objects of the same class.[41] This model of thinking the relationship between part and totality presupposes the direct connection between knowing and acting (Bergson's sensory-motor schema). The idea that a given particularity derives its meaning from a corresponding universality is, however, according to Benjamin based on a form of experience that is "virtually reduced to a nadir, to a minimum of significance" (*SW 1*, 101), and it cannot indeed account for those moments in which we have the feeling that something is exceptional and truly meaningful.[42] There is nothing particularly meaningful in recognizing an object (or oneself for that matter) as a member of a universal class or category, and noticing a sensuous similarity or even identity between two things or moments does not as such make for an experience charged with emotional resonance.

What marks off both melancholic contemplation and the experience of the *souvenir involontaire* in Benjamin's interpretation is that they do not just problematize but even *subvert* this relationship between part and totality (fragment and unity) and that they disrupt the supposed continuity between knowing and acting. In melancholic contemplation, a totality ("some enigmatic wisdom") is felt to derive its force of attraction from the very fact that it has seemingly migrated to an alienated part ("most simple object"). Similarly, in the case of the *souvenir involontaire*, a unity (a moment of the past) is experienced as overwhelming or moving only because it has somehow ended up as a fragment that, without any announcement and against all odds, washes up on the shores of the present and leaves the present powerless in front of it.[43] In both cases it is, in other words, only *because* it has become fragmentized that an initial unity or continuous totality is experienced as significant, and it is made meaningful *by virtue of* its capacity to deliver a shock to our ordinary sense of self and to "arrest" our normal actions. For Benjamin, melancholy contemplation and the *souvenir involontaire* illustrate how a process of depersonalization can at times become a token of a meaningful experience and how partialization can in some cases allow for something that was not significant as an original totality to *become* significant as a fragment. This is, of course, fully at odds with the assumptions of Simmel's *Lebensphilosophie* which, as we have seen, considers the creation of meaning to be a formative impulse that is at work *within* the overarching unity of life. While Simmel maintains that the constructs and forms that bring about meaning arise *from* the infinite variability and continuous totality of life ("life is at once itself and more than itself"), Benjamin considers life to be something that is still to *become* meaningful. For Simmel, therefore, life is marked by a "too much" vis-à-vis the forms and constructs that it creates ("life cannot enter into form at all"), whereas Benjamin suggests that life itself is "not enough": it can only *receive* meaning. For Benjamin, this process through which meaning is bestowed *onto* life originates in those very bits and pieces that seem *devoid* of life and it cannot for this reason be tied back to an underlying totality or overarching continuity.

This is why Benjamin attaches so much importance to ruins, material remains, residue, or detritus and to those conceptual personae that are fully at home within them (the ragpicker [*Lumpensammler*], the prostitute, the flâneur, etc.): the former are topoi that make one understand that an inconspicuous object can sometimes grant an initial unity a power that it lacks on its own, that is, the power to take leave of the thoroughly familiar and easily recognizable totality it once was.[44] Benjamin claims that it is only by that very token and on account of its fragmentized state that an original totality becomes "legible."[45] Such meaning is therefore inevitably experienced as dislocated (*entstellt*) or not in its proper place: it is discovered in an object where it quite clearly does not belong. *Unscheinbarkeit* denotes the (negative) ability of such an object to not-become-a-totality-in-its-own-right or "to interrupt its own context" and to thereby present a different but refracted unity that is experienced as external to that object itself. Inconspicuous objects are themselves exhausted by meaning, but it is precisely this quality that allows them to "actualize" a process of becoming-meaningful that is made *in*exhaustible through them. These *unscheinbare* objects allow that which they refer to (an "enigmatic wisdom," a former self) to resonate with an unexpected power to live on (*Nachleben*, *Nachgeschichte*) and with a dynamic of significance that the latter did not have on its own account. Melancholy contemplation and the *souvenir involontaire* are "determined by an astounding tenacity of intention" (O, 139) because they gain, from the very encounter with things that are not meaningful in themselves, a feeling that they therefore remain incomplete and a responsiveness to a highly improbable (but no less real) potential for significance.

"A Little History of Photography" (Contingency)

In all this, an important question remains to be looked at: why is it that *some* processes of fragmentation or depersonalization are charged with a sense of inexhaustible meaning and other ones are not? If in a meaningful experience neither the object that triggers it nor what it refers to can be regarded as meaningful in its own right, what is it then that brings about the *connection* between both that does create the possibility of a meaningful experience? The most evident answer is already ruled out from the outset: an object or experience is not made significant because the connection with the unity to which it refers seems natural and is easily discovered. Benjamin's notion of a "*non-sensuous*" (and non-sensical) similarity between an object and the refracted unity that it refers to inevitably makes the relation between the former and the latter external to them both: the meaning that inconspicuous objects become endowed with can properly speaking neither be regarded as a quality of their own nor as one of what they refer to, but it is located *in between* the two and it remains perpetually dislodged.[46] The true stakes of Benjamin's concept of *unscheinbar* revolve around the idea that because of this relational and dislocated nature of meaning, it cannot be regarded as an autonomous essence that rests in itself and, so to speak, remains dormant in specific experiences or objects until it happens to be discovered and is exposed. What strikes the eye and mind as "significant" does not derive this quality from something external that is being referred to in a direct manner, nor does it draw attention to any supposed importance of its own, but it highlights, first and foremost, a specific precariousness. Meaning, according to Benjamin, is a dynamic that takes place *against all odds*: it cannot fully present *itself* and therefore needs to be actively *produced* or *brought about*. This process of *becoming*-meaningful presupposes the creative interruption of an original unity and the subsequent construction of a relationship between two things that do not even sensuously resemble each other.[47]

It is only in the third prominent place where he takes recourse to the word *unscheinbar*, in his essay "Kleine Geschichte der Photographie" ("Little History of Photography," 1931), that Benjamin takes the time to properly identify and describe in more detail the place where this process takes shape, that is, the experience of the *subject* who encounters a moment of the past, object, or image and *makes* it meaningful in the process of actively responding to it. This idea and the accompanying plea for an empowerment and responsabilization of the spectator form the basis of his overall views on photography and cinema and his well-known theory of the mechanical production and reproduction of images. In these essays, the meaning of the notion of *unscheinbar* revolves around the third layer that was introduced in the Brecht essay, that is, transition, change, becoming-other.[48]

In the essay on photography, Benjamin describes how, upon looking at an early self-portrait of the photographer Karl Dauthendey and his fiancée (figure 15), he is struck most of all by the way in which it refers forward to the suicide, some years later, of the woman in the picture. Benjamin writes: "Or you turn up the picture of Dauthendey the photographer . . . from the time of his engagement to that woman whom he found one day, shortly after the birth of her sixth child, lying in the bedroom of his Moscow house with her veins slashed" (*SW 2*, 510). The reference to *unscheinbar* is part of a sentence a couple of lines further on in the text: "No matter how artful the photographer, no matter how carefully posed his subject, the beholder feels an irresistible urge to search such a picture for the tiny spark of contingency, of the here and now, with which reality has (so to speak) seared the subject,

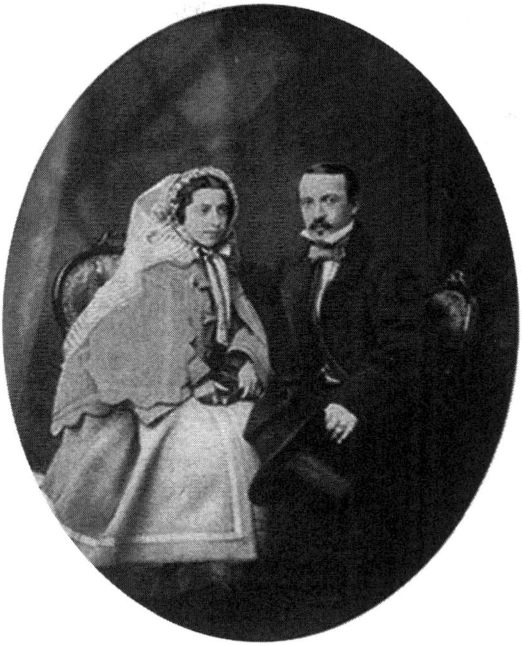

Figure 15. The photographer Karl Dauthendey and his wife, Miss Friedrich, after their first attendance at church. 1857.

to find the inconspicuous spot [*die unscheinbare Stelle*] where in the immediacy of that long-forgotten moment the future nests so eloquently that we, looking back, may rediscover it" (*SW 2*, 510; *GS II-1*, 371).

This description of how a photograph becomes meaningful in the eyes of a spectator mimics the ones that were central to Benjamin's views on melancholy contemplation and the *souvenir involontaire*: something that is clearly felt to be not fulfilled with meaning in its own right (the untimely death and violent suicide of a mother of six children) derives its sole significance from the way in which it can be encountered as a dislocated fragment or an alienated part that is, however, not meaningful in itself either (an "inconspicuous spot," the "long-forgotten moment"). This fragment, rather, produces meaning through its ability to not become one with the totality to which it most obviously belongs (a seemingly peaceful portrait of a man and his fiancée): it disrupts this easily recognizable unity, and it derives its significance precisely from not merely being a part of it and from thereby referring to a different, refracted unity that is clearly external to it (a life that was broken off prematurely). Similar to the examples of melancholy contemplation and the *souvenir involontaire*, meaning is located in the *connection* between the image and what it refers to, and this connection is described as highly arbitrary (the place where the image was "seared" by its reality is described as a "contingent spark"): there is no *necessary* link, let alone a relationship of sensuous similarity or identity, between a picture of a man and his fiancée and the violent suicide of the woman some years later.

It is important to Benjamin that, even though it would be nonsensical to claim that the image of the couple predicted the reality of the future death of the woman, the former does nevertheless, *in his mind*, refer forward to the latter.[49] For Benjamin, this paradox that images do not necessarily make sense when they produce meaning is not antithetical to the possibility that they have an overwhelming impact on the viewer's mind. This paradox, rather, even becomes constitutive of such a potential impact. For it is only this *excess* of meaning with regard to the image itself, clearly felt to be read *into* the photograph by the spectator, that can be considered to truly speak. It is this very residual significance itself, which obviously cannot be considered as an internal part of the image in its own right, which authenticates that it still remains worthy of our interest, even—and especially—after all attempts to reconstruct the original setting of the image or to interpret its initial unity of meaning have become exhausted. It is for this reason that Benjamin emphasizes that in certain images there "remains something that goes beyond testimony to the photographer's art, something that cannot be silenced, that fills you with an unruly desire to know what her name was, the woman who was alive there, who even now is still real and will never be wholly absorbed in 'art' " [*die da gelebt hat, die auch hier noch wirklich ist und niemals gänzlich in die 'Kunst' wird eingehen wollen*] (*SW* 2, 510; *GS II-1*, 370). What is crucial to Benjamin is that this "something that cannot be silenced" cannot speak on its own account and that it can only be made meaningful through the response of the viewer. For him, the creation of an image is to be seen as a starting point of an enduring process through which it gains meaning. This production of meaning takes place by virtue of its being connected with a network of facts and a set of associations and connotations that are obviously external to the image itself. Because the viewer is able to connect what is shown in a photographic image with what he himself knows, feels, and thinks, he is capable of helping the meaning of an image to go beyond its own limits, thereby granting its referent an improbable survival in the present and, in the case of past suffering, Benjamin might add, creating the possibility that it be recollected or mourned.[50] For Benjamin, that is to say, the active response to an image and the construction of its meaning involve a *transformation* or *change* of the refracted unity it refers to. The active response to a photograph comes together with the ability, on the part of the viewer, to release this refracted unity from being *merely* past and to rescue it from being a *mere* fragment. Disrupting the easily recognizable unity of an image and allowing a detail that is present in it to enter into his own mental and emotional world entails, according to Benjamin, that the viewer even becomes capable of fulfilling or redeeming that which the image refers to. This, of course, does not mean that the suicide of the fiancée can be undone or that the transience of her life could be somehow revoked. Still, while life's overall progression of annihilation cannot be unhinged altogether, Benjamin claims that it can be briefly interrupted. For, through his ability to recognize that the fiancée's death has "nested itself" in a "long-forgotten moment" that *was* captured by a camera, the viewer's active response is believed to redeem it from being a *mere* end point ("the woman who was . . . who even now is . . .").

However, there is more to Benjamin's discussion of Dauthendey's photograph than this. Because the confrontation with contingency enters wholly into the experience of encountering the photograph as a meaningful image, the feeling that it refers forward to the future of what it portrays is intrinsically linked to the sentiment that this future was not in itself necessary, that is to say, that nothing in the past that was captured by the photograph made its unhappy ending *unavoidable* or *inescapable*. The "interruptive" effect of the active response to the photograph itself, and the highly improbable character of the meaning that it yields, inevitably have an impact on what it is felt to convey, and they cannot but infect it with a sense of *openness*. Experiencing the similarity between the photograph of the couple and the future violent death of the fiancée *as* non-sensuous, and thereby remaining fully aware of how non-sensical this connection really is, increases the feeling that these future events were not at all preordained or endowed with a necessity that was proper to them. By that token, these very events become legible as contingent upon external circumstances and as not inevitable in their own right. What is most moving about Benjamin's description of Dauthendey's photograph is therefore that it shows how an active response to it in the present is experienced as being capable of injecting an irreducible feeling of *possibility* even into what seems utterly immune to change, that is, a fact of the past. In this way, it instills difference even into what is most determined of all, a moment in history: the violent death of the fiancée *was* not avoided in reality, but Benjamin nevertheless derives from Dauthendey's image the feeling that it *could have been* if the circumstances were other. The result of his attentiveness to what has remained inconspicuous in the image is a sentiment that no power in the past was able to turn this future violence, however real it may have been, into an event with an ineluctable character of its own. The discovery that a future moment of suffering is in a way already to be found within the image of an otherwise peaceful past is thus, on account of the experience of utter contingency and the improbability of this connection, capable of presenting even an untimely death as not fully closed off and internally complete ("the woman who was . . . who even now is . . . who will never be fully absorbed").

Benjamin's concept of the "inconspicuous spot" differs from the "tiny spark of contingency" that in the view of Roland Barthes produces a meaningful experience in a photograph. Barthes understands the *punctum* as the photographic image's "accident which pricks me (but also bruises me, is poignant to me)"[51] or as a "detail [that] is offered by chance and for nothing."[52] Like

Benjamin, Barthes maintains that the photographic image does not derive genuine meaning from the unity it naturally belongs to (the unary image, the *studium*), but only from the viewer's capacity to recognize in it a residual significance in the form of a different, refracted unity (*punctum, sense obtus*). The *punctum*, writes Barthes, "is an addition: it is what I add to the photograph and *what is nonetheless already there*."[53] However, the temporality that both authors see at work in this process of the image's meaningful disintegration differs in an important way. Benjamin emphasizes the viewer's "irresistible urge to *search*" (*den Zwang . . . zu suchen*) (*SW* 2, 510; *GS II-1*, 371, my emphasis) for the hidden meaning of an image, his productive role in the process of *making* it meaningful, and the *contingency* of the relation between the image and its meaning. For this reason, the viewer's initial acknowledgment of the being-past of the life in the image goes hand in hand, strangely enough, with the sense that his interruptive response can somehow save it from being *nothing but* past. On account of the contingency that is preserved in the experience, it even testifies to the inherent openness of the future and it restores the faith in a potential for change. Barthes, on the other hand, focuses on how the viewer is made power*less* in the process of being addressed by the *punctum*, and he describes how overwhelmingly *strong* this connection between the image and its unexpected meaning really is: "A detail overwhelms the entirety of my reading; it is an intense mutation of my interest, a fulguration."[54] "The detail," writes Barthes, moreover "[is allowed] to rise *of its own accord* into affective consciousness."[55] For this reason, the overwhelming experience that the *punctum* delivers always and necessarily comes together with the feeling that the death of the person that is portrayed was *unavoidable*: "By attesting that the object has been real . . . the photograph surreptitiously induces belief that it is alive . . . but by shifting this reality to the past ('this-has-been'), the photograph suggests that it is already dead."[56] It is crucial for Benjamin that the "tiny spark of contingency with which reality has (so to speak) seared the subject" makes a "long-forgotten past" mournable by allowing it to point forward to a merely *possible* future. For Roland Barthes, on the contrary, the *punctum* is first and foremost a confrontation with "what-has-been" and a moment that, remaining completely closed off from the present, presents death as an inescapable *necessity*. "The circle is closed, there is no escape," writes Barthes while contemplating a photograph of his deceased mother: "When it is painful, nothing in it can transform grief into mourning. . . . Not only is the Photograph never, in essence, a memory . . . but it actually blocks memory, quickly becomes a counter-memory."[57]

Conclusion

In crucial passages in Benjamin's writings the word *unscheinbar* denotes the ability of a moment in history, an object, or an image to not become a unity in its own right. For this reason, what is termed as such can according to Benjamin present a refracted view on a unity that remains external to that moment, object, or image itself. These views build on the idea that what is *unscheinbar* appeals to the viewer's active response and this precisely by displaying its own incompleteness: what is *unscheinbar* is experienced as something that is merely *potentially* meaningful and that needs to be actualized by something that it has no natural connection with. In this moment of actualization, the meaning of an initial unity undergoes an important alteration in that it is released from any sense of internal necessity or teleology.[58] On account of the contingency of the link between an inconspicuous phenomenon and the meaning that is created through it, the concept of *Unscheinbarkeit* denotes the strongest possible counterforce to what Benjamin calls "Fate" (*Schicksal*) or "myth."[59] As will be further developed in the next chapter, in his opinion, fate and myth are interwoven with the experience of "the false errant totality, the absolute totality" (*SW 1*, 340) of life as such in that they presuppose that moments, objects, images, or even human beings derive their meaning *solely* and *completely* from a unity to which they are supposed to *naturally* belong. On account of this necessary and natural connection between a phenomenon and the totality that supposedly determines its entire life, the experience of a fated or mythic force comes along with the sentiment that moments, objects, images, or human beings are complete in themselves and that there is nothing in them that remains open or invites a fulfillment or prolongation from without.[60] For this reason, what is fated is inevitably experienced as a closed-off unity in its own right and as something that, through the mythic force that is at work within it, actualizes only the possibilities that were preordained for it. Fate extinguishes everything that is still open to change and thus *merely* possible in a moment, object, image, or human being, and it brings them on display as entities that, on their own account and with an inherent necessity, are realizing a life that is a-priori determined.[61] What is encountered as fated cannot therefore be released from a form of *Schein* (semblance) (*SW 1*, 204) in that it has *internalized* life and closed itself off from any dynamic that, coming from outside, would interrupt this seeming autonomy.[62]

As stated at the outset of this discussion, Benjamin endorses the Platonic viewpoint that "truth is the content of beauty" (*O*, 31) and that it is therefore interwoven with a form of semblance through which it shines forth as a secret (beautiful semblance as "the necessary veiling of things for us" [*SW 1*, 351]). It was in this context that the word *unscheinbar* was used in a seemingly privative way ("unveiled, truth would prove to be infinitely inconspicuous" [*SW 1*, 351]). We can now understand, however, why Benjamin adds to this the idea that the mysterious unity in which truth becomes interwoven with beautiful semblance and seems to rest in itself as an autonomous totality cannot on its own account present truth as such: the dimension of beautiful semblance is what lures the eye of the viewer and what seduces him with the *promise* of truth (this is why Benjamin writes that "truth is beautiful" but "*only for whoever seeks it*" [O, 31, my emphasis]), but it cannot itself present anything that is truly meaningful. The seeming autonomy of what mysteriously appears to harbor truth needs therefore for its part to be interrupted by something that comes from without and presents it as not otherwise fulfilled and incomplete. This is what Benjamin calls the "expressionless" (*das Ausdruckslose*) which "shatters whatever still survives as the legacy of chaos in all beautiful semblance: the false, errant totality—the absolute totality. Only the expressionless completes [*vollendet*] the work, by shattering it into a thing of shards [*zum Stückwerk zerschlägt*], into a fragment of the true world [*Fragmente der wahren Welt*], into the torso of the symbol" (*SW 1*, 340; *GS I-1*, 181). What Benjamin elsewhere terms *unscheinbar* and what is further analyzed in his reading of Charlie Chaplin, thus comes together with all the qualities of what can also be called "expressionless": it denotes the ability to release a seemingly autonomous unity from itself by making manifest a fragment that does not derive its meaning from that original unity. This fragment can only create meaning (it "completes the work") by way of an enduring interruption of the totality in which it was initially experienced. The fragment thereby reveals this totality as structurally incomplete and unfulfilled on its own account and, by that token, as still awaiting the external movement of being-made-meaningful.

Chapter 5

✦

Charlie Chaplin

"Man Would Not Be the Noblest on Earth if He Were Not Too Noble for It"

The headlines of the newspapers on the day that Benjamin kills himself by overdosing on pills make it clear that a peril of an altogether different scale might have been resonating in his individual feelings of despair. *The Times* of September 26, 1940, for instance, reports that Britain's Royal Air Force (RAF) managed to bomb no less than two factories, a power station, a foundry, and a canal bridge in the heart of Berlin. For their part, at 4:30 in the afternoon, 100 German planes of the Luftwaffe have attacked the Spitfire factory in Woolston, Southampton, adding at least 30 factory workers to the list of casualties in the United Kingdom (the week before 1,300 people had been killed in London alone), with raids on the capital and other important British cities continuing for a long time to come. It seems that what started off as a military conflict between nation-states is now turning into a catastrophic event on a more cosmic scale, reducing the space for mutual understanding and harmony on both sides of the Channel to a vanishing point. This is how *The Daily Mail* puts it on the front page of their edition: "From many neutral sources yesterday came unimpeachable evidence of the shock with which the R.A.F.'s latest raids on Berlin came to a population that was always taught to regard itself as secure. The life of Berlin, like the life of London, is being painfully revolutionised by bombs."[1]

On the same day, however, in Copenhagen, the Danish King Christian X is celebrating his seventieth birthday. A famous photograph that is printed a day later in most international newspapers shows him firmly saddled on his horse, proudly parading the streets of the Danish capital and cheered on by hundreds of admirers and well-wishers. This is, indeed, quite an extraordinary event since, six months prior to that date, Denmark has been invaded by the Germans in a surprise attack. The king's daily and unaccompanied rides through the city have therefore become a symbol of the passive resistance of the Danes, since he feigns indifference and makes a show of failing to acknowledge the German occupiers.[2]

However seemingly at odds with each other they may be, these news reports on the day of Benjamin's death indicate elements that are crucial to understand both his life and work. For it has by now become a cliché that his philosophy is organized around the poles of hope and melancholy, resistance and despair, or, in Anson Rabinbach's words, Enlightenment and Apocalypse.[3] What is usually meant by this is that, while certain elements in Benjamin's work testify to a belief in the powers of man to think, act, and change (Benjamin's so-called activism), other elements in his work are at odds with such optimism since they refer to a more universal state of gloom (Benjamin's so-called mournfulness). The final chapter of this book, however, focuses on Benjamin's writings on Charlie Chaplin because a close reading of these fragments and paragraphs results in a more refined and nuanced approach of precisely these two *Grundgefühle*. Of Chaplin, that is, Benjamin writes that he "has become the greatest comic because he has incorporated into himself the deepest fears of his contemporaries" (*SW* 2, 792; *GS VI*, 103), but also that he is like an "angel of peace who is suited to this world / who attends to this world" (*SW* 2, 590; *GS IV*, 406, translation modified). What is at stake in Benjamin's interpretation of Chaplin is therefore not so much an indication of how he has incorporated elements of hope *alongside* elements of despair, but the chance to encounter points in his work, and in Benjamin's own work, where hope and despair have become *inseparable* from each other. Hope and despair, in other words, are to Benjamin not indications of two realities that exist independently from each other, but rather they are vectors that refer to one and the same reality, albeit from two different perspectives: in crucial places in the work of Chaplin and Benjamin, hope and despair are two different views on one and the same thing.

The Compass of Success ("A Caprice in the Workings of the Universe")

One way to start this analysis of Benjamin's views on Chaplin is to return to a short text written for the *Frankfurter Zeitung* in June 1932 and printed under the title "Ibizan Sequence." In one of its paragraphs Benjamin describes how he sets out to look for what he calls "the compass by which to determine all the winds, favorable and unfavorable, that play their games with human existence" and immediately adds to this the remark that "nothing remains but to define [the] meeting point [*Mitte*] [of these winds], the point of intersection [*Schnittpunkt*] of the axes, the site of complete inseparability of success and failure" (*SW* 2, 590; *GS IV*, 406, translation modified).[4] To understand how success and failure can become inseparable and, moreover, to indicate the essential difference between this concept of inseparability and that of mere identity (for it does not make sense to claim that success and failure can become one and the same thing), Benjamin attacks the "deeply rooted prejudice that willpower [*der Wille*] is the key to success" (*SW* 2, 589;

GS IV, 404).[5] This already illustrates at the outset that Benjamin's views on success result from his interest in "pure" means: in line with his descriptions of "politeness, sympathy, peaceableness, trust" as "subjective preconditions" for a "nonviolent resolution of conflict" (*SW 1*, 244, translation modified) or with his interpretation of friendliness as, as we have seen in the previous chapter, "a promise nothing short of messianic" (*SW 4*, 248), and in line, moreover, with his overall ideas on language and political action, Benjamin emphasizes, in this context as well, the importance of noninstrumental or non-teleological types of activity. "In general," he states, "what reveals the true nature of success is not the reasons that account for it" (*SW 2*, 589). What deserves to be called "success," therefore, neither refers to an end in its own right nor to a means to an end, but is to be understood as an indication of what, in the essay on violence, is called "unalloyed" means (*SW 1*, 244). This means that true success is neither something we can realize by striving towards it, nor a measure for the degree of perfection we have acquired in realizing other aims.

An important step in understanding this plea for a noninstrumental manner of acting entails the introduction of a *world*. One of the reasons why success "has very little to do with the willpower that pursues it" is that this line of argument presupposes that "success concern[s] only the individual" whereas it is in truth "also an expression of the fact that an individual's life intervenes in the structure of the world as a whole" (*SW 2*, 589; *GS IV*, 404–5).[6] Success, therefore, is always and necessarily a relational quality, denoting the active and reactive interactions that are set up between human beings and the world that surrounds them. This world, moreover, cannot be regarded as mere material for a human being's actions, lying in wait to be molded by his will. In an important formula, Benjamin summarizes it as follows: "Success, which some people so readily dismiss as the blind activity of chance, is the deepest expression for the contingencies for this world [*der tiefste Ausdruck für die Kontingenzen dieser Welt*]. Success is a caprice in the workings of the universe [*die Marotte des Weltgeschehens*]" (*SW 2*, 589; *GS IV*, 405, translation modified). It is for this reason, first of all, that success cannot be fully separated from failure: it can only become visible in a world that manifests itself as *not* fully controlled by human beings and, for that reason, it cannot but also expose that the human quest to objectify and instrumentalize the world is bound to fail. Success, however, indicates a situation in which, *in spite of* the world's ultimate uncontrollability, the position of a human being is not reduced to mere passivity: in success, a human being shows that he remains responsive to a fundamentally disorganized world, engaging with it in a meaningful way. This argument is further elaborated in a paragraph entitled "Practice" ("*Übung*") included in the same "Ibizan Sequence." Of importance to Benjamin's later view on cinema as a "training instrument" (*Übungsinstrument*), Benjamin describes in this paragraph an embodied process of learning that brings about a fundamental alertness to the world. In this sense, Benjamin disagrees with Simmel's view that an individual is *always already* open to the world that surrounds him and argues, instead, that such a "non-closedness" (*Unabgeschlossenheit*) needs to be actively created. In his "Ibizan Sequence," Benjamin connects such a responsiveness to a training process that includes an element of failed control and is therefore to be likened to "success conjured up by luck" (*Erfolg . . . die das Glück herbeiruft*): "The fact that in the morning the pupil knows by heart the contents of the book he has put under his pillow the night before, that the Lord inspires His own in their sleep, and that a pause is creative [*die Pause schöpferig ist*]—to make space [*dem Spielraum zu geben*] for such things to happen is the alpha and omega of all mastery, its hallmark" (*SW* 2, 590–91; *GS IV*, 406). With the example of the famous juggler Enrico Rastelli, Benjamin goes on to describe a manner of relating to the outside world and the objects within it where the latter are, rather than overpowered or controlled, received as an external force with which to dynamically and creatively engage. Rastelli, that is, does not *look* for the ball, but, to the contrary, his "stretched-out little finger *attracts* the ball [*rief . . . den Ball herbei*], which hops onto it like a bird" (*SW* 2, 591; *GS IV*, 406, my emphasis). This, however, "does not mean that either his body or the ball is 'in his power' but it enables the two to reach an understanding behind his back" (*SW* 2, 591; *GS IV*, 406).[7] Practice, therefore, denotes the diligence and hard work through which the body discovers capacities that are released from the mastery of reason and willpower. No longer controlled and unified by these faculties, the body allows, instead, "each of [the] limbs [to] act in accordance with their own rationality." Through practice, a body learns to shed an important part of its internal unity, while not, however, disintegrating into mere bits and pieces but in order to become a force that is open to the outside world and remains responsive to its variety of movements. Hence, for instance, the specific importance of the hand in reaching success through practice: "Practice is successful because the will abdicates its power once and for all inside the body, abdicates in favor of the organs—the hand, for instance" (*SW* 2, 591).

Second, Benjamin's formula that success is "the deepest expression for the contingencies for this world" makes clear that while the universe is lacking in any fundamental form of order or logic, it cannot be reduced to a state of mere arbitrariness either. The statement that success has nothing to do with "the blind activity of chance" (*Zufall*) but needs to be taken for a "caprice in the workings of the universe" indicates that the only element that somehow counterbalances the contingency of the world nevertheless shares in this very same contingency. For with the formula that success is a "caprice" Benjamin does not at all raise doubts about the possibility that the world could be encountered as meaningful in the first place. To the contrary, this formula describes the conditions of possibility for the expression of meaning, since it seems that, as I have described in the previous chapter, for Benjamin, contingency is not at all antithetical to meaningfulness: contingency, rather, enters into the structure of the expression of meaning *and*, moreover, it endows it with a succinct urgency of its own. For this last reason, the idea that an experience of contingency belongs to the heart of the expression of meaning does not entail the idea that meaning would be *itself* a category of contingency. Experiencing success as a "caprice in the workings of a (contingent) world" means that, in spite of a great number of possible responses to the world, one has nevertheless managed to find the one response that gets it exactly right. Upon entering into the expression of meaning, therefore, the experience of contingency undergoes an important change: the world is no longer experienced as *merely* contingent but it has, in fact, been charged with an unexpected form of necessity.[8] Success, in this manner, describes the perception that a world that is devoid of a principle of internal order has nonetheless catered to one's wishes. If the world is somehow encountered as meaningful, therefore, this has neither to do with the discovery of a form of teleology that suspends the contingency of the world from *within*, nor with the human faculty of reason that can, so to speak, resolve its contingencies from *without* (by way of, for instance, cognition or practical thinking), but with the ability to react in such a way *to* contingency that one brings into existence something that *exceeds* it: in a world that lacks a more universal type of lawfulness, one has seemingly succeeded in giving shape to a lawfulness of one's own. To illustrate this, Benjamin gives the example of serendipity: "This is why you can look for something for days, until you finally forget it; then, one day, when you are looking for something else, you suddenly find the first object. Your hand has, so to speak, taken the matter in hand and has joined forces with the object" (*SW* 2, 591; *GS IV*, 406–7).[9] In such instances, the world simultaneously expresses the two mutually exclusive qualities of indifference and generosity, without in any way allowing one of those qualities to mitigate the other: the world becomes manifest as foreign (the world is simply too large for me to take it all in, I should rather stop looking) *and* as profoundly familiar (still, for no apparent reason at all, I managed to act in such a way that the world gives me precisely what I want). This disparity illustrates that success presupposes *both* a sustained openness to an uncontrollable outside world *and* the surprising ability to nevertheless find fulfillment or completion within it.[10] Success, for this reason, does not just require an abdication of one's will: a genuine responsiveness to what cannot be controlled entails that one truly sets up a novel relationship with contingency and "has joined forces with the object."

The Origin of German Tragic Drama (Heroes and Antiheroes)

Taking a look at Benjamin's own writings with this "compass of success" in hand, we stumble upon an interesting paradox: the way Benjamin describes the tragic hero makes clear that he did not at all consider him a figure of success. The first reason for this is that, in encountering his life as predetermined, the tragic hero lacks all feeling for the contingency of this world.[11] In tragedy, the power of predetermination comes in at least two different forms. The first one is Fate (*Schicksal*). Benjamin's analysis runs parallel to Simmel's view that the presence of Fate in tragedy denotes "the resolution of the uncanniness of coincidence into necessity."[12] The tragic hero experiences life as a realm that is governed by the obscure yet inescapable force of Destiny. This explains why the tragic hero inhabits a mythical universe without a historical index and fights an essential ambiguity or lack of clarity that he experiences as universally present. "The object of tragedy is not history, but myth, and the tragic stature of the *dramatis personae*, derives from the prehistoric epoch of their existence—the past age of heroes" (*O*, 62). Fate "corresponds to the natural condition of the living" and to a "semblance" that is "not yet wholly dispelled" (*SW 1*, 204). Benjamin connects this fundamental ambiguity with an original condition of guilt (*Schuld*) and understands the hero as a person who takes this condition fully onto himself: "This guilt, which according to the ancient statutes falls upon men from without through misfortune, is taken over by a hero in the course of the tragic action and absorbed into himself [*in sein Inneres*]" (*O*, 131; *GS I*, 310). The tragic hero, in other words, encounters his own life as always already guilty and meets existence as a fight to extinguish this ancient curse: "Fate shows itself . . . in the view of life, as condemned, as having essentially first been condemned, and then become guilty" (*SW 1*, 204). For this reason, the tragic hero is haunted by what Benjamin calls "individual time," that is, by the idea that history can be fulfilled by the actions of a great individual (*SW 1*, 56). In this manner, however, the tragic hero jumps over history pure and proper and identifies himself with a super-historical task: in fighting off necessities that come from an unformed and obscure "elsewhere," he has closed himself off from *this* world and stands prepared to confront what can only be called a "demonic" power.

A second reason why the tragic hero cannot in Benjamin's view open himself up toward contingency has to do with something that Simmel associates with human existence *as such*, that is, the all-pervasive presence, in life, of a different type of inescapable necessity: death. For Simmel, human existence has a tragic structure to the extent that "death is related to life not like a possibility that at some point becomes reality, but rather . . . we . . . are always *such beings that will die*" (*R*, 71). In Benjamin's account, however puzzling it may seem, death's necessity is *not* a feature of human existence *as such* and it pertains only to that type of existence that has *become* tragic: the tragic hero does not experience the limits of his life as external to that life (this denotes, for Benjamin, the difference with Socrates) but he has fully internalized them, making death a dimension that is wholly present within life. In a certain manner, the tragic hero is always prepared to die and his death, for this reason, is not at all something that runs counter to his life: it has become a "power that is familiar, personal, and inherent in him. His life, indeed, unfolds from death, which is not its end but its form" (O, 114; *GS I*, 293; see also O, 136).[13] Like guilt, the inescapability of death has become so fully absorbed by, and in, the life of the tragic hero that it makes a genuinely "historical" existence impossible and results in an immunity vis-à-vis the openness and the possibilities that mark the immanent realm. In pitting the experience of an internalized death *against* a truly historical existence, Benjamin thus subverts the argument that underlies Simmel's interpretation of Rembrandt's portraits, where the intimate experience of one's own mortality is precisely considered as a feature *of* a truly historical existence and a condition *for* an "openness" to the world. For Benjamin, to the contrary, the experience that life and death can in no way be separated turns death into a suffocating presence. In tragic life, such a fully absorbed and all-pervasive death should in fact rather be called "an ironic immortality, ironic from an excess of determinacy. . . . In tragedy, the hero dies because no one can live in fulfilled time. He dies of immortality" (*SW 1*, 56).

When Benjamin emphasizes that the tragic hero emerges from these struggles on the winning side, moreover, this victory over the demonic should not be understood as a token of success either. Benjamin, to be sure, does state that "in tragedy . . . the head of genius lifted itself for the first time from the mist of guilt, for in tragedy demonic fate is breached" (*SW 1*, 203) and that "in tragic poetry the ancient curse which has been passed down from generation to generation, becomes the inner, self-discovered possession of the tragic character. And it is thus extinguished" (O, 126). Still, like guilt and death, this victory is fully absorbed into the life of the hero and for that reason does not involve a genuine "intervention in the structure of the world as whole." The ultimate clash between the tragic hero and the gods is by all means an event that "concern[s] only the individual" and when he "realizes that he is better than his gods" (O, 109) this does not result in any profound change within history: the "idea of a fulfilled historical time is never identical with the idea of an individual time. This feature naturally changes the meaning of fulfillment completely, and it is this that distinguishes tragic time from messianic time" (*SW 1*, 56). The indication of the absorption of this victory within the individual and, as a consequence, of an ultimate lack of success on the part of the hero, is his silence. This muteness reveals an inability to turn meaning into something that is communicable to other people: it is not played out in *this* (interpersonal) world but withdraws in a super-historical realm. The tragic hero does therefore not at all escape from the violence of the mythical world and his actions are "far from inaugurating a purer sphere" (*SW 1*, 249). His momentary victory over the demonic powers of fate does not result in a genuine "reconcil[iation] with the pure god" (*mit dem reinen Gott versöhnten*) (O, 109; *GS I*, 288) and it does not give rise to a truly just order: "There is no question of the 'moral world order' being restored; instead, the moral hero, still dumb, not yet of age—as such he is called a hero—wishes to raise himself by shaking that tormented world" (*SW 1*, 203; see also O, 109–10).

Benjamin's suggestion that the actions of the tragic hero do not deserve to be called "successful" because they do not have any genuine bearing on the contingencies of history is further illustrated by his understanding of the tragic hero's death as the primordial sacrifice that founds a mythically unified community. By unifying a novel people on the basis of a supposed sacrifice of a great individual, that is, the death of the tragic hero *extends* the powers of myth rather than *expelling* them in a turn toward immanence. "Tragic poetry is based on the idea of sacrifice . . . being at once a first and a final sacrifice. A final sacrifice in the sense of the atoning sacrifice [*Sühnopfers*] to gods who are upholding an ancient right; a first sacrifice in the sense of the representative action [*stellvertretenden Handlung*], in which new aspects of the life of the nation become manifest" (*O*, 106–7; *GS I*, 285).[14] The birth of such a new "nation" cannot for Benjamin entail the promise of true justice or genuinely historical and political emancipation because it simply translates the demonic power of fate into the no less demonic and mythic force of law: "The laws of fate—misfortune and guilt—are elevated by law to measures of the person" (*SW 1*, 203). Of key importance in this transition of the final sacrifice (that overthrows the powers of the gods) to the first sacrifice (that founds a divinized community) is the name of the tragic hero, which is endowed with a mythic power: "The tragic hero, in his immortality, does not save his life but only his name" (*O*, 136). In these early passages Benjamin already prepares the ground for his later analysis of the "reactionary" mass as an "impenetrable, compact entity" (*SW 3*, 129) where "the emotional element" and "the unmediated reactions" are a "determining factor." For when the death of the tragic hero endows him with quasi-divine characteristics, "invalidat[ing] the ancient rights of the Olympians" but not without simultaneously "offer[ing] up the hero to the unknown god as the first fruits of a new harvest of humanity," this can only lead to a pernicious movement in which a *Volk* internalizes the authority of a leader and thus mythologizes its own supposedly super-historical essence (*O*, 107).

A most cursory glance at Benjamin's oeuvre suffices to bring out that it devotes ample attention to *anti*heroes and, moreover, it is plain to see that it is to these that his heart really goes out. In Kafka's work, for instance, Benjamin discovers first and foremost "the figure of a failure" (*SW 3*, 327) because he deems him ultimately incapable of believing in the possibility that the historical could ever be fulfilled by anything absolute: Kafka "regarded his efforts as failures [*als verfehlt*] . . . and counted himself among those who were bound to fail [*die scheitern mußten*]. He did fail in this grandiose attempt to convert poetry into teachings, to turn it into a parable and restore to it that stability and inconspicuousness [*Unscheinbarkeit*] which, in the face of reason, seemed to him the only appropriate thing for it" (*SW 2*, 808; *GS II*, 427–28).[15] This failure to express the workings of something absolute within history is, however, a prime example of a failure that is inseparable from success. For, in crucial places of his work, Kafka lets go of this quest for the stability of religious teachings but in this very manner creates a space for "a whole group of creatures, [n]one of which have a firm place [*feste Stelle*] in the world, or firm, inalienable outlines," yet "for whom there may be hope" (*SW 2*, 798–99; *GS II*, 414–15).[16] Benjamin describes the confidence man from the story "Unmasking a Confidence Trickster," the fools from the story "Children on a Country Road" (both in the collection *Meditation*), and Karl Rossmann's neighbor from the novel *Amerika* as belonging to the class of the "assistants" (*Gehilfen*) who are *unfertig* and *ungeschickt* (*GS II*, 415). As such, he clearly places them in a realm that cannot be fully touched by either the powers of Fate or the all-pervasiveness of an internalized death. These assistants, however clumsy and half-witted they may be, are perpetually "*non*-prepared" to die but therefore grow capable of surviving in an unexpected way (*unfertig* means incompetent, but also "unfinished" or "unready"): however implausible and utopian it may sound, in the existence of these assistants, life and death do seem to part ways. What is more, these assistants are indifferent to the idea that they were "sent" by Destiny, but for this very reason they remain free to undergo the most awkward modifications (*ungeschickt* means unskilled but also "disordered," "uncalled-for," or "un-Fated"). They are, in other words, fully exposed to the contingencies and unexpected shifts and turns that mark a realm of constant transition, and their universe is "at once unfinished and everyday" (*SW 3*, 799). Kafka's assistants are "neither members of, nor strangers to, any of the other groups of figures, but, rather, messengers busy moving between them" (*SW 3*, 798), and they continuously take on the most surprising guises: "There is not one that is not either rising or falling, none that is not trading qualities with its enemy or neighbor, none that has not completed its period of time and yet is unripe, none that is not deeply exhausted and yet is only at the beginning of a long existence" (*SW 3*, 799). It is in such places, far removed from any context of heroism, that Kafka's work manages to point to the possibility of escaping the "excess of determinacy" that marks the tragic universe and warding off the mythic powers that come together with it: he "did not succumb to [the] temptation" to believe the "redemption promised by myth," and the powers of myth "cease to be invincible" (*SW 3*, 799).

Benjamin's opposition between Greek tragedy and the German *Trauerspiel* can also be clarified from this perspective. From the very first pages of his book on the *Trauerspiel* on, Benjamin emphasizes that "historical life . . . is its content, its true object" and that "in this it is different from tragedy. For the object of the latter is not history, but myth" (*O*, 62). The universe of the *Trauerspiel* is indeed to an extreme degree marked by contingency, since "the baroque knows no eschatology; and for this very reason it possesses no mechanism by which all earthly things are gathered in together and exalted before being consigned to their end" (*O*, 66). As a "representative of history," the sovereign, for instance, bears a crucial resemblance to the martyr, since "in the *Trauerspiel* monarch and martyr do not shake off their immanence"

(O, 67) and thereby remain oblivious to the tragic hero's super-historical task and his ideal of an ultimate redemption by way of "individual time." The ability to cope in the face of extreme danger, on the contrary, is about the highest mission to which a monarch can aspire, his "most important function" being "to avert . . . the state of emergency" (O, 65). It is no surprise, therefore, that Benjamin cuts the events that are described in the *Trauerspiel* loose from the all-determining presence of Fate and, when he describes it as a "drama of fate" (*Schicksalsdrama*), this has nothing to do with any heroic absorption of guilt and death. For in the *Trauerspiel* Fate becomes dispersed to the world at large and thereby loses its pseudo-transcendent ambivalence and mythic semblance: in the *Trauerspiel*, "destiny is not only divided among the characters, it is equally present among the objects [*es waltet gleichermaßen in den Dingen*]" (O, 132; *GS I*, 311). In the *Trauerspiel*, Fate does not simply *disappear* but, to the contrary, the necessity through which it makes itself felt is *heightened* to such a degree that it becomes tainted with the vicissitudes of *this* world and is gradually pushed into history. In the *Trauerspiel*, "everything intentional or accidental is so intensified [*sich steigert*] that the complexities betray, by their paradoxical vehemence [*paradoxe Heftigkeit*], that the action of this play has been inspired by fate" (O, 130; *GS I*, 308–9). The essential difference between such an intensified but "equally present" fate and the mythic presence of Fate in tragedy is that the former resists any and all attempts at internalization by a supposedly great individual. In externalizing Fate to the outside world and by granting it a visible presence within history, the *Trauerspiel* turns it into a presence that can be actively responded to by ordinary human beings. Benjamin's opposition between the transcendence of Fate and the immanence of history runs parallel to Simmel's idea that, as I have explained in the second chapter, in ordinary life, fate does not "descend" upon human beings but "rather . . . bursts out of them" (*R*, 102). In its turn toward immanence and history, that is, Fate loses its capital F and is tamed into the plural "fates": the pull of *das Schicksal* is expelled by the dynamic contingencies that color *die Schicksale* of a life played out in history and, rather than denoting an obscure and unformed *jenseits* (beyond), the latter indicate a profoundly accessible yet not fully controllable *diesseits* (here and now).[17] Similarly, in the *Trauerspiel*, guilt becomes a general condition that is shared by all and thus no longer triggers an individual quest for its final and complete annihilation through sacrifice: it is not "extinguished" but "worked out" (*wirkt . . . sich . . . aus*) (O, 132; *GS I*, 310) or, as Eli Friedlander puts it, it "runs its course": "Death, as the form of tragic life, is an individual destiny; in the *Trauerspiel* it frequently takes the form of a communal fate" (O, 136).[18] Thus voiding the ideal of an "individual time," the temporality that underlies the *Trauerspiel* is now no longer that of decisive action, final fulfillment, or ultimate completion through a supposedly absolute gesture, but it indicates an immanent force of repetition: the *Trauerspiel* "has no proper end" (O, 135). Having discovered fate as an irreducible presence within history that needs to be constantly reckoned with but that does not seek any grandiose and super-historical action, the *Trauerspiel*, in short, "has no individual hero, only constellations" (*O*, 132, translation modified).

Benjamin's emphasis on the importance of acknowledging the contingency of history does not merely underlie his views on the difference between tragedy and the *Trauerspiel*, but also his distinction between tragedy and comedy. For, in the "Ibizan Sequence," he stresses that it is first and foremost the *comic* figure who needs to be regarded as the antipode to the tragic hero. The comic figure "is quite unconcerned about destiny, myth or doom" and "in his eyes success is no lucky star [*Stern*], failure no unlucky star [*Unstern*]" (*SW 2*, 590; *GS IV*, 405).[19] The success of the comic figure cannot be released from his particular stance within a profoundly disorganized and chaotic universe, and nowhere does it transcend the level of "caprice": the "justice of comedy is the work not of heaven but of countless mistakes that end up producing an exact result, thanks to one last little error" (*SW 2*, 590; *GS IV*, 405).[20] The comic figure cannot for this reason lay claim to any profound knowledge ("the comic figure . . . is never wise") or to an intimate feeling for its underlying unity. Meeting the world as fragmented and in constant movement, the comic figure does not at all obtain a synthesis of the Great All, yet his position in the world is one of a precise and well-balanced "belonging": the comic figure "is a rogue, a simpleton, a fool, a poor devil. But whatever he is, the world fits him like a glove" (*SW 2*, 590; *GS IV*, 405).[21] According to Benjamin, an important concept to understand this strange success of the comic figure is its idiosyncrasy: "Th[e] caprice of the universe," writes Benjamin, "corresponds to idiosyncrasy in the individual." The term "idiosyncrasy" derives from the Greek words *idios* ("private," "not-shared"), *sun* ("together with"), and *krasis* ("mixture") and thus in fact denotes an oxymoron. Indeed, in opposition to the tragic hero, whose individual absorption of guilt and death closes him off from the surrounding world but in this very manner establishes a privileged relation with a demonic "beyond," the comic figure does reach a level of indifference vis-à-vis the powers of myth but thereby loses all claim to any heroism or greatness. This first movement of seeming isolation and diminution, however, is a precondition for a more fundamental form of syncretism, namely, for a capacity to interact or even "join forces with" the many objects and events of this world. Benjamin's formula that idiosyncrasy denotes an individualized but general contingency is therefore the exact mirror image of his definition of tragedy: in tragedy, man is similarly depicted as sharing in a general condition, but this condition is one of an inaccessible yet inescapable lawfulness ("In tragedy, the laws of fate—misfortune and guilt—are elevated by law to measures of the person"). The comic figure, in other words, encounters the world as lawless and deprived of an overarching organizing principle, yet he remains attentive to its many unexpected modifications and thereby produces "an exact result" that does nevertheless express a form of necessity. Meeting the universe as deprived of any underlying and synthesizing teleology, he ceaselessly confronts it with precision and an analytic sensitivity for its many partial movements and transitions. It is in this manner that Benjamin finally gives away why the determination of someone's success in fact requires a "compass": "The key to the comic figure's nature is a *mathematical* figure" (*SW* 2, 590; *GS IV*, 405, my emphasis).[22]

Charlie Chaplin ("Theme and Variations")

Since it is, of course, Charlie Chaplin who has brought perfection to the genre of comedy, it is no surprise that Benjamin describes him, in this same "Ibizan Sequence," as the "genius of failure" (*Geniefall der Erfolglosigkeit*) and thus, ultimately, as a paradoxical figure of success: his movie character is a "schlemiel [who] takes offense at nothing; he just stumbles over his own feet. He is the only angel of peace who is suited to this world / who attends to this world [*der einzige Friedensengel, der auf die Erde paßt*]" (*SW* 2, 590; *GS IV*, 406, translation modified). Slapstick is indeed, first and foremost, the art of feeling at home within a world that utterly lacks organization and of transforming the failure to control one's surroundings into a capacity to unexpectedly "join forces with" the most random objects. For this reason, Chaplin is the master of "pure" means and "non-teleological" acting: if things work out in the end, it is never the result of careful planning or instrumental rationality. In most cases, it is *thanks to* his clumsiness and not *in spite of* it that Chaplin gets what he wants. Chaplin's work is replete with scenes that illustrate such an embodied and intense feeling for contingency, but the many scenes of fights and chases are prime examples. Most of Chaplin's opponents are clearly much stronger than he is and his chances to win a one-to-one fight are slight at the most. In most cases, therefore, Chaplin can only achieve some kind of victory over his opponent with the help of objects, other human bodies, or the elements of nature he happens to stumble upon during the fight. The success of Chaplin, therefore, is indeed never more than a mere "caprice," involving the intervention of a disparate world that is at once encountered as both uncontrollable *and* cooperative.[23]

In a short text written in 1929, "Chaplin in Retrospect," Benjamin develops this line of argument further by stating that "Chaplin was the first to construct a film with a theme and variations—in short with the element of composition—and that all stands in complete opposition to films based on action and suspense" (*SW* 2, 222–23). In opposition to Friedrich Nietzsche, Benjamin emphasizes that the medium of music is marked by a power to resist the mythic instant of absorption and that it is therefore at odds with the pseudo-natural pull towards transcendence that marks tragedy: music shares a temporal dynamic with "the time of redemption . . . or of truth" (*SW* 1, 204) because it consists of a series of notes that inevitably requires a temporal sequence, and thus needs to be allowed to "run its course." For this reason, Benjamin's emphasis on the musical structure of Chaplin's films brings out a resemblance with the underlying temporality of the *Trauerspiele*. Chaplin's films dismiss the possibility of a final solution, decisive action, or ultimate completion and replace it by an immanent dynamic of repetition that results in a sustained interaction with the most random objects. About *The Circus* (1928), for instance, Benjamin writes that "the most wonderful part is the way the end of the film is structured [*die Komposition des Schlusses*]. He strews confetti over the happy couple, and you think: this is the end. Then you see him standing there when the circus procession starts off; he shuts the door behind everyone, and you think: This must be the end. Then you see him stuck in the rut of the circle earlier drawn by poverty, and you think: This must be the end. Then you see a close-up of his completely bedraggled form, sitting on a stone in the arena. Here you think the end is absolutely unavoidable, but then he gets up and you see him from behind, walking further and further away. . . . And now, at the only point where there's no break and you'd like to be able to follow him with your gaze forever—the film ends!" (*SW* 2, 199–200; *GS VI*, 138). At odds with the ideals of Aristotelian *poiesis* in which a firm plotline and the actions of the protagonist endow the story with a semblance of internal necessity leading up to an ultimate, cathartic conclusion ("films based on action and suspense"), Chaplin's experiments with slapstick release events and scenes to a certain extent from an overarching narrative, and they play with the anticipation of a final ending. In this manner, the unity of the events that are depicted in such films is no longer anchored in the unity of something that seems, in fact, to preexist the depicted events themselves. The continuity of Chaplin's films, rather, builds itself up step by step and it cannot therefore be separated from a more fundamental *dis*continuity: it depends on specific instants that open up an unanticipated course of events and the actor's capacity to respond to them in a creative way.

Still, Chaplin is not simply your average slapstick artist: he renewed the genre from within by turning this physical interaction with random objects into a medium of *expression*. Chaplin's biographer David Robinson puts it as follows: the slapstick films that were common in his day (like the works of Sennett and the Keystone comedians) were "created from without; anecdote and situations were *explained* in pantomime and gesture. Chaplin's comedy was created from within. What the audience saw in him was the expression of thoughts and feelings, and the comedy lay in the relation of those thoughts and feelings to the things that happened around him. The crucial point of Chaplin's comedy was not the comic occurrence itself, but Chaplin's relationship and attitude to it."[24] It is for *this* reason that Benjamin singles out Chaplin among the other movie stars of his time and considers him the "genius of failure." To further understand this argument, Benjamin's statement that Chaplin, unlike other comic figures, has "releas[ed] every conviction" (*Preisgabe jedweder Überzeugung*) (*SW* 2, 590; *GS IV*, 406, translation modified) is important. Benjamin's term *Über-zeugung* suggests the superlative (*Über*) of an "act of creation" (*Zeugung*), thereby indicating that the convictions of comic figures are not results (they are not the outcome of a rational argumentation) but beginnings: these convictions come from nowhere but still—and this is what is comic about them—they invent and produce a universe of their own. The comic dimension in Gustave Flaubert's *Bouvard and Pécuchet*, for instance, is derived from the entirely gratuitous manner in which they "test every conviction" (*Annahme jedweder Überzeugung*) (*SW* 2, 590; *GS IV*, 405), the most irreconcilable convictions all of a sudden, and without any underlying reason, being accepted as dead certainties. Chaplin does not use *convictions* as elements to build up such a comic universe but *emotion*, turning the expression of feeling (and even sentiment) into the superlative of an act of creation, that is, into an *Über-zeugung*.[25] His interactions with the outside world, that is, do not simply *extend* the latter's chaos, but they also *interrupt* it and bring *something genuinely new into the picture*: an emotional dimension that is fully at odds with the universe from which it nevertheless arises. Benjamin states that Chaplin "has become the greatest comic because he has incorporated into himself the deepest fears of his contemporaries" (*SW* 2, 792) and refers to "the feminine impact of the little tramp portrayed by Chaplin / So much luster [wrapped around] so much shabbiness" (*SW* 2, 792; *GS VI*, 103, translation modified).[26]

Chaplin's genius does indeed lie in his ability to extract poetry from a world that is nevertheless encountered as disenchanted and forlorn, using its very indifference as an instrument to conjure up beauty. For Chaplin, therefore, the expression of emotion is inseparable from the expression of something that *resists* emotion, that is, the indifferent course of an external world that simply "runs its course." This disparity is what marks a scene in *The Kid* (1921) as one of the most moving scenes he has shot. Chaplin is violently restrained by a policeman and assistant while the little boy he has been taking care of is brutally taken away to a county orphanage. Chaplin manages to struggle free and escapes to the roof. However, what starts as a chase, with Chaplin running away from the policeman, suddenly changes into its opposite, a search: from a distance, Chaplin spots the car with the little boy and, making his way across roofs, meets it at the exact moment that it passes by (figure 16). The timing of this interaction between Chaplin and the car is perfect, resulting in the impression that it was not so much Chaplin who was looking for the car as the car who had been driving toward him all along.

The same disparity of emotion and *absence* of emotion underlies the romantic element in Chaplin's most famous feature films and gives them their true expressive resonance. For in those cases where there is a chance that Chaplin does manage to get the girl in the end, this is only on account of a series of coincidences and accidents, without which he, in some cases, would not even have been recognized in the first place. In the final scene of *The Gold Rush* (1925), for instance, Chaplin, who has become a millionaire, is putting

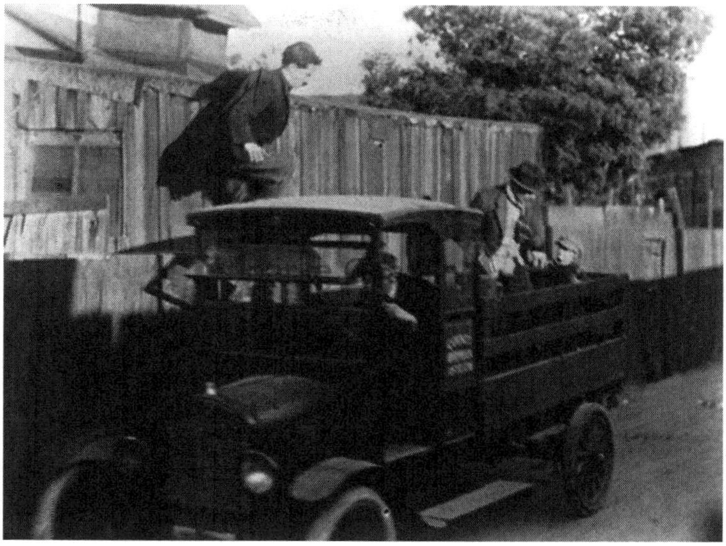

Figure 16. Charlie Chaplin, from the film *The Kid.* 1921.

on his old clothes again to pose for a journalist but suddenly slips and falls from the deck of the ship, landing at the feet of his lost love. Similarly, in the famous closing scene of *City Lights* (1931), Chaplin is tramping down the avenue when he accidentally spots the girl whose eye operation he had somehow managed to pay for. Although her sight has now been restored, she would not have been able to recognize Chaplin as her anonymous benefactor save for a coin she gently pushes in the palm of his hand, thereby recognizing the shape of his fingers and the texture of his skin. When Chaplin does manage to find the girl of his dreams in the end, therefore, he has the whole world to thank, if it were not for the fact that this same world had just been exposed as an altogether uncaring and anonymous environment.[27]

"Fate and Character" (Charlie Chaplin)

In the essay "Fate and Character," Benjamin describes the main protagonist in a comedy of character as someone "whom, if we were confronted by his actions in life instead of by his person on the stage, we would call a scoundrel [*Schurken*]" (*SW 1*, 205; *GS II*, 177). For Benjamin, the *actions* of such people are not really of interest, for these are "interesting only in so far as they reflect the light of *character*" (*SW 1*, 205, my emphasis). The concept of "character" is an important one in Benjamin's writings and, apart from his analysis of Chaplin, it underlies his views on, for instance, Dostoevsky's *The Idiot* and the protagonists in the stories of Robert Walser. The concept of character once again makes clear that, unlike Simmel, Benjamin grants the category of the individual at most a secondary significance. Any sense of a "deeper" self or inner-I, that is to say, is alien to the mental universe of characters, who cannot shake off a seeming superficiality and shallowness. Characters do not build up a unified ego through a spontaneous openness to the world's events, and their identities are not "continuous streams of becoming" that take shape in an intimate dialogue with their surroundings. Instead, the lives of characters are lived out *at odds with* their environments, and it is *they themselves* who thereby become a draw to other things. "Every event," Benjamin writes in a note about Prince Myshkin that would fit Chaplin equally well, "however remote from him it appears to be, seems to gravitate toward him, and this process in which all things and people gravitate toward this one center [*dieses Gravitieren aller Dinge und Menschen gegen den Einen*] constitutes the content of the novel" (*SW 1*, 79; *GS II*, 238). Most remarkable about characters is therefore that they are difficult to identify with on account of a lack of psychological profundity. They are "completely unapproachable" and "emanate an order at whose center we find a solitude that is almost absolute" (*SW 1*, 79). Molière, for instance, "excludes psychological analysis from his work" and "far from making [character] traits comprehensible, [his dramas] depict them with an intensifying crassness" (*SW 1*, 205; *GS II*, 177–78).[28] The comic character, for Benjamin, therefore does not derive its singularity from an inner psychological constitution or dynamic unity but, to the contrary, from the sustained and unique manner in which it continues to create its very own universe. A character, one could say, does not cease to produce the world anew according to its very own idiosyncrasies. As Eli Friedlander puts it, "character would be reflected in the unity of world that persons of character inhabit, in how they open their surroundings of life in a specifically coherent way. Persons of character have a transformative effect on their surroundings by making things happen at their own pace."[29] In this sense, characters manage to live out their inability to adapt and, so to speak, they stubbornly refuse to meet reality merely on its own conditions. Their reactions to the world are not streamlined by social norms or moral values, nor even by "ordinary" psychological motivations, but they gain a consistency through this very heterogeneity. These reactions are interruptive, but they endure *as* interruptions because they do not refer back to an underlying totality or system of assumptions. Marked by one, intensified character trait, comic figures unify their surroundings on account of an irreplaceable perspective that, in a way, obliges the world to follow *their* terms rather than the other way around. "Characters develop in [Molière's protagonists] like a sun [*sonnenhaft*], in the brilliance of its single trait [*im Glanz seines einzigen Zuges*], which allows no other to remain visible in its proximity" (*SW 1*, 205; *GS II*, 178).

In the earlier mentioned "Chaplin in Retrospect" Benjamin describes Chaplin as someone whose "mask of noninvolvement turns him into a fairground marionette" (*SW* 2, 222; *GS III*, 157).[30] Such a formula suggests that Benjamin does indeed consider Chaplin's screen personae as "characters," that is, as constituted by the movement in which a single, intensified character trait both isolates a figure ("noninvolvement") and connects it to an outside in a surprising way ("fairground marionette"). Moreover, in a fragment that will be of importance later on in this chapter, "Hitler's Diminished Masculinity," Benjamin specifies that "it would be wrong to interpret the figure of Chaplin in a purely psychological light" since it is thanks to his "outfit [*Ausstaffierung*], the cane and bowler hat" that his character is revealed: "Rarely do such popular figures fail to carry with them sundry properties or emblems that, from without, set the proper tone for them" (*SW* 2, 793; *GS VI*, 104, translation modified).[31] Both the walking stick and hat are objects that are released from their normal practical function and take on a mediating role between Chaplin and his immediate surroundings. The walking stick, for instance, is not used to reestablish contact with the firm ground under Chaplin's feet but, on the contrary, it introduces an element of instability and improvisation and seeks out the most random objects: it is a rare thing for it to touch the ground and, instead, it most often ends up as a prop for the most awkward movements and interactions (in *The Gold Rush*, for instance, Chaplin uses it to keep his trousers up while dancing). Chaplin's bowler hat is the most interesting object in this context. As David Robinson writes, in classical slapstick films "it was enough to bump into a tree to be funny. When Chaplin bumped into a tree, however, it was not the collision that was funny, but the fact that he raised his hat to the tree in a reflex gesture of apology."[32] The bowler hat is indeed first and foremost indicative of an extraordinary form of "docility" (*Gefügigkeit*) (*SW* 2, 792; *GS VI*, 103) and no character trait is more intensely expressed in Chaplin's actions. It is, therefore, politeness (*Höflichkeit*) that needs to be regarded as the "single trait" that *both* isolates Chaplin (*idios*, "mask of noninvolvement") *and* allows him to open up an internally consistent world (*sun-krasis*, "fairground marionette").

Politeness (An "Alert Openness to the Extreme, the Comic, the Private and the Surprising Aspects in a Situation")

Benjamin's views on politeness and the fundamental difference with Henri Bergson's take on this topic will provide the necessary background to understand what is at stake here. Moreover, the comparison between both will allow for a further analysis of the opposition between Benjamin's thinking on the one hand and *Lebensphilosophie* on the other. In a short paragraph in the "Ibizan Sequence," Benjamin connects "the advanced school of politeness" (*die Hohe Schule der Höflichkeit*) to "an alert openness to the extreme, the comic, the private and the surprising aspects in a situation" and thus describes it as a specific manner of being-in-the-world (*SW* 2, 588; *GS IV*,

402).[33] For Benjamin, politeness indicates the ability to not simply *resolve* a given conflict but to *extend* it in such a manner that the focus is shifted away from its insurmountability: politeness "is an agreeable way of enabling us to trade away [*hinwegzutäuschen*] the cruelty of the conflict raging between the opposing parties" (*SW* 2, 587; *GS IV*, 402, translation modified).[34] Politeness, consequentially, entails first of all a movement of distanciation and even forgetfulness on the part of the individual: Benjamin likens a polite attitude in the face of conflict to a game of solitaire and adds that "patience [*Geduld*] is in any case at the heart of politeness [*das Kernstück der Höflichkeit*] and, of all the virtues, is perhaps the only one that politeness adopts without modification" (*SW* 2, 588; *GS IV*, 402–3).[35] For this reason, politeness cannot be regarded as an instrument to bring about justice: it is "anything but a rigorous moral prescription" and, instead, it refers "merely [to] the representation of a morality that has been annulled" (*SW* 2, 587; *GS IV*, 402).[36] Through politeness, in other words, one does not immediately seek to solve a problem and rather than looking for the easiest way to bring a conflict to an end, one *suspends* such a pragmatic stance and takes the time to allow certain things to follow their own pace. Politeness, hence, inevitably includes "the representation of the fact that th[e] struggle is unresolved" (*SW* 2, 587; *GS IV*, 402).[37] Still, it is in this very element of non-immediacy that the importance of politeness can be found. For politeness is a prime example of a "pure" means or of noninstrumental behavior; that is, it refers to a manner of acting that achieves something by *interrupting* the very quest for a solution. For Benjamin, namely, politeness is "the true mediator" (*das wahrhaft Mittlere*): deferring the urge to simply reconcile the struggling parties, it musters the ingenuity that is needed to come up with entirely novel and unexpected perspectives. Because politeness originates in a deeply felt awareness that the situation with which one has to deal includes an element of unresolved injustice (it is the "product of the conflict between morality and the struggle for existence"), it adjourns the spontaneous impulse to look for solutions that are solely and directly modeled on the present state of affairs. Politeness, in other words, brings to the fore a capacity to reinvent a given condition: "It widens the conflict past all bounds, while at the same time granting entry—as helpers, mediators, and conciliators—to all those forces and authorities that it had excluded" (*SW* 2, 587; *GS IV*, 402).[38] In politeness, hence, the first movement of seeming distanciation is complemented by the ability to approach the world with an unrelenting attentiveness to what had hitherto been overlooked. Politeness indicates an active patience that gains mastery over a given conflict by first "sitting it out": politeness makes palpable a way of acting, but only at the instant when all parties are forced to admit their own inability to resolve the conflict. "Anyone who practices this will be able to seize the reins in a negotiation, and ultimately also gain control of the interests at stake" (*SW* 2, 588; *GS IV*, 402).[39] Politeness is the sign of a situation that can suddenly be rejuvenated through a specific intervention, but only when it had seemingly reached a complete deadlock. This explains why Benjamin criticizes the common viewpoint that politeness refers to the ability to follow, or worse, to internalize certain customary rules and agreed-upon conventions. "Politeness is everything when it frees itself from convention [*Konvention*]. . . . If a negotiation room is entirely surrounded by the barriers of convention . . . then true politeness comes into its own, since it tears down these barriers" (*SW 2*, 587; *GS IV*, 402).[40] In thus destroying convention, politeness shows itself as nothing less than an act of genuine "creation." Politeness, that is, indicates the ability to interrupt the power of the already known and the well-adjusted, conjuring the truly "new" in a situation that had seemingly closed itself off from all possibility of change. It testifies to the fact that, in keeping one constant eye on external elements that can mediate the conflict, one has managed to create for oneself an attitude of mental sturdiness and even stubbornness. In politeness, one simply refuses to play the game of reality merely on its own terms. Politeness, hence, is never less than a genuine addition to an otherwise hopeless situation. It entails, writes Benjamin in conclusion, "a real chance for the underdog" (*SW 2*, 588; *GS IV*, 403).[41]

Bergson's views on politeness are not only much closer to the commonsensical view, they are also steeped in a view of life that is akin to Simmel's *Lebensphilosophie*. They remain at odds with Benjamin's ideas on almost all counts. In 1885 and 1892, Bergson was invited to give the graduation speech in a lycée in Clermont-Ferrand and at the Lycée Henri-IV in Paris. Choosing for both occasions the issue of politeness as the topic of his speech, it is clear from the outset that in Bergson's mind, this quality could not be further removed from the context of comedy. Politeness, and especially what he calls "the highest form of politeness, politeness of the heart,"[42] is what for Bergson marks the true essence of the ideal of *humanitas*, and it indicates "this deepened science of the human heart that nourishes itself with an attentive study of the classics and which allows kindness, aligned with acuteness, to effortlessly move around the thousand detours of irritations and narcissisms."[43] In this manner, running counter to Benjamin's views, Bergson argues that politeness has nothing to do with an *ability* to *act* since it indicates, first and foremost, an *agility* of *thought* ("a type of intellectual flexibility") that is exemplified by philosophers like Plato and Socrates.[44] One of the main differences with Benjamin's views on politeness consists in the clear pedagogical and moral value that Bergson attaches to such an attitude: whereas Benjamin emphasizes that politeness entails "the representation of a morality that has been *annulled*" and that it is, as a consequence, a "product of the *conflict* between morality and the struggle for existence" (my emphases), for Bergson, to the contrary, it "would extend justice and kindness beyond the tangible world"[45] and numbers among "the great reconciliators of spirits and hearts."[46] This is an important element since, whereas Benjamin underlines a fundamental *dis*continuity with the world in which we live, Bergson draws attention to a supposed *continuity* between both ("would extend").

For Benjamin, that is, politeness originates in an attitude of suspension and draws on a space that has managed to retain a form of distance with regard to this world; for Bergson, to the contrary, politeness emerges *from* this world and it "arises *naturally* from the harmony and alignment of minds."[47] A second important point of difference is that Benjamin understands politeness as a twofold movement that results in the expression of *difference* (it "*widens* the conflict past all bounds" and is "the representation of the fact that the struggle is *unresolved*" [my emphasis]) since it combines a first moment of general equanimity with a second moment of precise intervention, introducing something genuinely new and unexpected. Bergson's view reverses this completely, since he ultimately seeks the expression of an *equality*: his idea of politeness does indicate, first, an ability to adapt to the different interests and sometimes even opposed viewpoints of other people, but this is only important when, in a second moment, it allows for the expression of the equality of all human beings. "What pleases us [in the polite person] is the ease with which he circulates among feelings and ideas; it is perhaps also the ability he has, when talking to us, to make us believe that he is not the same to everyone; for what is characteristic to this very polite man is to prefer each of his friends to the other ones, and to thus succeed in loving them all in the same way."[48] Bergson's model, as a consequence, is an organic one that is based on the *natural* resemblances between human beings and the innate capacity to respect them.[49] Benjamin, to the contrary, understands politeness as a capacity to truly confront the differences between human beings and to make them productive for a sustained attentiveness to the outsider. Very illuminating in this regard are the last words of Bergson's speech and Benjamin's essay: Bergson ends with an appeal to "the greatness of the Nation" (*la grandeur de la Patrie*)[50] whereas Benjamin's closes with "a real chance for the underdog." For Bergson, namely, politeness has nothing to do with a feeling for what is excluded since it is evidence, to the contrary, of the irreducible presence of ideals that are rooted fully within the natural core of humanity. It is, therefore, chief among the ideals of French Enlightenment: "It seems therefore that politeness, in all its forms . . . introduces us to an ideal republic, a true community of spirits where freedom would be the liberation of minds, equality a just distribution of considerations, and brotherhood a delicate sympathy with the sufferings of sensitivity."[51]

It is clear that, from Bergson's perspective, Chaplin's screen personae are but impolite and maladjusted fools. Agility of thought is about the last quality with which one would associate Chaplin's screen personae, and in his films a deeply felt affinity for a fellow human being only arises in a romantic context, that is, when it involves a relationship with a single individual (*The Kid* is a rare exception). The high-strung ideals of universal freedom, equality, and justice that Bergson reads into politeness are never conjured up in any of Chaplin's movies (with the sole exception of two movies that Benjamin could not have seen, *The Great Dictator* and *Monsieur Verdoux*) and, as perpetual outsiders who come most fully into their own when left all by themselves in an anonymous ditch alongside the road, the ambitious "ideal republic" that Bergson already sees looming on the horizon is rather far removed from the preoccupations of Chaplin's protagonists. Moreover, numerous different scenes illustrate that the "luster" of Chaplin's screen personae bears no resemblance whatsoever to any innate goodness or natural innocence or to an innate sense of the shared qualities between human beings. In *The Tramp* (1915), for instance, Chaplin's first impulse after chasing away a robber is to keep the girl's money himself, and in *City Lights*, upon spotting a cigarette butt on the sidewalk, the tramp brutally and without further ado pushes away another tramp to get at it. Still, it is not wrong to consider a type of humanism as central to Chaplin's art and, as Benjamin suggests, this results from the manner in which a sustained politeness can bring about "a real chance for the underdog." For Chaplin's politeness is first and foremost a type of action or, to be precise, a gesture. It has nothing to do with a flexibility of the mind but, rather, with the *in*flexibility of one physical response: the act of raising his bowler hat is stubbornly repeated and does not adapt itself to the situation. In this manner, Chaplin makes clear that politeness cannot be simply identified with a natural ability to affirm the uniqueness of one's interlocutor and accustom oneself spontaneously to it. In fact, the politeness that is expressed by and embodied in this gesture lacks the infinite variability that Bergson and Simmel associate with the dynamic of life, and it has taken on the obstinacy of a mechanical and non-differentiating repetition. It is precisely in this manner, however, that this action is endowed with the power to interrupt that Benjamin, in other contexts as well, connects to the concept of "gesture" (*Gestus*).[52] With the gesture of raising his hat in a quasi-mechanical manner, Chaplin disrupts the context of meaning in which the object that is greeted is usually encountered: the simple act of raising his hat to it adds a layer of being to an otherwise insignificant object. This does not mean that such an object gains a sudden importance or that politeness brings out an unsuspected value in it that had been overlooked. It is illustrative, in this regard, that Chaplin does not just raise his hat to human beings but also to inanimate objects. In these cases, the gesture of raising one's hat in greeting exposes all the more clearly that this added quality is something that the object in question *does not in fact deserve*.[53] By this token, such a gesture makes manifest that what it adds is no match for ordinary life and that it, therefore, brings into existence a way of being that remains genuinely "new": the act of raising his hat to a thoroughly familiar object acknowledges its presence in a manner that resists a more overarching context of meaning. For this reason, politeness is indeed an act of true "creation" or renewal, adding something to life that it will not and cannot ever fully internalize or appropriate: this gesture is an action that completes something (it entails a genuine moment of recognition), but it is bound to remain in "excess" vis-à-vis the object to which it was directed. This is why Benjamin calls politeness the "true mediator" that does not at all seek to dissolve difference but acknowledges it and makes it productive: by way of this constant repetition, the act of raising a hat recasts the most insignificant object time and again, with each instance conjuring, out of nowhere, the stubborn presence of something that remains irreducible to ordinary life. It is in this manner that politeness might entail "a real chance for the underdog": it does not show that the underdog is, in truth, just like the "normal" citizen but, to the contrary, it makes manifest, time and again, the irreducible gap that separates both. Politeness, therefore, does indeed inevitably originate in the feeling that "the struggle is unresolved": still, for the very reason that it *starts* with this intensified feeling that existence is a struggle, it installs the chance that it might *end up* with something altogether different. For, while pushing the immediate aim of true justice out of sight and thereby representing "a morality that has been annulled," it results in a prolonged yet continuously novel approach to *this* world. Politeness encounters the surrounding world again and again as imperfect but, in this movement, also discovers it as something that can still be *changed*. Politeness, therefore, might not deliver the underdog safely to the doorstep of "the greatness of the Nation" but, in the very act of shattering this "ideal republic" from within, it works up the attitude to persevere in a stubborn rejection of the status quo.

Spiel-Raum ("Body and Image Space")

This intensified, "single trait" of politeness and the concomitant, repeated gesture that again and again refuses to meet reality solely on its terms are tokens of the more fundamental paradox that Chaplin defamiliarizes the world precisely by interacting with it. In this, Chaplin's way of dealing with the world is akin to experiences and phenomena that Benjamin elsewhere describes with concepts like allegory and citability. Often, that is, Chaplin conjoins the act of affirming the simple presence of a given object directly with a response that is completely off the mark and clearly does not "fit" the object in question. Such a movement provides proof, again, that a disparity belongs at the heart of Chaplin's creative reception of the surrounding world. For, in Chaplin's disconnected response to a certain object, it is not so much the case that the object is confused with something else as that it is simultaneously placed into two very different contexts of meaning. Such a transformation of the way of being of a given object, therefore, does not entail the mere *annihilation* of the old one but its *dislocation* and the *addition* of a new one. The capacity to reinvent an object cannot, as a consequence, be separated from a moment of genuine "creation." In this context, *The Gold Rush* is the most intriguing of Chaplin's films. The signature scene for such a transformation-through-disparity is the one where Chaplin and a fellow gold-seeker are locked inside a cabin in the middle of the mountains. Since

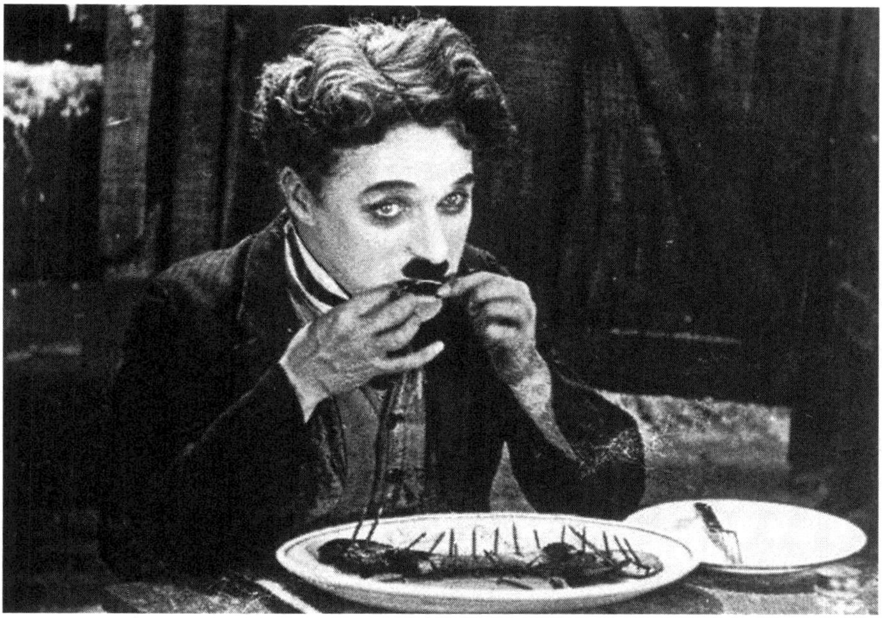

Figure 17. Charlie Chaplin, from the film *The Gold Rush*. 1925.

they are starving and cannot leave to get food, they see no alternative but to boil their own shoes and start eating them. What gives this scene its splendor is the fact that Chaplin manages to get away with the impossible: he is, in fact, successful in presenting the shoe as a tasty dish and this *solely* by way of his manner of interacting with it (see figure 17). Chaplin, so to speak, *acts* the tastiness of the shoe *into existence* since, unlike the scene where Chaplin's friend is so hungry that he starts hallucinating and mistakes Chaplin for a chicken, no special effects are used. It is, in other words, on account of something that is external to the shoe itself (Chaplin's gestures and facial expressions) that its leather cover takes on the presence of the skin on a piece of meat, that its nails are expressive of fish bones, and that its strings have seemingly been turned into spaghetti. For the cover, nails, and strings of the shoe remain at all times visible as exactly what they are. Such a change-by-way-of-disparity is also at stake in Benjamin's concept of *Spiel-Raum*. This concept refers to the fact that the response to a given phenomenon cannot be regarded as merely secondary, since it is only there that the space is created for the phenomenon in question to take on a second, and added, presence.[54] Such an active reaction denotes a moment of productivity, since it is only then that the object is given the necessary space to become more than a mere thing. Illustrative of this phenomenon is the scene, again in *The Gold Rush*, where Chaplin brings two buns and forks together to create the "fiction" of two dancing legs. What is most interesting in this scene is that, here as well, the newly assembled element is turned into a convincing presence and that human longing (Chaplin is now no longer hungry but he is being set up by the woman of his dreams) is thus expressed as an act of creation: rather than merely indicating lack or the absence of its object (food, a loved one), human desire is discovered as an ability to produce something that, although it is not an actual thing, cannot be regarded as a no-thing either. Such phenomena denote what Gilles Deleuze has, in a different context, called "the powers of the false" since they involve "the paradox of an enduring interval in the moment itself."[55] In both the scene with the shoe and the one with the buns, indeed, fiction creates a novel reality of its own and "something becomes all the more real because [one] has been better at inventing."[56]

On account of this change-through-disparity, the statement that Chaplin expresses politeness as a character trait does not mean that Chaplin's screen personae are polite at all times, everywhere and to everyone. On the contrary, in many scenes, Chaplin manifests rather rude and impolite behavior. Still, strange as it may sound, his politeness and impoliteness are not in conflict with each other because they both originate from the same place, namely, in the idiosyncrasy that marks all characters: Chaplin's impoliteness indicates a capacity to remain strangely unaffected by immediate surroundings and to thereby open the world in entirely novel terms. One specific scene in *The Gold Rush* is a case in point. Chaplin, starving again, pretends he is frozen stiff and is kindly taken in by someone who cooks him a lovely dinner and goes through all kinds of pains to bring him back to life and to make him feel comfortable. Chaplin, however, behaves in a very rude manner, treats his host as a waiter, and bosses him around, demanding more food and coffee. In no way mistakable for polite behavior, this impoliteness can nevertheless not be understood outside of the context of Chaplin's politeness. Both of these attitudes, that is, testify to the same sustained ability to illuminate a world that is fully one's own. However distinct it is from politeness, this impoliteness, as a consequence, is just as much inseparable from it.

In a short fragment that was written in 1935, Benjamin connects the significance of Chaplin's films to the fact that they reveal that cinema, because of the still images by which it is constituted, is the art of discontinuous movement. "Discontinuous images replace one another in a continuous sequence. A theory of film would need to take account of both of these facts. . . . Concerning [the] significance [of discontinuity] we have at least one important pointer. It is the fact that Chaplin's films have met with the greatest success of all, up to now" (*SW 3*, 94; *GS I*, 1040).[57] Most illustrative of this discontinuity are the strange, jerky movements that characterize Chaplin's way of moving on screen. For Benjamin, these movements can no longer be regarded as qualities of a natural body (*physis*) since they belong to a mechanized one: "Chaplin's unique significance lies in the fact that, in his work, the human being is integrated into the film image by way of his gestures—that is, his bodily and mental posture" (*SW 3*, 94; *GS I*, 1040).[58] For Benjamin, Chaplin "could not have made an impact on stage" because this specific type of moving discontinuously inevitably involves the intervention of a machine: the camera "integrates" Chaplin's natural movements to truly re-produce them, that is, to create them anew and thereby modify them into movements that a merely natural body would not normally produce. "Whether it is his walk, the way he handles his cane, or the way he raises his hat— [it is] always the same jerky sequence of tiny movements [which] applies the law of the cinematic image sequence to human motorial functions" (*SW 3*, 94; *GS I*, 1040).[59] With this argument, first of all, Benjamin formulates an interesting response to opponents of Chaplin who attack him for a supposed inability to truly experiment with the medium of film. From the 1940s on Chaplin has been criticized for being old-fashioned and for never having understood film as a medium of its own because of the stability of his camera and his reluctance to "intervene" in the filmed events.[60] In Benjamin's view, on the contrary, Chaplin does not simply use technology to record a world that remains external to it, but he creates a novel reality in which the "actual" world and its mechanized reproduction have become inseparably entwined (Benjamin's concepts of "body and image space" and "one hundred percent image space" are the best description of such a condition). In this account, Chaplin's camera is not at all passive since he uses it, first, to divide natural movements into discontinuous instants (analytic stage) in order to then reassemble these instants, putting them together again to form a novel and not-merely-natural continuity (synthetic stage). "The innovation of Chaplin's gestures is that he dissects [*zerfällt*] the expressive movements of human beings into a series of minute innervations [*eine Folge kleinster Innervationen*]. Each single movement he makes is composed of a succession of staccato bits of movement" (*SW 3*, 94; *GS I*, 1040).[61]

The relevance of this mechanized process of dividing-up and reassembling again can be borne out by referring to Benjamin's ideas about the assembly line. Emphasizing that the assembly line and the medium of film "came into being at roughly the same time" and that "the social significance of the one cannot be fully understood without that of the other" (*SW 3*, 94), Benjamin's argument seems to be that, on account of the *dis*continuity of the movements of its images, film is capable of turning the *continuous* movement of the assembly line (which, to be sure, is alienating) against itself. This might explain why he mentions that "the assembly line, which plays such a fundamental role in the process of production, is in a sense represented by the filmstrip in the process of consumption" (*SW 3*, 94; *GS I*, 1040).[62] Film, that is, injects a moment of welcome interruption and disruption into the very core of a continuity-gone-awry. This argument can be illustrated most clearly in the famous scene where Chaplin interacts with an assembly line in *Modern Times* (1936). The jerky movements of Chaplin's body do not simply *repeat* the movement of the assembly line but they mimic it, that is, they share in it, extend it, and thereby *master* it. For the movement of the assembly line, when taken over by Chaplin's body, is turned into a choreography with a beauty of its own: released from its practical function, the movement of the assembly line communicates itself freely to other bodies, undergoing a change with each transition. The mimetic repetition of movement, that is, is capable of undoing it from its most alienating features and, in fact, comes together with a novel type of embodied attentiveness that Benjamin calls, here and elsewhere, innervation.[63] "Innervation" is the term for a presence of mind that cannot be regarded as a merely natural faculty, since it is triggered by an uncontrollable external stimulus that interrupts the continuity of thought. Closely related to the notion of distraction, it is to be understood as an ability of man to "join forces" with the machine.[64] Rather than detaching himself from such mimetic movements, therefore, Benjamin emphasizes the need to "turn them into habits" and it is clearly for this reason that Chaplin's cinema can be endowed with revolutionary powers. It is, moreover, only this type of embodied presence of mind which will allow us to understand the genius of Chaplin's *The Great Dictator*.

"Hitler's Diminished Masculinity" (Mustache)

Less than three weeks after Benjamin's suicide, on October 15, 1940, *The Great Dictator* hits American movie theaters. Six years earlier, however, in August 1934, Benjamin had written a short fragment, entitled "Hitler's Diminished Masculinity," that already draws on a comparison between Charlie Chaplin and Adolf Hitler and reads like an uncanny prefiguration of Chaplin's masterpiece. Most uncanny of all, moreover, is that, in bringing together two personae that have (apart from their little mustache) no sensuous similarity to each other, Benjamin was capable of not only identifying the historical power which in his time posed the most acute threat to world peace, that is, fascism, but also of highlighting that this threat and the horror to which it has led could, at that moment, still have been warded off.

The fragment starts from an analysis of innervation: even though Chaplin and Hitler do not truly resemble one another, Chaplin's discontinuous and "staccato" way of moving would be a most opportune manner of rendering present Hitler's persona. "Every inch of Chaplin can produce the Führer" (*jeder Zoll von Chaplin [kann] den Führer Machen*) (*SW* 2, 792; *GS VI*, 103, translation modified). By describing this discontinuous manner of acting so clearly as a form of creation ("produce" rather than "become"), Benjamin suggests that the relation between Hitler and Chaplin is not just that of model and copy: Chaplin does not just *repeat* the movements of the Führer, but he *modifies* them and this by "dissecting" his expressive movements. It is for this reason that Chaplin's powers of innervation can be taken for an embodied form of attentiveness and criticism: in not allowing his own body to become visible as a unity in its own right ("every inch" has its own expressivity), Chaplin's manner of moving entails the sharpest antidote to the godlike appearance of Hitler. The discontinuity of Chaplin's movements has an interruptive effect that divests such pseudo-transcendent appearances of the semblance of seriousness or grandeur with which they resonate: "Chaplin shows up the comedy of Hitler's gravity" (*SW 2*, 792; *GS VI*, 103).[65] Benjamin's ideas, despite having been written years before the production of *The Great Dictator*, set up the interpretative framework that helps understand that film. In *The Great Dictator* Chaplin unmasks Hitler not by merely imitating him, nor by displaying a heroic counterforce that would be even stronger than fascism, but by *actively disintegrating* the fake sense of immanent unity and continuity (aura) that Hitler was building up around his own person. The displacement of Hitler's gestures in Chaplin's fragmentized mimicry thus makes him *legible* for what he truly is: it both highlights *and* dispels the almost mythical semblance of his invulnerability: "The poor devil wants to be taken seriously, and instantly must call upon all hell / Chaplin's docility is apparent to all eyes; Hitler's only to those of his bosses" (*SW 2*, 792).

At least two of Benjamin's statements are illustrative in this regard, the first one being that Chaplin "explicates himself allegorically" (*legt sich selbst allegorisch aus*) (*SW 3*, 94; *GS I-3*, 1047, translation modified).[66] In his *Trauerspiel* book, Benjamin emphasizes the crucial difference between allegory and symbol. Whereas the latter is a token for a (fake) continuity between transcendence and immanence, the former opens up the field of history and allows for an experience of its contingencies. The symbol indicates a "unity of the material and the transcendental object" that is "distorted into a relationship between appearance and essence" and underlies a form of romanticism where the "beautiful is supposed to merge with the divine in an unbroken whole" (*O*, 160). The symbol, therefore, belongs to the realm of myth and its temporality is that of "individual time": it presupposes the possibility of an ultimate fulfillment of history. Allegory, to the contrary, embraces the very vicissitudes of our world and expresses them through a movement of fragmentation. It exposes precisely these things that "lack all symbolic freedom," that is, "everything about history that, from the very beginning, has been untimely, sorrowful, unsuccessful" (*O*, 166). To be sure, the world that is opened up by allegory is usually not a beautiful sight since it has a marked propensity for "decline." Still, in bringing about an annihilation of the false ideal of immediate redemption of and within history, it confronts the immanence of the world and discovers a genuinely "historical time" that is required for change to become possible and thinkable. Chaplin's discontinuous movements thus relate to the continuity of Hitler's movements like allegory relates to symbol: they entail a fragmentation of its supposed self-sufficiency and its pseudo-natural semblance of transcendence.[67]

A second important statement in this context is that Chaplin's "clothes are impermeable to every blow of Fate" (*SW 2*, 199; *GS VI*, 137).[68] With this

Benjamin first of all implicitly states the obvious: Chaplin lacks all features that would make him fit to qualify for a hero. None of his gestures takes on the weight of the absolute and, as mentioned, he encounters the world as a sphere of possibility rather than as one that is determined from within by necessity and lawfulness.[69] This indifference to the power of fate is borne out by the fact that, in Chaplin's films, guilt is expressed as nothing but an external element. Fully at odds with the hero's sentiment that guilt is a mythic and ahistorical feature that can be absorbed and appropriated by a single individual, in Chaplin's films guilt, and its expression in law, is a purely historical presence that comes and goes without further ado. Instead of experiencing the natural pull of a life that has "essentially first been condemned," Chaplin understands guilt as an element of *this* world alone that, moreover, wears the easily identifiable mask of one of his foremost antagonists: the policeman. Guilt, then, is only present when Chaplin is chased by a policeman, and it disappears completely when he is set free: it becomes an object for play, and the policeman is just another person with whom to play hide-and-seek. A token of this is the ease with which, in Chaplin's films, innocence can be turned into guilt and vice versa.[70] Both in *City Lights* and *Modern Times*, for instance, Chaplin is arrested and actually put into prison while the audience is fully aware that he is innocent of the crime of which he is suspected (he is mistaken for, respectively, a burglar and a revolutionary). Similarly, in Chaplin's films, a wrongdoing simply does not exist when it is not found out or it disappears from sight when he is capable of escaping from the police. In this manner, in *The Kid*, for instance, Chaplin's scheme of having the young boy throw a brick through people's windows in order to make money as a window-setter, loses all sense of illicitness after the policeman has been shaken off in a chase.[71]

Second, the claim that Chaplin's "clothes are impermeable to every blow of fate" is intriguing because it not only reveals something about Chaplin's (non-)relation to Fate but, connected to this, it also reveals something about the significance of his clothes in this context. Benjamin describes Chaplin's clothes as follows: "The fashion keynote for Hitler is not the image of the military man, but that of the gentleman in easy circumstances. The feudal emblems of authority are out of date; there remained only men's fashions. Chaplin, too, looks to men's fashions. He does this in order to take the master caste at its word" (*SW* 2, 792; *GS VI*, 104).[72] In this way, he gives Chaplin a face that must have been easily recognizable to the German audiences of his time: a proletarized middle-class man and member of the impoverished bourgeoisie, which was described by Siegfried Kracauer with the concept *Die Angestellten* ("the salaried masses"). It is this class which, unable to grasp the mechanism behind its own downfall, is in hindsight believed to have brought Hitler to power. "His bowler hat, which no longer sits so securely on his head, betrays the fact that the rule of the bourgeoisie is tottering [*die Herrschaft der Bourgeoisie wackelt*]" (*SW* 2, 793; *GS VI*, 104). It is for this reason that

Benjamin's understanding of Chaplin's clothes as an immunization against Fate has a profound truth to it. For in describing the Tramp in this manner, Benjamin shows how Chaplin gives expression to a specific class that is desperately in need of being represented while at the same time curing it of any belief in a Fated or super-historical power. In Benjamin's view, Chaplin's screen personae do exemplify a more universal or shared layer of being but, paradoxically, only on account of the visibility of the very specificity of their situation and social standing: "With his art, Chaplin confirms the old insight that only an imaginative world that is firmly grounded in a society, a nation, a place will succeed in evoking the great, uninterrupted, yet highly differentiated resonance that exists between nations. In Russia, people wept when they saw *The Pilgrim*, in Germany, people are interested in the theoretical implications of his comedies; in England, they like his sense of humor" (*SW 2*, 223; *GS III*, 159).[73] The particularities that identify the Tramp's social status (his signature suit, walking stick, and bowler hat) "succeed in evoking" a more general communality for the very reason that they are neither made absolute (fetishized) nor merely relativized (ridiculed). They are, to be precise, described as being both graceful *and* comical at the same time: "Wet through, sweaty, in clothes far too small for him, Chaplin is the embodiment of Goethe's *aperçu*: Man would not be the noblest on earth if he were not too noble for it" (*SW 199*; *GS VI*, 138, translation modified).[74] In this formula, Benjamin makes clear that Chaplin neither simply disenchants the image with which his audiences identify nor inflates it with an overblown importance or pseudo-transcendence. It is on account of this tension that Chaplin's gags gain a redeeming potential: the combination of their poetic and comic effect presents the audiences with a safe way to preserve their self-esteem, while at the same time warning them against weighty meanings that their imaginary selves cannot carry. In this context Benjamin quotes Philippe Soupault's statement that "the undeniable superiority of Chaplin's films is based on the fact that they are imbued with a poetry that everyone encounters in life, admittedly without always being conscious of it" (Philippe Soupault, quoted in *SW 2*, 222). In Benjamin's mind, Chaplin thus understands both that his movies will only have a more widely shared dimension if they speak to the "non-shared" situation of the audience and that this specificity cannot *itself* be universalized. Chaplin is aware of the reactionary tendency that creeps up behind all attempts to essentialize one's own specific situation (the *Volk* or "compact" mass) and he understands the fundamental paradox that human beings can only grasp themselves truly as members of a shared community if they also see themselves as different from one another: "Hitler's following to be compared with Chaplin's public / Chaplin—the plowshare that cuts through the masses; laughter loosens up the mass / the ground of the Third Reich is stamped down hard and firm, and no more grass grows there" (*SW 2*, 792).

For this context, *The Great Dictator* is, of course, Chaplin's most relevant film. A remark by Gilles Deleuze is especially interesting in this regard. In his *Cinema 1: The Movement-Image*, he writes that "the difference between the little Jewish barber and the dictator is as slight as that between their two mustaches. However, two situations arise from this which are infinitely far apart, as opposable as those of the victim and the executioner."[75] For Deleuze, this denotes that in Chaplin's later films "it is a case of two states of society, two opposable Societies, one of which makes the slight difference between men into the instrument of an infinite distance between situations (tyranny), and the other which would make the slight difference between men the variable of a great situation of community and communality (Democracy)."[76] Benjamin's view on Chaplin runs parallel to Deleuze's reading, interpreting the difference between tyranny and democracy as the opposition between myth and history or, put differently, between a (compact) mass that seeks the Fated authority of absolute ideals and an (open) mass that embraces the contingency of the immanent world and the inherent difference between human beings. From Benjamin's point of view, the very inconspicuousness of the feature that is shared by the Jewish barber and the dictator Hynkel, their mustache, would obtain a redemptive function: by presenting the common trait between both as something insignificant, the essential difference between them is highlighted. The inconspicuous presence of the mustache in the Jewish barber and Hynkel results in a clear-cut affirmation of the contingency of history that reminds one of the redemptive "spark of contingency" that Benjamin discovered in Dauthendey's photograph: although the Jewish barber does represent the very people who will end up voting a brutal dictator into power, on account of the nonsensical link between them, this event, although a historical fact, is expressed as avoidable and non-Fated.

That the "resonance that exists between nations" is "great" and "uninterrupted" but also "highly differentiated" is, however strange it may sound, exemplified in the two scenes where Chaplin does proclaim the universality of mankind in an immediate manner. For both the famous speech in *The Great Dictator* and the one in *Monsieur Verdoux* (1947) revolve around an appeal to a form of humanism that does situate itself *jenseits* all differences. In *The Great Dictator*, for instance, the Jewish barber who has accidentally ended up on the speech stand in dictator Hynkel's stead even conjures a supposedly natural continuity between immanence and transcendence by quoting the seventeenth chapter of the Gospel according to Luke ("The Kingdom of God is within man—not one man, not a group of men but in all man!") (see figure 18). Similarly, appearing in court to be condemned for the many murders he has committed, Henri Verdoux appeals to an ideal of universal pacifism, blaming the world at large for its active encouragement of uncondemned violence on a much bigger scale than his own ("Has it not blown unsuspecting women and little children to pieces? And done it very scientifically? As a mass killer, I am an amateur by comparison"). Verdoux, as well, ends his talk by drawing attention to an immediate presence of the divine within man (to the priest's "May the Lord have mercy on your soul," Verdoux replies "Why

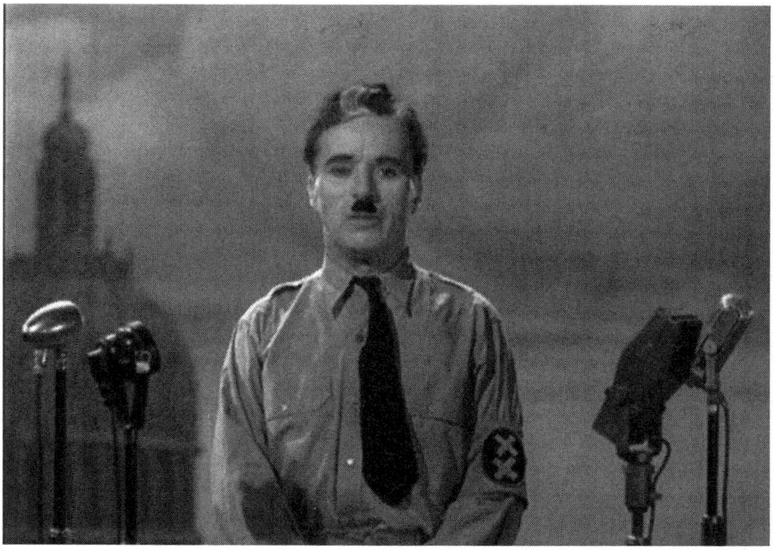

Figure 18. Charlie Chaplin, from the end of the film *The Great Dictator*. 1940.

not. After all, it belongs to Him"). Still, for all the criticism that has been raised against them, neither of these two speeches has anything to do with the mythic belief in ultimate fulfillment or with the temporality of "individual time."[77] The Jewish barber's speech is a *critique* of the godlike aspirations of the dictator, and Henri Verdoux's reconciliation with his death sentence has nothing in common with heroic sacrifice. That they are, instead, the very antithesis of myth, in spite of their appeal to universality and absoluteness, is a consequence of the fact that both of these speeches display the utopian nature of these ideals: in so clearly idealizing humanism and pacifism, these speeches make manifest an urgency that far surpasses the supposedly "realistic" goals of normal political action. In such a manner, these ideals become manifest as more than a mere aim for this world and as more weighty than the goals that can be attained through instrumental reason. This is what Benjamin has in mind with his concept of "pure ends" and the idea that true justice can never be considered a direct aim for human actions. For him, "it is never reason that decides . . . on the justness of ends" (*SW 1*, 247), thereby clearly affirming that certain ideals retain an imperative significance (and even a chance to become actual) despite their being not immediately accessible to the human mind.[78] In this manner, success is once again expressed as having become inseparable from failure: for it is precisely by putting them in the mouth of a dictator and a murderer that Chaplin saves the purity of his ideals and thus appeals to the only thing that can genuinely be called justice.

Two Concluding Remarks

"Always Lagging Half a Step Behind"

Simmel's fear that his spiritual legacy will be all but obliterated by the very people who consider themselves his heirs is not without grounds. Not a few of his insights are among the most contested philosophical ideas of the twentieth century. The Frankfurt school, post-Freudian psychoanalysis, postmodern thought, and deconstructionism have joined forces in battling the view that life spontaneously renews itself and that individual identity designates a unique, continuous, and unified existence. It is therefore rather paradoxical that the name Georg Simmel shows up most regularly in an academic discipline that seems otherwise almost wholly at odds with his metaphysical views of life and individual identity: modern, progressive, and leftist sociology. This surprising presence can partly be explained by the fact that Simmel takes recourse to conceptual personae that indicate the blind spots of most of the other philosophers of life. The main proponents of *Lebensphilosophie* pit the supposed purity of life against history and thereby expose themselves to a rather facile appropriation by reactionary and right-wing ideologues. Ludwig Klages, for instance, connects the recapitulation of the continuity of "life *as such*" (*das Leben selbst*) with an "experience of resemblance" (*Ähnlichkeitserlebnis*) and the "falling away of restraints" (*Fortfall der Hemmungen*).[1] Simmel, to the contrary, immunizes himself against such perilous ideas in that he highlights the meaningful and irreducible presence of what inevitably remains different and resists uniformization. In his essay on the stranger, for instance, he emphasizes that no social relationship can do away with the feeling that the very elements that one holds as unique are always shared by others as well. Strangeness is for this reason deemed "insurmountable" since it indicates that what we consider as irreplaceable is always touched by a "contingency" that will not be resolved. The stranger stands for an ultimate "generality" that is "probably not absent in any relation," since he makes manifest that the commonalities that underlie a given group or collective are never theirs alone. "Similarity, harmony, and nearness," Simmel summarizes, "are accompanied by the feeling that they are not really the unique property of this particular relationship: they are . . . something which potentially prevails between the partners and an indeterminate number of others, and therefore gives the relation . . . no inner and exclusive necessity."[2] Consequentially, in his essay on "Secrecy and Secret Societies," he describes how societal relations necessarily presuppose a *distance* between individuals that can be mediated but not entirely overcome. Rather than in any ontological "mystery" that would supposedly underlie the shared essence of a homogeneous *Volk*, Simmel is interested in the "secret" that clings to individuals who acknowledge their being different from each other and interact in a dynamic manner. Far from unknow*able*, these secrets indicate that certain elements about the life of one's peers are bound to remain simply *unknown* for the main reason that it is impossible to read another person's intentions and beliefs. Because the intimate thoughts of an individual cannot become public in their totality, no one can fully reconstruct the mental life of another human being from his social appearance and behavior alone. "The strenuous organizing forms which appear to be the real constructors of society," writes Simmel, "must be continually disturbed, unbalanced, and detached by individualistic and irregular forces, in order that their reaction and development may gain vitality by alternate concession and resistance."[3]

In Simmel's view this unstable and dynamic character of society at large is, though inseparable from social and historical conditions, ultimately to be understood as the expression of an all-encompassing principle of life. Therefore, to understand the irreducible presence of an "outside" vis-à-vis society he takes recourse to an overall concept of unity and continuity that plays itself out in a societal and historical setting. In his essay on the poor, for instance, Simmel considers the obligation to assist the poor to be a fundamental feature of every social community. The assistance of the poor indicates, first and foremost, a specific interaction with those elements that a given collectivity cannot fully identify with but nevertheless needs to appropriate. "The poor person," writes Simmel, "stands undoubtedly *outside* the group, inasmuch as he is a mere object of the actions of the collectivity; but being outside, in this case, is only . . . a particular form of being inside."[4] The irreducible presence of the poor thus indicates in the first place how life in general is marked by boundaries that do inspire the most different forms of interaction but will not themselves ever go away. In Simmel's view, social boundaries are in the end expressions of boundaries that are inscribed within the very heart of the continuity of life in general. "The unified act of life [*Der einheitliche Akt des Lebens*]," he writes, "includes both boundedness and the transcendence of boundary, despite the fact that this, considered as a whole, seems to present a logical contradiction" (*VoL*, 3; *GSG 16*, 215).[5] For this reason, Simmel attaches the possibility of justice, be it historical, moral, social, or political, to the sustained consideration of elements that need to be both encountered as "different" and actively integrated. In his view, it is vital to "accept" poverty as "an official and unchangeable fact" without thereby forgetting that it is "the *moral* task of man . . . to overcome himself."[6]

In his biographical writings, Benjamin turns to this same figure of the poor. A brief comparison between his and Simmel's views brings out a crucial difference between the philosophical frameworks of both thinkers. Benjamin's short remark on the poor revolves around a description of a sense of social suffocation.[7] Calling his native neighborhoods in Berlin's Old and New West a "ghetto" and himself a "prisoner," he describes his first attempt to break through the "obstinacy and self-satisfaction" of the class into which he was born (*SW 3*, 404). The earliest battles of this social revolution, it seems, were fought in the city streets of late nineteenth-century Berlin. While going out to run errands, Walter refuses to be taken by his mother's hand and deliberately keeps a distance. "I had, in fact, formed the habit of always lagging a half-step behind her [*die Gewohnheit . . . immer um einen halben Schritt zurückzublei-ben*]. It was as if I were determined never to form a united front with anyone, not even my mother" (*SW 3*, 404; *GS IV*, 287). Benjamin connects this desire to emancipate himself from his social surroundings to a growing fascination with the anonymity of the big city and a yearning for those who make its streets their home, in the first place prostitutes. "There could be no doubt," he writes, "that an idea (unfortunately, an illusory idea) of repudiating my mother, those like her, and the social class to which we both belonged was at the bottom of that unparalleled excitement which drove me to accost a whore in the street" (*SW 3*, 404).

The main difference between Simmel's account of the poor and that of Benjamin is that Benjamin does away with the explanatory value of any over-arching principle of life. In his view, the position of the poor only gains true legibility from within merely societal and historical structures. In Benjamin's short remark the poor wear the clear traces of a specific social class, that is, they are "beggars" or "poorly paid" but never merely "poor" (*SW 3*, 404). In *The Arcades Project*, therefore, Benjamin describes the concept of culture that also underlies Simmel's philosophy as something that "has . . . favored the cause of barbarism" because it puts forward an ideal of universal integra-tion in which aesthetic, scientific, and ethical values lose their independence and become visible as "elements in the development of human nature beyond its natural state" (*AP*, 480). Like Adorno, Benjamin takes Simmel to task for a lack of mediation between the concreteness of historical and social-economic analyses on the one hand, and the explanatory weight that is given to general and all-encompassing concepts on the other. As a consequence, social boundaries cannot in his view be considered an immanent presence within whatever unity or continuity of life since they are determined by *social* conditions.

Benjamin's views on the poor, moreover, are not at all motivated by the attempt to include even the "outside" as an "inside" but, vice versa, by the ongoing task to disrupt the "inside" in such a manner that it brings forth something that cannot be recuperated in any way. Benjamin, that is, does not connect the *appearance* of the poor to an "unchangeable *fact*" but seeks ever-new ways to experience their very *dis*appearance as a utopian *possibil-ity*. "As long as there is still one beggar around," Benjamin writes in *The Arcades Project*, "there will still be myth" (*AP*, 400). The drive to constantly break through the boundaries of one's own social class exposes the current state of affairs as but one of many potential situations. Benjamin's messianic presuppositions understand this endeavor to continuously interrupt and "lag behind" as constitutive of a power of redemption.

Underlying the differences between Simmel and Benjamin are antithetical views of memory, recollection, and time. In an early text on memory and recollection, Aristotle sets up an important distinction that is relevant for our own discussion. Aristotle's analysis starts from a seemingly rather banal insight: when we have a memory of a given event, we know we are dealing with something that is no longer the case ("No one would say that he remembers the present").[8] For this reason, memory is always entangled with "a time elapsed," and "the consciousness of 'formerly'": it is a function of that "organ whereby [we] perceive time."[9] Aristotle understands memories as pictures that manage to survive after the events they depict have passed away. In his view, such pictures preserve a "likeness" of the past.[10] This allows all animals with memory to relate to something that they nevertheless experience as no longer present. Aristotle writes: "One might as well suppose it possible also to see or hear that which is not present. In reply, we suggest that this very thing is quite conceivable, nay, actually occurs in experience."[11]

Simmel's thought sketches out a philosophy of memory along the same lines: it is steeped in the idea that a continuous totality underlies an individualized existence and thereby permits the individual to identify with experiences that he knows to have passed. "It is the nature of life to be at every moment there as a *totality*," writes Simmel. As a consequence, the past of an individual is truly "collected" (*gesammelt*) in or "narrated" (*erzählt*) by the present (*R*, 7). Simmel's philosophy is indebted to what Benjamin, in his essay on the Swiss-German writer Johann Peter Hebel, calls "an experientially [*erfahren*] grounded metaphysics" (*SW 1*, 430). Simmel is fascinated by the idea that, on both the individual and collective level, a wide variety of different elements can be contracted into one lived unity. To indicate such a "highly dialectical relationship between two opposite poles, a constant one and a variable one" (*SW 1*, 430), Benjamin gives the example of the passing of fifty years that, in Hebel's story "Unexpected Reunion," indicates the mourning period of a miner's wife after the disappearance of her fiancé. Benjamin quotes Hebel's description of such a dynamically contracted unity in toto:

> In the meantime the city of Lisbon in Portugal was destroyed by an earthquake, and the Seven Years War came and went, and the emperor Francis I died, and the Society of Jesus was banned, and Poland was partitioned, and the empress Maria Theresa died, and Struensee was executed, and America gained its freedom, and the combined French and Spanish forces failed to capture Gibraltar. The Turks locked up General Stein in the Veterani cave in Hungary, and the emperor

> Joseph died, too. King Gustav of Sweden conquered Russian Finland, and the French Revolution and the long wars broke out, and the emperor Leopold II went to his grave. Napoleon conquered Prussia and the English bombarded Copenhagen, and the farmers sowed and reaped. The miller ground his corn, and the smiths hammered, and the miners dug for metal ore in their subterranean workshop. But in 1809, when the miners in Falun . . . (Hebel, quoted in *SW 1*, 430)

The old woman in Hebel's story exemplifies a key element of Simmel's overall philosophy. In spite of the abrupt loss of her beloved, the emotional life of the miner's widow has managed to retain a deeply felt continuity. The succession of the many events that have occurred throughout the period of fifty years is of no concern to her. Her mental life, that is, remains consistently colored and unified by her memories of a lover who has disappeared long ago. "He is my fiancé," Hebel has her say, "whom I have mourned for fifty years."[12]

Of course, the faculty of memory to unify our existence cannot be considered infallible. It is at this moment that recollection comes into play. Aristotle describes it as follows: "When [after an interval of obliviscence] one recovers some scientific knowledge which [one] had before, or some perception, or some other experience . . . this recovery may amount to a recollection of any of the things aforesaid."[13] Recollection indicates the attempt to make a forgotten past usable for our current existence. This forces our mind to start precisely there: not in the past, but in the *present*. Recollection, that is to say, is not dependent on the "knowing contemplation" (*theoria*) of mnemonic tokens or pictures of the past but on a not-yet-knowing and active *quest*.[14] In Aristotle's view, recollection refers to a specifically human "investigation" (*zêtêsis*) of one's surroundings and the ability to "think together" (*sullogismos*) a series of mental associations.[15] Because recollection seeks a past that was not hitherto accessible, it has little to do with a seemingly natural continuity between the past and present. Recollection, rather, is steeped in a feeling of *dis*continuity. It involves the ability to interrupt one's ordinary course of activity and "deliberate" about the correct strategy to bring back the past.[16] Strategies of recollection, moreover, allow human beings to go beyond the immediate "likeness" of things and they establish a connection between elements that do not directly resemble each other (Aristotle's example is an associative chain that goes swiftly from the word "milk" to "Autumn"). This ability to "deliberate" and return an otherwise inaccessible past is described with the same word (*bouleuesthai*) that, in Aristotle's *Nicomachean Ethics*, indicates the preparation of moral and decisive action. As a consequence, recollection does not so much indicate the sentiment that things of the past have survived over time as the altogether different awareness that something new is yet to begin. "When one wishes to recollect, this is what [an individual] will do: he will try to obtain a beginning of movement whose sequel shall be the movement which he desires to reawaken. . . . One must get hold of a starting-point [*dei de labesthai archês*]."[17]

Benjamin's is a philosophy of recollection and not of memory. Because his view of life is steeped in an awareness of unending transience, it appeals neither to mnemonic tokens nor to pictures that manage to spontaneously survive over time. Of much greater importance to Benjamin is, instead, the ceaseless quest for a new "starting point." Concepts like the dialectical image, now-time, or weak messianic power are genuine "actualizations" of the past and, hence, first and foremost indications of a specific investment in the *present*. Such concepts refer to a "rejuvenating" force that can be discovered in what is at hand and not to the "time elapsed," or "the consciousness of 'formerly'" that inevitably introduces lack and incompleteness into memory. The rejuvenating power of recollection may not be capable of recovering an overall continuity with the past, but it does briefly interrupt an otherwise all-consuming dynamic of disappearance. In Benjamin's view, therefore, recollection does not indicate the sheer *absence* of forgetfulness, but the fact that forgetfulness has been made operative. For it is only because human beings can briefly "forget" life's "eternal passing away" that recollection is charged with the significance of a "task." In such forms of recollection, forgetfulness is briefly made to overcome the even more fundamental forgetfulness that is the transience of life as such. After the example of Nietzsche and Valéry, Benjamin considers a specific form of forgetfulness to be a human capability and even the condition of genuine action. For only "active" forgetfulness can counteract the otherwise unbearable awareness that nothing is meant to last anyway.

Sharing in this very awareness of transience, forgetfulness allows for the distinctly human capacity to always start anew and regain the novel and ever-fresh perspective that makes true change possible. As we have seen, Benjamin connects Proust's *mémoire involontaire*, for instance, with "a Penelope *work* of forgetting" that is a "counterpart" to memory and not its "likeness" (*SW* 2, 238, my emphasis). While it cannot bring to a full stop "the day['s] unravel[ing] what the night has woven," in this recollection-cum-forgetfulness we are nevertheless taught to pay attention, time and again, to the "few fringes of the carpet of lived existence . . . [that] [e]ach morning we hold in our hands, usually weakly and loosely." In this manner, recollection and forgetfulness work together to preserve images that would not be able to survive on their own—images that are truly "without a place" and for this reason prepare the ground for genuine innovation, that is, utopian images of "happiness" (*SW* 2, 238–39). In Benjamin's view, neither individual nor collective recollection refers to the spontaneous survival of the past. Instead, recollection denotes an active intervention that, for the shortest moment, prevents it from passing away. Only in such an interruptive and redemptive moment is the past allowed to remain "pure" and acquire meaning, and this always only in relation to the present. In *The Arcades Project*, Benjamin describes this faculty to "rejuvenate" the past as the ability to "recognize the new once again [*das Neue wiedererkennen*]" (*AP*, 390; *GS V*, 493). Recollection is neither directed toward historical elements that have managed to live on nor toward elements in the present which retain a likeness with the past. It is, rather, inseparable from a historical form of forgetfulness that takes as its object the unending progress of time itself: collective recollection cannot overcome the past's "being essentially dead," but it approaches it with an interest that nevertheless remains "vital" (*AP*, 363).

Recollection lays out the path for the recovery of age-old dreams and wish-images that have never been realized in history but, precisely for this reason, gain a sharpness and urgency. Benjamin's philosophy is therefore not exemplified by the old widow in Hebel's story "Unexpected Reunion" but by her lost fiancé. Fifty years after his disappearance, miners retrieve the dead body of the young boy and find that it has remained exactly like it was before. "A good three hundred ell below ground level," Hebel writes, "they dug up the dead body of a young boy from within the rubble and vitriol water. It was completely covered by iced vitriol but otherwise unexpired and unchanged, in such a manner that one could still fully make out his facial traits and age, as if he had died only an hour before or had fallen asleep a bit during work."[18] The fiancé's body has withstood the passage of time and shows no signs of aging whatsoever, as if it has been frozen in an eternally suspended "now-time." It is this suspension of the passage of time that, after fifty years of uninterrupted mourning, reanimates the old widow's hope of an "unexpected reunion" with her beloved. "As he was laid to rest in his grave at the cemetery," Hebel writes, "she said: 'Sleep well now, another day or ten in the cool wedding bed, and don't allow time to grow long on you [*laß dir die Zeit nicht lang werden*]. There is little left for me to do and I will soon be there with you, soon daytime will come again. What the earth has once returned, she won't keep to herself the second time.' "[19]

"The best way out," writes Robert Frost, "is always through," though not without immediately adding that there might in fact not be another one ("I can see no way out but through"). From Benjamin's perspective, the all-consuming forgetfulness that is inscribed within the transience of life as such knows no counter-principle. Still, Benjamin's descriptions of the interruptive power of inconspicuous objects, images, events, and a "character" like Charlie Chaplin's Tramp reveal that forgetfulness can be turned against itself. Inconspicuousness is precisely that: a genuine more-than-life that embodies the limits to life's all-encompassing forgetfulness but which is located within the heart of forgetfulness itself. For this reason, in his essay on Dostoevsky's *The Idiot*, Benjamin draws attention to the difference between the "eternity of nature" (*das ewige der Natur*) and the "infinity" (*Unendlichkeit*) of an "immortal life" (*unsterbliche Leben*) (*SW 1*, 80; *GS II*, 239). While the eternity of nature indicates unending disappearance, an infinite and immortal life dislodges this empty repetition of the same. However inconspicuous and seemingly devoid of importance Prince Myshkin's life may be, for Benjamin it simultaneously indicates the highest form of significance. No underlying or overarching principle of life renders the Prince a meaningful or memorable presence: his existence has, in fact, "no monument or memorial, or perhaps even any testimony," and even his "individuality" is "secondary" (*SW 1*, 80). Therefore, however, the Prince is forever spared the fate to be included in any of life's projects and developments. His existence is thus always already on the path to be forgotten and left out but, for no other reason, it "points to something in the nature of the unforgettable itself, something that makes it unforgettable" (*SW 1*, 80).

NOTES

Introduction

1. See *GS VI*, 215; and Howard Eiland and Michael W. Jennings, *Walter Benjamin: A Critical Life* (Cambridge, Mass.: Harvard University Press, 2014), 47. For more information on Simmel's difficulties obtaining a permanent academic position, see Lewis Coser, "The Stranger in the Academy," in *Georg Simmel*, ed. Lewis A. Coser (Englewood Cliffs, N.J.: Prentice-Hall, 1965), 37–39; and Kurt Gassen and Michael Landmann, "Bausteine zur Biographie," in *Buch des Dankes an Georg Simmel*, ed. Kurt Gassen and Michael Landmann (Berlin: Duncker und Humblot, 1958), 11–33.

2. Quoted in Gassen and Landmann, "Bausteine zur Biographie," 13. For more on Simmel and World War I, see Patrick Watier, "The War Writings of Georg Simmel," in *Theory, Culture & Society* 8, no. 3 (1991): 219–33. See also the statement made by Simmel's son, Hans Simmel, that "he had the feeling that the largest part of his life work had come to nothing." In Hans Simmel, "Auszüge aus den Lebenserinnerungen," in *Ästhetik und Soziologie um die Jahrhundertwende: Georg Simmel*, ed. Hannes Böhringer and Karlfried Gründer (Frankfurt am Main: Vittorio Klostermann, 1976), 267.

3. Karl Kraus, *The Last Days of Mankind*, trans. Fred Bridgham and Edward Timms (New Haven, Conn.: Yale University Press, 2015), 500, translation modified.

4. Eiland and Jennings, *Walter Benjamin: A Critical Life*, 47. Simmel's influence on Benjamin is either mentioned or hinted at by other writers as well, chief among them some of his most intimate friends like Adorno and Scholem. See Theodor Adorno, "A Portrait of Walter Benjamin," in *Prisms*, trans. Samuel Weber and Shierry Weber (Cambridge, Mass.: MIT Press, 1997), 231; and Gershom Scholem, *Walter Benjamin: The Story of a Friendship*, trans. Harry Zohn (London: Faber and Faber, 1982), 15. However, as David Frisby notes, "the relation between Benjamin's work and that of Simmel has not been systematically explored" (in David Frisby, *Simmel and Since: Essays on Georg Simmel's Social Theory* [London: Routledge, 1992], 143n43). Frisby's own work, most notably his *Fragments of Modernity: Theories of Modernity in the Work of Simmel, Kracauer and Benjamin*, is an important step in this direction. His texts, however, focus on sociological rather than philosophical issues, and on theories of modernity rather than on religious and metaphysical concepts, and therefore leave important issues unmentioned. The same goes for Micko Marian, *Walter Benjamin und Georg Simmel* (Wiesbaden: Harrassowitz Verlag, 2010). Other texts that focus mainly on the sociological stakes and on theories of modernity are Ann T. Martinez, "Walter Benjamin: A Sociologist in the Path of Simmel," *Humboldt Journal of Social Relations* 12, no. 1 (1984–85): 114–31; Gerard Raulet,

"Simmel et ses héritiers," *Information sur les Sciences Sociales* 25, no. 4 (1986): 845–59; Frederic Jameson, "The Theoretical Hesitation: Benjamin's Sociological Predecessor," *Critical Inquiry* 25, no. 2 (Winter 1999): 267–88; Ulrich Lehmann, *Tigersprung: Fashion in Modernity* (Cambridge, Mass.: MIT Press, 2000), 125–278 (see also note 115, p. 463); Fabio d'Andrea, "Redemption in a Fragment: Simmel and Benjamin," *Simmel Studies* 14 (2004): 39–55; and Ingo Meyer, "Benjamin, Adorno und in Hintergrund der Dritte," *Simmel Studies* 15 (2005): 63–115.

5. See Georg Simmel, "The Law of the Individual" (*VoL*, 100–154). Simmel argues in favor of an internal unity and continuity that gathers all of the lived experiences and moments of an individual's life. It is only this internal totality that can be called the ultimate reality of the individual's life. Simmel writes: "Th[e] inner knowledge of the identity of the individual amid full variability evidently extending into the deepest level is a fundamental fact in the face of which, for the present, all analytic conceptualizations fail" (*VoL*, 139). See also chapter 2 of the present volume.

6. See, among other texts, Georg Simmel, "Sociological Aesthetics" (translated in Georg Simmel, *The Conflict in Modern Culture and Other Essays*, ed. and trans. K. P. Etzkorn [New York: Teachers, 1968], 68–80); Georg Simmel, "Sociology of the Senses" (*SoC*, 109–20); and Georg Simmel, "The Metropolis and Mental Life" (*SoC*, 174–85). Simmel argues that the relation between sensory perception and the social life of human beings is one of mutual determination and that the specificity of one's environment (historically, socially, politically) has an essential impact on one's perceptual faculties.

7. See Georg Simmel, *The Philosophy of Money*, ed. David Frisby, trans. Tom Bottomore and David Frisby (London: Routledge, 2004), 429–32. Simmel criticizes the Marxist view on the relationship between value and labor for disregarding the fact that concepts such as "utility" (of a product) and "intensity" (of labor) are not as clear-cut as is often believed. This criticism is quoted by Benjamin in *The Arcades Project* and opposes the view of Karl Korsch. In the passages of his book on Marx that are quoted by Benjamin, Korsch attacks "those minor followers in the wake of the great scientific founders of political economy" who are "no longer accustomed to such audacity of scientific thought" and "must be reminded of the fact that [the] 'violent abstraction' [for which they criticize Marxism] results not from . . . economic science but from the real character of capitalist commodity production." Benjamin's added line "This in opposition to Simmel" suggests that he believes Simmel's ideas to be exposed to Korsch's criticism (*AP*, 660–61, 664).

8. See Georg Simmel, *Sechzehn Vorlesungen gehalten an der Berliner Universität* (*GSG* 9, 8–226). Simmel retains Kant's discovery of the subject's world-constituting faculties but emphasizes that the intellect is actively involved in all the other faculties and that it displays an overarching power. See also Andrea Staiti, *Husserl's Transcendental Phenomenology: Nature, Spirit, and Life* (Cambridge: Cambridge University Press, 2014), 55–62.

9. For the argument that Simmel's interest in *Lebensphilosophie* did not just underlie the later stage of his writing, see Nitzan Lebovic, "Simmel's Apple: The Image of Living Time," in *Georg Simmel in Translation: Interdisciplinary Border Crossings in Culture and Modernity*, ed. David Kim (Cambridge: Cambridge

Scholars, 2009), 190–91; and Rudolph H. Weingartner, *Experience and Culture: The Philosophy of Georg Simmel* (Middletown, Conn.: Wesleyan University Press, 1960).

10. See Siegfried Kracauer, "Georg Simmel," in *The Mass Ornament: Weimar Essays*, ed. and trans. Thomas Y. Levin (Cambridge, Mass.: Harvard University Press, 1995), 225; and Max Horkheimer, "Lebensphilosophie: Bergson, Simmel, Dilthey," in *Gesammelte Schriften*, vol. 10: *Nachgelassene Schriften 1914–1931*, ed. Alfred Schmidt (Frankfurt am Main: Fischer Taschenbuch Verlag, 1990), 287–95.

11. Georg Simmel, "The Philosophy of Landscape," *Theory, Culture & Society* 24, no. 7/8 (2007): 22.

12. For the view that the "more-than-life" is immanent to life, see, for example, *VoL*, 14: "The logical difficulty raised by the statement that life is at once itself and more than itself is only a problem of expression." For this issue, see also Josef Bleicher, "From Kant to Goethe: Georg Simmel on the Way to 'Leben,'" *Theory, Culture & Society* 24, no. 6 (2007): 139–58, especially the connection with Goethe's philosophy of life as analyzed on p. 152: "Its inhering moment of meaningful self-organization and directional development through cycles of polarity relates it to Bergson's conception rather more than to Nietzsche's, and it is one Simmel seems to operate with also." See also Josef Bleicher, "Leben," *Theory, Culture & Society* 23, no. 2–3 (2006): 343–45.

13. See also the statement that a given value "become[s] [a] manifestation of culture to us inasmuch as we interpret [it] as [an] intensified display of natural vitality and potential, intensified beyond the level of development, fullness and differentiation that would be achieved by their mere nature" (*SoC*, 36).

14. For a first suggestion of this ambiguous relationship with philosophy of life, see Donald N. Levine, "*Soziologie* and *Lebensanschauung*: Two Approaches to Synthesizing 'Kant' and 'Goethe' in Simmel's Work," *Theory, Culture & Society* 29, no. 7/8 (2012): 40. Levine is justified in warning against "the label 'vitalism' as an adequate representation of Simmel's philosophy" because he "rejects the Bergsonian view of form as inherently antagonistic to life." See also Turo-Kimmo Lehtonen and Olli Pyyhtinen, "On Simmel's Conception of Philosophy," *Continental Philosophy Review* 41 (2008): 315: "It is . . . the definition of life simultaneously as more life and more-than-life that crucially separates Simmel's philosophy of life from his predecessors."

15. See, for instance, Simmel's views on landscape: "Nature, which in its deep being and meaning knows nothing of individuality, is transfigured into an individuated 'landscape' by the human gaze that divides things up and forms the separated parts into specific unities" (Simmel, "Philosophy of Landscape," 22). For a systematic analysis of the entirety of Simmel's work that focuses on the duality between life and form, see Levine, "*Soziologie* and *Lebensanschauung*," 26–52. My own interpretation is fully in line with Levine's suggestion that Simmel's sociology and his metaphysical insights need to be read side by side and presuppose the same conceptual framework.

16. See also the statement that life's aspiration to "determine and manifest itself beyond all forms, in its naked immediacy" is "unattainable" (*SoC*, 90). See also Simmel's statement that "where the expression of life . . . offers itself . . . in a nakedness free from form, absolutely nothing that is actually comprehensible results" (*SoC*,

103). For a further understanding of these ideas and Simmel's duality between objective and subjective culture, see Karl Mannheim, "Soul and Culture," *Theory, Culture & Society* 29, no. 7/8 (2012): 286–301; and David Kettler, "Introduction to 'Soul and Culture,'" *Theory, Culture & Society* 29, no. 7/8 (2012): 279–85.

17. See, for example, respectively Georg Simmel, "Die Gegensätze des Lebens und die Religion" (*GSG 7*, 295–303); Simmel, "The Metropolis and Mental Life" (*SoC*, 174–85); Simmel, "Deutschlands innere Wandlung" (*GSG 15*, 273–85); and Simmel, "Zum Problem des Naturalismus" (*GSG 20*, 220–48).

18. See also the following claim in the book on Rembrandt: "It seems to me beyond doubt that death *inhabits* life from the onset." Simmel goes on to describe it as "one of its elements" and a "*character indelebilis*" (a permanent mark) (*R*, 71–72). These ideas had a big influence on Heidegger's *Being and Time*; see, for example, the reference to Simmel's *View of Life* in Martin Heidegger, *Being and Time*, trans. Joan Stambaugh (Albany: State University of New York Press, 1996), 408n6. Heidegger criticizes Simmel for insufficiently distinguishing the biological (ontic) and the existential (ontological). See also Olli Pyyhtinen, "Life, Death and Individuation: Simmel on the Problem of Life Itself," *Theory, Culture & Society* 29, no. 7/8 (2012): 78–100. Pyyhtinen's reading focuses on the idea that Simmel's views on death presuppose a biological view of life. My own view runs counter to this: it is precisely on account of the immanent presence of death within life that its dynamic of change can be modified into the "more-than-life" that constitutes culture. See also Gadamer's reference to the influence of Simmel on Heidegger, quoted in Isabelle Darmon and Carlos Frade, "Beneath and Beyond the Fragments: The Charms of Simmel's Philosophical Path for Contemporary Subjectivities," *Theory, Culture & Society* 29, no. 7/8 (2012): 214.

19. In his book on Rembrandt, for instance, he puts it as follows: "Death is related to life not like a possibility that at some point becomes reality, but rather our life only becomes life as we know it, and is only formed as it is, in that we . . . are always such beings that will die" (*R*, 71).

20. See also Levine, "*Soziologie* and *Lebensanschauung*," 40. For the overall relationship with Bergson, see Gregor Fitzi, *Soziale Erfahrung und Lebensphilosophie: Georg Simmels Beziehung zu Henri Bergson* (Konstanz: UVK Verlagsgesellschaft, 2002).

21. For an interpretation of this concept of repetition, see, for instance, Beatrice Hanssen, "The Turn to Natural History," in *Walter Benjamin's Other History: Of Stones, Animals, Human Beings and Angels* (Berkeley: University of California Press, 1998), 49–65; and Peter Osborne, "Small-Scale Histories, Large-Scale Defeats," in *Walter Benjamin's Philosophy: Destruction and Experience*, ed. Andrew Benjamin and Peter Osborne (London: Routledge, 1994), 82–85. For Benjamin's criticism of historicism, see Beatrice Hanssen, "Philosophy at Its Origin: Walter Benjamin's Prologue to the *Ursprung des deutschen Trauerspiels*," *MLN* 110, no. 4 (1995): 786–816; and her "The Epistemo-Critical Prologue Reconsidered," in *Walter Benjamin's Other History*, 24–48. For its relevance for Benjamin's reading of modernity as hell, see Susan Buck-Morss, *The Dialectics of Seeing: Walter Benjamin and the Arcades Project* (Cambridge, Mass.: MIT Press, 1989), 96–109. See also Sigrid Weigel's ideas on the theme of a "secularization of the historical" in Benjamin's work in *Walter Benjamin: Images, the*

Creaturely and the Holy (Stanford, Calif.: Stanford University Press, 2013), 11–14.

22. See also Stéphane Symons, "Walter Benjamin and the 'Highly Productive Use of the Human Being's Self-Alienation,'" in *The Aesthetic Ground of Critical Theory: New Readings of Benjamin and Adorno*, ed. Nathan Ross (Lanham, Md.: Rowman and Littlefield, 2015), 99–110.

23. See also Beatrice Hanssen's plea for an "ethico-theological response to the creatural" in her *Walter Benjamin's Other History*, 162; and Eric Santner's discussion of this concept in his *On Creaturely Life: Rilke, Benjamin, Sebald* (Chicago: University of Chicago Press, 2006), 25–27.

24. In 1913–14 Benjamin attends a course taught by Heinrich Rickert that introduces him to Bergson's theory of time. Like Simmel, Bergson connects the temporal flow with a dynamic of change. As Peter Fenves notes, Benjamin is not impressed by what he hears (unlike Heidegger, who attends the same course) and writes to a friend: "I sit here and nibble on a sausage" (see Peter Fenves, *The Messianic Reduction: Walter Benjamin and the Shape of Time* [Stanford, Calif.: Stanford University Press, 2011], 6).

25. For an interesting elaboration of a "longing for the One" (a return to the totality of life as such) in Simmel, see Darmon and Frade, "Beneath and Beyond the Fragments," 197–217. See also Simmel's important essay "Sociological Aesthetics" and the assertion that "every point conceals the possibility of being released into absolute aesthetic significance. To the adequately trained eye, the *total* beauty, the *total* meaning of the world as a whole radiates from every single point" (*GSG 5*, 199). Compare with analyses that emphasize Simmel's sensibility for the *fragment* and a *loss* of unity; see, for example, Deena Weinstein and Michael A. Weinstein's interpretation of Simmel as a *bricoleur* in "Georg Simmel: Sociological Flâneur Bricoleur," *Theory, Culture & Society* 8, no. 3 (1991): 151–68.

26. Simmel's overall philosophy of art illustrates this process. For him "art . . . draws its meaning and its claim precisely from the fact that it is life's Other, the deliverance from its praxis, its contingency" (*VoL*, 52). This otherness, however, indicates the very site from which art derives its capacity to actively bring about meaning and significance: art "produces an ideal world where it no longer adapts to the vital order, but instead itself determines or discerns an order to which life . . . must adapt" (*VoL*, 42).

27. See, for example, Andrew Benjamin, "The Absolute as Translatability: Working through Walter Benjamin on Language," in *Walter Benjamin and Romanticism*, ed. Beatrice Hanssen and Andrew Benjamin (New York: Continuum, 2002), 116: "The Fall becomes the moment staging the presence of the Absolute in terms that are, in the end, proper to it: namely, the necessary impossibility of the Absolute's actualization. With the Fall there is a retention of the Absolute. Never present as itself, it is only ever present within—perhaps also as—the symbol of the non-communicable. Moreover, the Fall has its own topology. Fundamental to it is the spacing that it sets in place. . . . Its communication—understood as the immediacy of its presence—would entail the elimination of spacing and thus the refusal of the plurality of languages."

28. See Benjamin's views on divine violence and revolutionary violence and the claim that "if the rule of myth is broken occasionally in the present age, the

coming age is not so unimaginably remote that an attack on law is altogether futile. But if the existence of violence outside the law, as pure immediate violence, is assured, this furnishes proof that revolutionary violence, the highest manifestation of unalloyed violence by man, is possible, and shows by what means" (*SW 1*, 252).

29. For a clear elaboration of these ideas, see Sigrid Weigel, "The Artwork as Breach of a Beyond: On the Dialectic of Divine and Human Order in Walter Benjamin's 'Goethe's Elective Affinities,'" in *Walter Benjamin and Romanticism*, 197–206; and Eli Friedlander, *Walter Benjamin: A Philosophical Portrait* (Cambridge, Mass.: Harvard University Press, 2012), 56–59. See also chapter 4 of the present volume.

30. Simmel quoted by David Frisby in "Preface to the Third Edition," *PhoM*, xxiv.

31. In this regard, it would be very interesting to compare the relation between Simmel and Benjamin with the relation between Bergson and Bachelard. See, for example, Gaston Bachelard, *La Dialectique de la durée* (Paris: Presses Universitaires de France, 2006), 7–9: "Continuity—or continuities . . . are to be constructed. . . . In the end, the continuity of duration does not present itself to us as an immediate given [*une donnée immédiate*] but as a problem. . . . Pure thought needs to start with a refusal of life" (my translation). For the relationship between Simmel and Bergson, see Fitzi, *Soziale Erfahrung und Lebensphilosophie*. On pp. 275–77, Fitzi analyses the parallels between Simmel and Bergson's views on duration.

32. For another illustration of Benjamin's argument that the duration of the past needs to be *constructed* (in a poem, for instance), see his essay on Hölderlin and the claim that "quite in opposition to 'fleeting time,' to the 'ephemeral ones,' that which persists—duration in the form of time and men [*das Beharrende, die Dauer in der Gestalt der Zeit und der Menschen*]—has been developed in the new version of these lines. The phrase 'turning of time' plainly captures the instant of persistence as well, the moment of inner plasticity of time" (*SW 1*, 31; *GS II*, 119). For an excellent analysis of this paragraph and Benjamin's concept of "plastic" time, see Peter Fenves, *The Messianic Reduction*, 18–43. See also the "Two Concluding Remarks" in the present volume and the difference between memory and recollection.

33. See Hanssen, "Philosophy at Its Origin."

34. See, for example, the work of Susan Buck-Morss and Andrew Benjamin, "Boredom and Distraction: The Moods of Modernity," in *Walter Benjamin and History*, ed. Andrew Benjamin (London: Continuum, 2005), 156–70; Irving Wohlfarth, "Et Cetera: The Historian as Chiffonnier," *New German Critique* 39 (1986): 142–68; and Rebecca Comay, "The Sickness of Tradition: Between Melancholia and Fetishism," in *Walter Benjamin and History*, ed. Andrew Benjamin, 88–101.

35. In *The Messianic Reduction*, Peter Fenves casts the distinction between Benjamin's philosophical thought and phenomenology along the same lines, arguing convincingly that Benjamin rejects the possibility of a "pure phenomenology" (Husserl) and "pure receptivity" through which phenomena are believed to give themselves "as they are." Benjamin understands such a supposedly "natural" attitude where a world of substantial things is believed to affect the perceiving

subject in a direct manner as "mythological" and argues for the necessity to "turn it off" (44–78).

36. Walter Benjamin, *The Correspondence of Walter Benjamin, 1910–1940*, ed. Gershom Scholem and Theodor Adorno, trans. Manfred R. Jacobson and Evelyn R. Jacobson (Chicago: University of Chicago Press, 1994), 106.

37. Georg Simmel, "The Problem of Historical Time," in *Essays on Interpretation in Social Science*, ed. and trans. Guy Oakes (Manchester: Manchester University Press, 1980), 138.

38. "The historical image which we actually *have* at our disposal on the basis of our research and the hypothetical constructions of our imagination consists of discontinuous, partial images . . . which, in a certain sense, revolve around a central concept" (Simmel, "The Problem of Historical Time," 138).

39. Ibid., 141.

40. Ibid.

41. Ibid., 143–42.

42. Ibid., 143.

43. Ibid., 144. Not a few of Simmel's famous students have taken issue with what they consider to be his relativism or "impressionism"; see, for example, Karl Mannheim, "Georg Simmel als Philosoph," in *Georg Lukács, Karl Mannheim und der Sonntagskreis*, ed. Eva Karádi and Erzsesbet Vezér (Frankfurt am Main: Vervuert, 1988); and Georg Lukács, "Georg Simmel," *Theory, Culture & Society* 8, no. 3 (1991): 145–50. The majority of Simmel scholars, however, identifies this impressionism as one of the strongest (and most original) elements in his work; see, for example, Otthein Rammstedt, "On Simmel's Aesthetics: Argumentation in the Journal *Jugend*, 1897–1906," *Theory, Culture & Society* 8, no. 3 (1991): 125–44; and David Frisby, *Sociological Impressionism: A Reassessment of Georg Simmel's Social Theory* (London: Routledge, 2013).

44. For an excellent discussion of Benjamin's ideas about historical time (and some brief references to the relationship with Simmel's reflections on the same topic), see Peter Fenves, *The Messianic Reduction*, 103–24. Throughout the book Fenves focuses on the concept of the "shape of time" to indicate the interruptive power that is at stake in our discussion as well. See, for example, Fenves's description of the moment when the "circular or cycloid character of the 'eternal return of the same' is . . . broken open—without time taking on a telos in the process" (243).

45. The tragic hero, for instance, is believed to experience the absolute power of death and guilt as immanent to life. Unable to truly interrupt the continuity of life, he cannot bring about a moment of genuine redemption (*SW 1*, 56). See also chapter 5 of the present volume.

46. Georg Simmel, "The Picture Frame," in *Theory, Culture & Society* 11, no. 1 (1994): 11–17.

47. See Sigrid Weigel, "Benjamin's 'World of Universal and Integral Actuality' and 'Body- and Image-Space': Traces through Benjamin's Writings," in *Body- and Image-Space: Re-Reading Walter Benjamin*, trans. Georgina Paul with Rachel McNicholl and Jeremy Gaines (London: Routledge, 1996), 3–15 and 16–29.

48. See also Buck-Morss, *The Dialectics of Seeing*, 195.

49. See Symons, "Walter Benjamin and the 'Highly Productive Use of the Human Being's Self-Alienation.' "

Chapter 1

1. [*empfand die Häßlichkeit so scharf, weil sie sich von dem Hintergrunde seines Schönheitsideales abhob*].

2. [*Seinem ganzen Liebesempfinden, soweit er dichterisch gestaltet hat liegt ein Gedanke zu Grunde: Der Gegensatz seiner Persönlichkeit gegen die der Geliebten*].

3. "Before everything, it is as if the soulful and the bodily essence of the human being recognize their unity again, after the long separation that was forced upon them by the transcendent nature of the soul" (*GSG 12*, 114).

4. "From this sublation of all mutual strangeness and contingency in the essential elements [*dieser Aufhebung aller gegenseitigen Fremdheit und Zufälligkeit der Wesenselemente*] arises the feeling that these figures have an existence that is internally complete [*einer in sich vollkomenen Existenz*]. What is deemed titanic in them, that which is released from empirical conditions and relations, is not the overpowering violence of their force, but a closure of the internal-external essence [*jene Geschlossenheit des innerlich-aüßeren Wesens*], the absence of which is what makes up the specifically fragmentary nature of our existence" (*GSG 12*, 117).

5. See also Anthony Hughes's description of the *Pietà* as "a carving of extreme restraint" in Anthony Hughes, *Michelangelo*, trans. Sophie Behr and Pierre Clertant (London: Phaidon, 1997), 19. For a further analysis of this work, see Michael Hirst and Jill Dunkerton, *The Young Michelangelo: Making and Meaning* (London: National Gallery, 1994), 47–55.

6. [*unberührt by allem Menschlich-Fragmentarischen*] [*seiner Ganzheit*] [*aus seinem einheitlichen Zentrum*].

7. [*eine anschaulich logische Konzequenz*] [*von einem inneren Gesetz betstimmten Lebens*].

8. Their lives are "disclosed in their proper movements, released of all the appearances that are caused by the This and That of the world" [*offenbart in ihren Eigenschwingungen, gelöst von all den Erscheinungsweisen, zu denen das Dies und Das der Welt sie veranlaßt*] (*GSG 12*, 131).

9. [*Gegensatz*] [*Einsamkeit des plastischen Werkes*] [*Einsamkeit der dargestellten Wesen*] [*etwas ganz anderes*].

10. [*plastischen Wesens*] [*porenlos gegen die Welt außerhalb ihrer abgeschlossen*]. Simmel is after a description of the manner in which Michelangelo's figures do not seemingly refer the spectator's gaze back or forward to anything that lies beyond them, but seemingly present themselves as fully self-sustaining: "These sculptures [are] formations of life that are situated in other realms of being entirely beyond the issue of being or non-being [*ganz jenseits der Frage nach Sein oder Nichtsein in anderen Sphären der Existenz stehen*]. They *are* what they *present* in that they are truly immediate and are not just legitimized by [the reference to] something that lies behind them. They do not imitate something that, outside of this imitation, could perhaps very well be different" (*GSG 12*, 119).

11. [*Die Grenzen der Welt, in denen die plastische Gestalt lebt, ihr idealer Raum, sind nichts weiter und nichts anderes als die Grenzen ihres Körpers selbst, außerhalb dieser ist keine Welt mehr, mit der sie zu tun hätte*].

12. [*sie sind was sie darstellen*] [*Der Mensch der Plastik und sein Beschauer . . . können nie von derselben Luft umfangen sein*].

13. [*das religiöse Gefühl [transponiert sich] in das Irdische hinein*].

14. [*gilt . . . eigentlich keinem Transzendenten*] [*eine Erlösung die von keinem Gotte kommt*] [*ein Schicksal aus den Mächten des Lebens*]. Michelangelo's longing, adds Simmel, "is nourished by the power sources of all worldly dimensions" [*genährt von den Kraftquellen aus allen weltlichen Dimensionen*] (*GSG 12*, 126).

15. [*Es war die Schicksalformel seiner Seele, die ganze Fülle des Unendlichen der ganzen Fülle des Endlichen abzufordern*]. Simmel adds that Michelangelo's "spirit is motivated by a goal that is essentially finite, but has now become . . . an unreachable, ideal goal" [*dem Geiste schwebst jetzt ein Ziel vor, das seinem Wesen nach endlich ist, aber nun ist es . . . ein Unerreichbares, ein ideelles Ziel*] (*GSG 12*, 126).

16. [*ein höchst persönliches, aus dem eigensten Verhängnis heraus lebendes Dasein*] [*einem allgemeinsten, durch die Menschheit als ganze hinwebenden Lose*].

17. See also chapter 3 and the difference between the concepts of the universal and the general.

18. [*selbstgenugsamen, eigengesetzlichen äußeren Form des Lebens*].

19. Types and forms cannot be released from "shared premises [*gemeinsame Voraussetzungen*] making comparison possible—a shared standard [*gemeinsamer Maßstab*] that in our case means in particular a shared idea of the human [*gemeinsame Idee des Menschlichen*] of which, so to speak, some quantum is contained in each personality that, however differently arranged, permits all of these incompatible forms to be infused and governed by a sense of common style and universal type [*das Gefühl eines gleichen Stiles und allgemeiner Typen*]" (*R*, 89; *GSG 15*, 424, translation modified).

20. [*An die Stelle jener individualistischen Zuspitzung der Erscheinung . . . setzte er die klassische, überindividuelle, auf das Typische gehende Stilisierung*]. In Simmel's view, Renaissance art is indicative of a Platonism-cum-individuation ("The Renaissance supplemented Platonism . . . with the element of individuality" [*R*, 89]).

21. [*daß der Mensch eine Individualität ist, . . . ist aus der Summe seiner angebbaren Eigenschaften zusammenzusetzen*].

22. This duality between what I term individuation and individualization is elaborated upon in various places in Simmel's work, most notably in his essays "Germanic and Classical Romanic Style," "Individualism," and "Goethe and Youth." See *Theory, Culture & Society* 24, no. 7/8 (2007): 47–52, 66–71, 85–90.

23. [*zu gesondertem So-Sein herausgelöst*] [*fertig*].

24. [*absolut getrennt*].

25. [*Lebensprozeß in zeitlicher Entwicklung*] [*ein resultathaftes So-Sein*] [*ein zeitloses . . . Definitivum*].

26. [*dem Druck eines allgemeinen Schicksals, in dem alle inhaltlich angebbaren Elemente augelöst sind*] [*Es lastet auf ihnen und es erschüttert sie das Leben als Ganzes, das Leben als Schicksal überhaupt*]. Compare with Benjamin's ideas on the tragic hero and Fate and, most notably, his claim that "the tragic hero dies of immortality"; see chapter 5. For an elaborate discussion of the concept of Fate in the work of Simmel, see Robert William Button, "Fate, Experience and Tragedy in Simmel's Dialogue with Modernity," *Theory, Culture & Society* 29, no. 7/8 (2012): 53–77. Surprisingly, Button does not mention the essay on Michelangelo which would nevertheless illustrate his main claims about the connection between Fate and tragedy.

27. "In the figures of Michelangelo, a felt or metaphysical reality *of life as such* [*eine gefühlte oder metaphysische Wirklichkeit des Lebens als solchen*] is brought to expression for the first time—of life, which, to be sure, develops into various meanings, stages and fates, but, ultimately, possesses a unity that cannot be described by words [*eine letzte, mit Worten nicht beschreibbare Einheit*], in which the opposition between soul and body has evaporated in the same manner as individual manners of existing and behaving" (*GSG 12*, 116).

28. [*das anthropomorphe Aufblasen des eigenen Loses zum Weltfatum*] [*das geniale metaphysische Fühlen des Weltwesens*].

29. [*dumpf und brennend, lastend und bohrend über der Menschheit und dem Menschen*] [*Sie ergreift uns wie die Drehung der Erde, die uns mit sich herumwirbelt, ein Los*] [*erfaßt . . . uns wie eine objective, durch die Welt hindurch waltende Kraft*]. The same distinction between Fate (*Schicksal*) and fates (*Schicksale*) underlies Sigmund Freud's distinction between "instinct" (*Instinkt*) and "drive" (*Trieb*) in an essay that was written around the time when Simmel wrote his second essay on Michelangelo, "Drives and Their Vicissitudes" ("Triebe und Triebschicksale," 1915). Whereas instincts are determined by nature, that is, by a universal and ahistorical principle of necessity that runs counter to individual freedom, drives play themselves out in the realm of history and are therefore individualized and marked by an irreducible openness and potential for change.

30. See *GSG 12*, 117, but compare, however, to *R*, 74–76.

31. [*als ein Teil ihres Seins in dieses eingeschlossen*] [*wie ihr Sein in ihre Sehnsucht*].

32. Simmel understands Michelangelo's *Sehnsucht* as "inescapable" (*notwendig*) (*GSG 12*, 133) and as something that "originates from the deepest foundations of his nature" (*GSG 12*, 133).

33. [*vernichtende Schicksal ihres Lebenswillens*] [*[S]ie sind von vornherein mit diesem Problem und Bedürfnis eines Absoluten, eines allen irdischen Maßstäben entzogenen Daseins geschlagen*] [*die Erfüllung ihres Seins ist die Vernichtung ihres Seins*].

34. [*[D]ie Elemente von Schicksal und Freiheit . . . [sind] hier näher, einheitlicher, zu entschiedenerer Äquivalenz zusammengerückt, als in irgend einer anderen Kunst*].

35. For a discussion of the slaves, see also Hughes, *Michelangelo*, 161–62.

36. [*wie mühsam und kämpfend aus dem Marmorblock heraus[steigen]*].

37. [*an das irdisch-persönliche Dasein wird die absolute Forderung gestellt, die objektiven Werte erfüllen sich mit subjektivem Leben—aber eben damit wird dieses der zufälligen Subjektivität der egozentrischen Zuständlichkeit enthoben*].

38. [*dem ewigen Verderben . . . das ihn erwartet*].

39. [*die rein innere Qual: ein solcher zu sein, der die Hölle verdient*] [*ein von außen drohendes Geschick*] [*die logische, kontinuierliche Entwicklung der irdischen Beschaffenheit*].

40. According to Simmel, the "pride" of the Renaissance individual "lies not in the first place in consciousness [*Bewußtsein*], but rather immediately in the person's being [*unmittelbar im Sein der Person*]" (*R*, 123; *GSG 15*, 467).

41. In his essay on Rodin, Simmel formulates it as follows: "With regard to the bodies of Michelangelo one does not at all get the idea, that they could also move differently [*der Gedanke, daß sie sich auch anders bewegen könnten*]; and

vice versa, the progress of the soul, so to speak the formula that is spelled out by the movement [*der seelische Vorgang, sozusagen der Satz, den die Bewegung aussagt*], cannot have another subject than this [specific] body" (*GSG 14*, 336). See chapter 3.

Chapter 2

1. For background information on the context in which Simmel wrote his essay on Rembrandt, see Uta Kösser, "Simmels Rembrandt," *Simmel Studies* 13, no. 2 (2003): 457. For an interesting summary of the main arguments, see Graeme Gilloch, "The Faces of Amsterdam: Rembrandt, Simmel and the Painting of Modern Lives," *Episteme* 4 (2010): 233–58; and Alois Kölbl, *Das Leben der Form: Georg Simmels kunstphilosophisches Versug über Rembrandt* (Vienna: Böhlau, 1998). For a general introduction and broad positioning in Simmel's overall oeuvre, see Karen Lang, "Simmel's *Rembrandt* and *The View of Life*," in *New Approaches to Neo-Kantianism*, ed. Nicolas de Warren and Andrea Staiti (Cambridge: Cambridge University Press, 2015), 186–202.

2. Following Schiller, Simmel puts it as follows: "Through the morning door of beauty you entered the land of knowledge" (Simmel quoted in *R*, xii). The translators of the Rembrandt book, for their part, describe the book as "a series of reflections for which Rembrandt's *work*, but not his life or the conditions in which that work came into being, is the occasion . . . It is the object before us—its meaning, its significance—not the historical context, nor even the psychological state or motivations, or the intentions of its creator, that must be the prime focus of our attention" (*R*, xii).

3. [*eine unendliche kontinuierliche Vielheit sich erstreckenden Leben*].

4. "The life of each person who is a bearer [of life] does not have its totality in the sum of its particular moments [*der Summe seiner einzelnen Momente*] (nor does one know how that sum is to be arrived at)" (*R*, 161; *GSG 15*, 514, translation modified).

5. For similar ideas in Bergson, see, for instance, his *Creative Evolution*, trans. Arthur Mitchell (Whitefish, Mont.: Kessinger, 2003), 3–6; and Henri Bergson, *The Creative Mind: An Introduction to Metaphysics*, trans. Mabelle L. Andison (New York: Dover Books, 2007), 124–25.

6. "When we think, we are only a vessel of contents [*Gefäß von Inhalten*] or, more accurately, the existence [*Dasein*] of contents; we cannot grasp the gestative or generative process [*den tragenden oder zeugenden Prozeß*] because it is already content in the moment when it is grasped. And yet we know it—with a consciousness sui generis, existing only for it and nothing else—as the ultimate reality of this very thinking [*die letzte Realität eben dieses Denkens*], as against the ideal, conceptually expressible contents" (*VoL*, 120; *GSG 16*, 377). As Simmel puts it in the Rembrandt book, "life does not reserve a somehow separable 'purity' and being for itself beyond the beats of its pulse [*eine irgend abtrennbare "Reinheit" und Fürsichsein jenseits seiner Pulsschläge vor*]," but it does not "remain in the sphere of diversity [*in dem Gebiet der Mannigfaltigkeiten*]" either (*R*, 6; *GSG 15*, 314).

7. [*ausschließlich in der Bewegung durch all diese Entgegengesetztheiten*]. Life is "an absolute continuity in which there is no assemblage of fragments or parts [*eine absolute Kontinuität in der es zusammensetzende Stücke oder Teile*

nicht gibt]," it has the "incomparable form" (*unvergleichbare Form*) of a "steady stream" (*stetiger Fluß*) that cannot be "further deduced" and remains "a basic given that cannot be constructed [*eine fundamentale, unkonstruierbare Tatsache*]" (*R*, 6; *GSG 15*, 314, translation modified).

8. For an extensive elaboration of Simmel's ideas about the relationality of the self and the connection between his formal sociology and the concept of individual lawfulness, see Monica Lee and Daniel Silver, "Simmel's Law of the Individual and the Ethics of the Relational Self," *Theory, Culture & Society* 29, no. 7/8 (2012): 124–45.

9. "Where we perceive life, and not a frozen cross-section that only offers a content but not the function of life as such, we constantly perceive a *becoming* (for otherwise it could not be life)" (*R*, 35).

10. Rembrandt's most profound portraits grasp the identity or "soul" of a person not from "a fixed state of total perfection [that] is attained within a particular moment in time [*einem bestimmten Zeitpunkt*] that now persists," but "rather contract the totality of a steady development. And this contraction [*Zusammenfassung*] is not that of an abstracting concept, but rather that of a specific viewing for which concepts are . . . inadequate" (*R*, 36; *GSG 15*, 356–57, translation modified).

11. See also Simmel's idea that social interactions are inevitably spatially embedded (in "The Sociology of Space," *SoC*, 137–70). See also Frank J. Lechner, "Simmel on Social Space," in *Theory, Culture & Society* 8, no. 3 (1991): 195–201.

12. [*[D]as Leben [ist] dasjenige, was in jedem Augenblick über sich hinaus will, über sich hinaus greift*]. For the same idea, see also: "It is the essence of life to reach and radiate beyond itself [*über sich hinauszugreifen, hinauszustrahlen*] without losing its unity; to surround itself, as it were, with a sphere beyond that which is primarily tangible. Its unity always remains bound to its center in that it interacts with, pervades, and melts into the sphere of others [*indem sie mit der Sphäre anderer wechselwirkt, sich durchdringt, verschmilzt*]" (*R*, 45; *GSG 15*, 368–69).

13. As Simon Schama puts it in his groundbreaking study of Rembrandt, they are "*caught*" within this stream of becoming; Simon Schama, *Rembrandt's Eyes* (New York: Knopf, 1999), 341, my emphasis. Simmel puts it as follows: "Each figure is viewed as having emerged from, or emerging out of, the fleeting rhythm of life, fate, development [*ein in der flutenden Rhythmik von Leben, Schicksal, Entwicklung, gewordenes oder werdendes*]. It is, so to speak, not the form in its current state that Rembrandt presents, but, rather, the totality of life that has been lived up to this moment, and is viewed from the perspective of [this moment] [*das gerade bis zu diesem Augenblick gelebte, von ihm her gesehene Gesamtleben*]" (*R*, 36; *GSG 15*, 356, translation modified).

14. "We see the whole person [*den ganzen Menschen*] and not a moment of his life from which we deduced earlier moments. For life *is* immediately nothing other than the past becoming present [*das Leben ist unmittelbar gar nichts anderes, als die Gegenwart werdende Vergangenheit*], and where we really see life, only a pure prejudice will allow us to claim that one merely sees the frozen present moment [*den starren Punkt der Gegenwart*]" (*R*, 34; *GSG 15*, 353). See also Simmel's claim that the life of an individual "transforms itself at each

moment, but remains at all times a unity in which character and history are not internally divided [*eine Einheit, in der Charakter und Geschichte such innerlich nicht scheiden*]" (*R*, 79; *GSG 15*, 411).

15. "Rembrandt collects its past into [the] here and now, not so much a fruitful moment but a moment of harvesting [*nicht sowohl ein fruchtbarer, als ein erntender Moment*]. Just as it is the nature of life to be at every moment there as a *totality* [*Wie es das Wesen des Lebens ist, in jedem Augenblick ganz da zu sein*] . . . so it is the nature of Rembrandt's movement of expression [*das Wesen der Rembrandtschen Ausdrucksbewegung*] to let us feel the whole sequence of its moments in a single feeling [*das ganze Nacheinander ihrer Momente in der Einmaligkeit eines einzelnen fühlen zu lassen*]" (*R*, 7; *GSG 15*, 315, translation modified). See also Ute Faath, *Mehr-als-Kunst: Zur Kunstphilosophie Georg Simmels* (Würzburg: Königshausen und Neumann, 1998), 148–54; and Kölbl, *Das Leben der Form*, 41–57.

16. See also his statement that it is not an "*object* that seduces us but . . . exclusively our own urge, breaking forth from our inner self and in this moment representing the ego" (*VoL*, 106).

17. [*das Ergreifen eines Ganzen durch eine einheitliche Funktion*] [*ein Augenblick, in dem sie sich zu einer Totalität zusammenschließen*]. See also the following sentence: "At once the order is now reversed: this unity does not come from the combined parts, but the parts from the whole [*diese Einheit kommt nicht aus den zusammengefaßten Teilen, sondern die Teile aus der Einheit*]" (*VoL*, 128; *GSG 16*, 386–87, translation modified).

18. In "The Law of the Individual" Simmel writes: "Though the external aspects of our behavior may show relatively sharp boundaries with respect to one another, life is not assembled [*zusammengesetzt*] inwardly from a lie, then a courageous decision, then a licentious act, then an act of beneficence, etc.—rather, it is a steady gliding where every instant represents the perpetually self-creating, transforming whole, where no part has sharp boundaries with another and where each reveals its meaning only within that whole and seen from its viewpoint" (*VoL*, 128; *GSG 16*, 387).

19. [*verschmilzt . . . mit der Sphäre anderer*].

20. This issue can shed light on the reason why Michelangelo, as is noted by Giorgio Vasari, was critical with regard to the artistic merits of portraiture.

21. In his essay on the face, Simmel uses the same categories he would later use, in the Rembrandt book and his final essays, to analyze the openness of the life of an individual. "There is no other thing which, staying so absolutely in place, seems to reach beyond it [*über ihn hinauszustrecken*] to such an extent; the eye penetrates, it withdraws, it circles a room, it wanders, it reaches as though behind the wanted object and pulls it toward itself." In Georg Simmel, "The Aesthetic Significance of the Face," trans. Lore Ferguson, in *Georg Simmel, 1858–1919*, ed. Kurt H. Wolff (Columbus: Ohio State University Press, 1959), 281 (*GSG 7*, 41).

22. For Simmel, the face indicates "the closest unity which, though composed of these particularities, transcends each of them and comes into being exclusively through their co-operation [*Wechselwirkung*]," in Simmel, "The Aesthetic Significance of the Face," 277, translation modified (*GSG 7*, 37). In *A Thousand Plateaus*, Gilles Deleuze and Félix Guattari develop a philosophy of the face (and landscape) that is fully at odds with that of Simmel. Whereas Simmel's interest

in the face ultimately revolves around an interest in the double issue of meaning (as a relational unity) and subjectivity (as the uniqueness of a life), Deleuze and Guattari's interest in the face revolves around the need to *escape* from precisely the "despotism" of signification and the "authoritarianism" of subjectivity (180). In their writings, as well, the concept of the face denotes a relational unity between different particularities that have seemingly nothing in common: "We could say that the face holds within its rectangle or circle a whole set of traits, *faciality traits*, which it subsumes and places at the service of signifiance and subjectification" (188). However, their analysis is aimed at exploring the "condition of possibility" (180) of the face in order to learn how to "dismantle" (188) this unity and "set *faciality traits* free like birds" (189). In *Cinema 1: The Movement-Image*, this view underlies Deleuze's interest in the close-up ("the close-up is by itself face" [88]) and in the work of filmmakers like Griffith, Eisenstein, and Dreyer where it is used to "tear the image away from spatio-temporal coordinates" (96) in order to bring to expression the purity of an "affect." Deleuze and Guattari thus disconnect the face from what is considered to be specifically human and unique to the individual ("There is even something absolutely inhuman about the face" [*A Thousand Plateaus*, 170]). Instead, they emphasize that the relational unity that is termed "face" is always "engendered by an *abstract machine of faciality* [*visagéité*]" (168) that can just as well be effectuated on other things or even (and preferably) eluded. "If human beings have a destiny, it is rather to escape the face, to dismantle the face and facializations, to become imperceptible, to become clandestine . . . by strange true becomings . . . that make *faciality traits* themselves finally elude the organization of the face" (171). The quotations from *A Thousand Plateaus* come from Gilles Deleuze and Félix Guattari, *A Thousand Plateaus: Capitalism and Schizophrenia*, trans. Brian Massumi (Minneapolis: University of Minnesota Press, 1998); while those from *Cinema 1* come from Gilles Deleuze, *Cinema 1: The Movement-Image*, trans. Hugh Tomlinson and Barbara Habberjam (London: Athlone, 1986).

23. On the general issue of symmetry in Michelangelo, see, for instance, James Hall's reference to the "abstract angular symmetry" in the Florentine *Pietà* in *Michelangelo and the Reinvention of the Human Body* (New York: Farrar, Straus and Giroux, 2005), 208.

24. "Sculpture, which presents the halves of the face symmetrically, is defined to a more general or typical style that lacks ultimate individual differentiation; painting, on the other hand . . . reveals from the beginning a more individualistic nature," in Simmel, "The Aesthetic Significance of the Face," 279 (*GSG* 7, 40).

25. [*ohne dies durch die Verallgemeinerung zu einem Typus zu erkaufen*].

26. The idea that Rembrandt's art lacks the feeling for a cosmic essence and thus exposes the gap between the historical and the absolute casts light on Simmel's criticism of Julius Langbehn's book *Rembrandt as Educator* (1890). Langbehn uses Rembrandt (and Nietzsche) to back up a reactionary appeal to the *Volk* and race. Simmel's review takes Langbehn's book to task for its inflation of metaphysical idea(l)s (see Faath, *Mehr-als-Kunst*, 77–81; and Jacques le Rider, "Rembrandt de Langbehn à Simmel: Du clair-obscur de l'âme allemande aux couleurs de la modernité," *Société* 44 [1994]: 145–55). For more on the gap between history and the absolute in Rembrandt (and the difference with the Renaissance): "For the Renaissance individual, nature was of a unified ideal

being . . . out of which grows the variety of individuals without detaching from this rootstock [*aus dem die Mannigfaltigkeit der Individuen herauswächst, ohne sich von diesem Wurzelgrund zu lösen*]. Herein, individualization finds its limit; one signified by those common features of form. Such an idea of 'nature' is completely foreign to Rembrandt. The nature, which he also seeks, is that of the single being" (*R*, 87–88; *GSG 15*, 422). "In that Rembrandt's figures keep [their] unity and self-assured continuity, they . . . pay the price of failing to actually arouse the feeling of the cosmic within us [*nicht eigentlich das Gefühl des Kosmischen in uns zu wecken*]" (*R*, 107; *GSG 15*, 448). "The 'great human themes' [*der Menschheit große Gegenstände*] . . . appear to the artist to be a detour in the life which is lived for its own sake [*ein Umweg des um seiner selbst willen lebenden Lebens*], a detour which life in its purest concentration avoids" (*R*, 109; *GSG 15*, 450).

27. About Rembrandt's portraits in general, Simmel writes: "Rembrandt made clear that out of the innermost life of a person his appearance can be developed into a convincingly necessary form [*zu einer überzeugend notwendigen Form*] that in no way borrows this development from a universal law [*keineswegs aus einer allgemeinen Gesetzlichkeit entlehnt*]" (*R*, 65–66; *GSG 15*, 394, translation modified). As Schama puts it, by way of Rembrandt's portrait Jan Six steps "out of the anonymous darkness [and] into the cordial, warming light of recognition" (in *Rembrandt's Eyes*, 578).

28. For an overview of Rembrandt's etchings of beggars, see Gary Schwartz, *Het Rembrandt boek*, trans. Loekie Schwartz and Paul Van Calster (Antwerp: Mercatorfonds, 2006), 286–89.

29. "It [remains] undeniable that the naturalistic artwork deduces its operational significance from something that is not art" (*GSG 8*, 410). See also Faath, *Mehr-als-Kunst*, 145–47; and Kölbl, *Das Leben der Form*, 105–8.

30. [*sich sekundär and das Wirklichsein der Dinge knüpfen*] [*bloß inhaltliche Qualitäten*].

31. "Reality as such," writes Simmel, "is something metaphysical: the senses cannot give it to us, but, vice versa, it is something that we give to the senses, a relationship between spirit and the inexpressible mystery of being, not a specific, perceivable quality of things, but a meaningfulness that transcends the sum of its qualities" (*[D]ie Wirklichkeit als solche sei etwas Metaphysisches: die Sinne können sie uns nicht geben, sondern umgekehrt ist sie etwas, was wir den Sinnen geben, eine Beziehung des Geistes zu dem unaussprechlichen Geheimnis des Seins, keine besondere, anschauliche Eigenschaft der Dinge, sondern eine Bedeutung, die über die Summe ihrer Eigenschaften kommt*) (*GSG 8*, 407).

32. [*eine Sache der Sinne*] [*etwas Abstraktes [welches] jenseits der Oberfläche der Dinge liegt*].

33. [*Die Seele . . . die dem Kunstwerk Sinn und Halt gibt, . . . lebt wirklich nur in diesem, nicht hinter ihm*].

34. In Simmel's view, Rembrandt discovers "the presentation [*Darstellung*] of the totality of a human life" as "truly a *painterly* [problem] [*wirklich [ein] malerisches [Problem]*], not . . . [a] psychological or metaphysical or anecdotal problem" (*R*, 12; *GSG 15*, 322, translation modified, my emphasis). Simmel summarizes it as follows: "That which the categories of intellect can express only in a contradictory and highly incomplete fashion [*ganz widerspruchsvoll und mit ihnen nur höchst unvollkommen ausdrückbar*] is here *artistically* accomplished

[*künstlerisch gekonnt*]: the figures' living process of becoming what they are has been shaped into *a purely visual construct without any literary or non-artistic association* [*ein rein anschauliches Gebilde, ohne jede literarische oder außerkünstlerische Assoziation*]" (R, 14; *GSG 15*, 325, translation modified, my emphasis). "We see," writes Simmel, "insofar as we see artistically [*insoweit wir künstlerisch sehen*], neither the human being beyond the paint spots through which he is indicated, nor the paint spots beyond the human being whom they indicate, but rather a novel construct [*neues Gebilde*]" (*R*, 82–83; *GSG 15*, 415, translation modified).

35. [*dem Menschen insoweit er empirische Wirklichkeit ist*] [*dem Menschen insoweit er Kunstwerk ist*].

36. [*im höchsten Maße individualistisch, ohne realistisch zu sein*]. Simmel does not hold back in calling it a "miracle" (*das Wunder*) "that a number of paint spots composed side by side receive an internally coherent life that is something other than that represented under the category of reality [*ein zentral zusammengehaltenes Leben . . . welches ein anderes ist, als das unter der Kategorie der Wirklichkeit vorgestellte*]" (*R*, 83; *GSG 15*, 415–16, translation modified). "Once it has absorbed what it wants from worldly reality [*aus der Wirklichkeitswelt in sich hineingenommen*] and the material has become art [*ist dieser Stoff erst einmal Kunst geworden*]," he writes, "then this form can never become a bridge across which we return to [worldly] reality" (*R*, 22; *GSG 15*, 337).

37. Simmel argues that "in direct opposition to the practice of life, [art] interprets the external [looks] of a human being through what is internal to him" (*[i]m direkten Gegensatz zur Praxis des Lebens interpretiert [die Kunst] das Aeußere des Menschen durch sein Inneres*) (*GSG 15*, 325).

38. "In many respects going into details and individualization are mutually exclusive [*in weiter Erstreckung schließen Detaillierung und Individualisierung sich gegenseitig aus*]" (*R*, 50; *GSG 15*, 375). "The individuality of the construct as a whole [i.e., of the painting] [*Die Individualität des Gebildes als Ganzen*] [and] [its] singularity that is thus brought about [*seine dadurch entstehende Einzigkeit*] will in any case be favored by the absence of details" (*R*, 51; *GSG 15*, 376, translation modified).

39. [*[N]ur die Totalität des Menschen . . . ist das Einzige, alles Einzelne an ihm ist ein Allgemeines*].

40. [*das oft so Grenzverwischende, Vibrierende, Verundeutlichende in Rembrandt's Malweise*] [*einem Träger seiner Individualisierungstendenz*].

41. [*[D]ie Einzigkeit des reinen Werdens*] [*Qualitäten, die sind oder werden*]. In some of Rembrandt's works, it is "as though the life of [the] person were admittedly absolutely his own, and not detachable from him, yet raised above all *particularities* that one may say about him" (*als wäre das Leben dieser Person, zwar absolut eigenstes und von ihr nicht lösbar, über alles Einzelne, das man über sie aussagen mag, hinausgehoben*) (*R*, 91; *GSG 15*, 427, translation modified). Similar to how the "mood" of a landscape has nothing to do with any "universal literary-lyrical emotional concepts" because it is too specific for words, the vividness of Rembrandt's works therefore eludes the grasp of linguistic concepts without, however, retreating into an abstract, mysterious, inaccessible, or ambiguous realm. His images, that is to say, do teach us something important

about the sitters but this knowledge is "immediate" and cannot be grasped "conceptually" (*R*, 66). Rembrandt's portraits allow the beholder to relate to an individual-become-paint but the "knowledge" that is gained *of* the sitter and *by* the beholder is not of the order of "universal mental concepts [*allgemein seelischen Begriffen*] [which tell us, for instance, that] a person is clever or stupid, generous or petty, good-natured or malicious, and so on" (*R*, 66; *GSG 15*, 394, translation modified).

42. Such an experience can, according to Simmel, be likened to the puzzling feeling with which we are sometimes overcome when a person we were previously unfamiliar with suddenly walks into our room: "In this very first moment we do not know particular facts about him. . . . Nevertheless, we still know a tremendous amount: the person, and that which is unmistakable about the person. The bodily uniqueness upon which this first presence fixes is a symbol, or perhaps more than a symbol, of this" (*R*, 66). Simmel thus understands a portrait more as a sudden encounter between painter, sitter, and beholder than as a mere object created by an artist: it is more a movement or event than a *thing*.

43. Schama, *Rembrandt's Eyes*, 557. For a different reading of the painting as a scene of immodesty, see Albert Blankert, "Looking at Rembrandt, Past and Present," in *Rembrandt: A Genius and His Impact*, ed. Albert Blankert (Melbourne: National Gallery of Victoria, 1997), 36.

44. "Life [here] flows into the concept of perfection and [for that reason] . . . forces it . . . to stretch itself so far into infinity [*dem Unendlichen zu, zu spannen*] that perfection here at least does not dismiss the human fatelike possibility of failure [*die menschliche, schicksalsmäßige Möglichkeit des Mißlingens*], as something it does not understand at all" (*R*, 86; *GSG 15*, 420, translation modified). See also Simmel's statement that "Rembrandt's style of painting . . . creates the illusion that one could follow the movement of his hand, the particular strokes [*die einzelnen Pinselstriche*]" and thereby makes it tangible that a work "in all its supra-subjectivity and closedness [*in all seiner Übersubjektivität und Geschlossenheit*] [nevertheless] grows together, as it were, out of the soulful artistic impulses or even imponderables [*aus den seelisch malerischen Impulsen oder auch Imponderabilien . . . zusammenwächst*]" (*R*, 85; *GSG 15*, 418, translation modified). "With Rembrandt we never have the feeling, not even in his most superior and absolutely 'perfect' works, that they had detached themselves absolutely from the ground of life that is at the mercy of chance and fate [*der Chance und dem Schicksal ausgelieferten Boden des Lebens*], nor that they dwell in a perfection that has elevated itself from the possibility of a being-different [*Möglichkeit eines Andersseins*]" (*R*, 85; *GSG 15*, 419, translation modified).

45. [*die Einheit des Innern mit dem Äußeren [war] unmittelbares Erlebnis*] [*Indem er diese eigene Einheit immer neu in künstlerische Formen objektivierte, gewann er gleichsam die allgemeine Formel solcher Einheit überhaupt in immer vollerem Maße*].

46. [*sein Künstlertum als solches*] [*die Realität seines Subjekts*].

47. [*zurücktritt . . . aus der Verwebung mit der Welt*] [*[brengen] nur sich selbst zum Ausdruck*].

48. [*die Beziehung zu den aüßeren Objekten als solchen ihn gleichgültig geworden ist*] [*das [er] zwar nur noch sich selbst [ausspricht], aber sich selbst als Künstler*].

49. [*sein ganzes und letztes Wesen [ist] völlig in sein Künstlertum aufgegangen*] [*sein Künstlertum [hat] sich völlig in die Subjektivität seines Lebens transformiert*].

50. Simmel's analysis of the self-portraits casts light, once again, on the reasons why he constructs his book on Rembrandt for an important part around the opposition with Michelangelo. In the essay on Michelangelo, he mentions that, near the end of his life, the Renaissance master was left with feelings of failure and internal incompleteness that are wholly at odds with the ideals of the "absolute callings" and "objective values" that, throughout his artistic life, had motivated the manner in which he portrayed the existence of *other* human beings (*GSG 12*, 130). This downright antagonism between a personal confrontation with internal fragmentation on the one hand and a commitment to the Renaissance ideal of displaying a human existence as internally fulfilled on the other can explain why Michelangelo never embraced the format of the self-portrait. No painted self-portrait of Michelangelo has been identified, and the one place into which he, according to some at least, did smuggle his own likeness shows quite clearly that, unlike Rembrandt, Michelangelo did not believe in the aesthetic significance of the face and the wondrous capacity of an artwork to "transfigure" a lived lack of completion into a seemingly unified and soulful image of the self. The flayed skin that is held by the hands of Saint Bartholomew in the *Last Judgment* and which supposedly carries the traits of Michelangelo himself is shown off as the scalp of a freshly killed animal, leaving no place at all for any genuinely individualizing features and depleting all the life a human face can possibly contain. For the issue of self-portraiture in Michelangelo's work, see Michael Hirst, *Michelangelo and His Drawings* (New Haven, Conn.: Yale University Press, 1988), 11–12. For a different interpretation, questioning the thesis of Michelangelo's crypto-self portrait, see Hughes, *Michelangelo*, 254.

51. [*solche Wesen . . . die sich jenseits des Lebens stellen können*]. Simmel starts from the surprising yet fundamental idea that "viewed overall, man is the least teleological creature [*der Mensch [ist] das am wenigsten teleologische Wesen*]" (*VoL*, 29; *GSG 16*, 250) and that it is for this reason that he is the most "free" of all creatures: "Freedom means precisely the capacity to break through purposiveness [*die Möglichkeit, die Zweckmäßigkeit zu durchbrechen*]" (*VoL*, 27; *GSG 16*, 248). Simmel develops a striking conceptual duality in which the very anonymity and blindness of the regenerative dynamic of mere life, on account of the automatism of its movement, is termed purposiveful or teleological, and the distinctly human form of life is termed non-purposiveful or genuinely free.

52. See also Simmel's statement that "they do not have to fight against invisible forces which drag them along as the fate of human life in general, and as [something that], nevertheless, [remains] beyond [the grasp of] the opposing individuals. In all those Rembrandtian figures—who frequently represent petit-bourgeois, poorly bred Jewish, intellectually insignificant persons—is something sovereign that, however, does not inhabit their consciousness, but rather the artist's conception of them. He has shown how in the ideal image of each human being there dwells a freedom and self-esteem as soon as the moment, grasped in the picture, really grows out of the continuity of his life" (*R*, 104).

53. [*der Aufhebung jener Unheimlichkeit des Zufälligen in ein Notwendiges*], in Georg Simmel, "The Problem of Fate," *Theory, Culture & Society* 27, no. 7/8 (2007): 83 (*GSG 12*, 489–90, translation modified).

54. [*einem großsprecherischen Mißbrauch des Wortes*], Simmel, "The Problem of Fate," 81 (*GSG 12*, 486).

55. Compare with Benjamin's views on Chaplin; see chapter 5.

56. [*Es schwebt nicht als das Menschenschicksal überhaupt über ihnen und läßt sich nur auf den einzelnen nieder, sondern es bricht aus ihnen selbst hervor*] "The intimacy [*Die Intimität*] that characterizes all Rembrandt's presentations exists here also between the human being and his fate, however dull and ordinary, however wearisome or fragile it may be: it is not a confrontation with fate, but its proximity which characterizes the human being" (*R*, 103; *GSG 15*, 442, translation modified).

57. [*weil [das Individuum] durch eine gewisse Affinität diejenigen Ereignisse ausgewählt hat*], in Simmel, "The Problem of Fate," 82 (*GSG 12*, 488).

58. [*dem unheimlichen Gefühl, daß das ganz Notwendige unseres Lebens doch noch irgendwie ein Zufälliges sei*], in Simmel, "The Problem of Fate," 83 (*GSG 12*, 489). See also the statement that "Particular 'fates' [*Die einzelnen "Schicksale"*] are essentially determined [*bestimmt*] from without (i.e., the objective factor appears in them as the predominant one); their totality, however, 'the destiny' of every man [*"das Schicksal" jedes Menschen*], is determined by *his* nature" (*VoL*, 80; *GSG 16*, 322).

59. [*wir heben also die Zufälligkeit auf, die zwischen den Ereignissen und dem eigenen Sinn unseres Lebens besteht*], in Simmel, "The Problem of Fate," 81 (*GSG 12*, 486, translation modified). In a fateful moment, what "fits into [the] meaning [of [the] core self] [*[dem] Sinn [jenes zentralen Ichs] sich einfügt*] and thereby acquires a new significance [*von ihm aus eine neue Bedeutung . . . gewinnt*]" can just as well be experienced from an entirely different perspective, that is, as a "mere event that is merely coincidental with respect to [that] inner meaning [*ein bloßes Geschehen . . . das zu der innerlichen Bedeutung jenes zentralen Ichs bloß zufällig ist*]," in Simmel, "The Problem of Fate," 82 (*GSG 12*, 487, translation modified).

60. [*dem bloß Geschehenden und dem Zwecksinn*], in Simmel, "The Problem of Fate," 82 (*GSG 12*, 487–88).

61. [*läßt irgendetwas Dunkles, Unauflösbares in dieser Welt bestehen*], in Simmel, "The Problem of Fate," 83 (*GSG 12*, 489).

62. Simmel, "The Problem of Fate," 83.

63. [*nicht bis ins Letzte assimiliert ist*], in Simmel, "The Problem of Fate," 83 (*GSG 12*, 489, translation modified). For a different interpraton of the concept of Fate in Simmel's writings, see Button, "Fate, Experience and Tragedy in Simmel's Dialogue with Modernity." Though Button mentions the essential shifts that the concept of Fate undergoes when it is translated from a metaphysical into a sociological and historical context, he emphasizes the connection with tragedy and pathos to such an extent that he obfuscates the *non*-tragic experience of fates that Simmel highlights in important places of his work.

64. [*der religiösen Darstellung*] [*der Darstellung des Religiösen*].

65. "In Rembrandt's case it was the artistic process rather than personal existence—the manner of conceiving and creating [*die Art des Konzipierens und Schaffens*]—which gave the work its all-pervasive religious quality [*die religiöse Durchdrungenheit*]" (*R*, 134; *GSG 15*, 481, translation modified).

66. In Rembrandt's paintings, religiosity "belongs only to a life that runs its own course [*[ein] in sich selbst ablaufenden Leben*], irrespective of the external

or internal event through which this is manifested" (*R*, 116; *GSG 15*, 458, translation modified), and it denotes "a soulful life itself, streaming from a deep individual productivity and sense of responsibility [*ein seelisches Leben selbst, aus einer tiefsten individuellen Produktivität und Selbstverantwortlichkeit strömend*]" (*R*, 111; *GSG 15*, 451, translation modified).

67. It has nothing whatsoever to do with any form of "mysticism," and this "rising of the soul beyond itself [*dieses Aufschwellen der Seele über sich selbst*] is quite foreign to Rembrandt" (*R*, 116; *GSG 15*, 458).

68. [*die Besonderheit des Lebens insoweit es religiös ist*].

69. Pious people "would live in this state of piety even when no God existed or was believed in" (*R*, 127).

70. This issue underlies a large part of Simmel's philosophy of religion. An English translation of Simmel's most important texts on religion can be found in Georg Simmel, *Essays on Religion*, ed. and trans. Horst Jürgen Helle and Ludwig Nieder (New Haven, Conn.: Yale University Press, 1997). It is also mentioned in the "Introduction to Philosophical Culture" (1911; *SoC*, 35) and "The Conflict of Modern Culture" (1918; *SoC*, 87–88). For an excellent analysis of the stakes of Simmel's philosophy of religion, see John McCole, "Georg Simmel and the Philosophy of Religion," *New German Critique* 94 (2005): 8–35.

71. [*das Religiös-Einzigartige aber jener Rembrandtschen Menschen*] [*die Frage des Diesseits und Jenseits*] [*da es ausschließlich Sache des seelischen Seins ist*].

72. [*ließ die Erscheinung im Zusammenhang des Irdischen ungestört*].

73. In such lives, "from the start a religious mood in the pure sense is available as the foundation of life or the coloring of the foundations of life [*eine im reinen Sinne religiöse Gestimmtheit als Lebensgrundlage oder als Färbung der Lebensgrundlagen*], a dynamic . . . that is immediately purely religious and on its own basis pervades or draws into itself the internal core of life and its external manifestations [*von sich aus das Innere des Lebens und seine Äußerungen durchdringt oder in sich einzieht*]" (*R*, 120; *GSG 15*, 462–63, translation modified). According to Simmel, Rembrandt's religious paintings are the best possible illustrations of such a piety because "the singular visible existence attaches itself to the religious [*das singulär anschauliche Dasein sich dem religiösen verknüpft*]" (*R*, 120; *GSG 15*, 463, translation modified).

74. [*das Äußerliche, ja Banale der Erscheinungen [ist] religiös durchgeistet*].

75. [*dieses schwache, wie schwankende Wesen [ist] doch das einzig wirklich feste*].

76. For Simmel on Rembrandt's use of light, see *R*, 138–41.

77. For an interpretation of this portrait that mentions its "religious" qualities, see Schwartz, *Het Rembrandt boek*, 227. In one of his final essays, "Death and Immortality," Simmel tentatively argues in favor of a conception of immortality that is relevant in this context. The crux of the argument revolves around the connection between, on the one hand, the "limitless contingency of our entire empirical life" and, on the other, "an intensive endlessness that is projected in the time-dimension as immortality" (*VoL*, 76–77). With regard to the first issue, Simmel starts from the idea that the relationship between our innate and individual characteristics and the historical circumstances in which we are to lead our lives is "a pure game of chance" (*VoL*, 77). Some people have the luck to be born with genes that are exactly fit for the circumstances in which they live their life,

while other people are not so lucky. However, this very contingency introduces a surplus of non-actualized possibilities in our existence that are "by no means nothing" (*VoL*, 76). Irrespective of what comes "completely to expression and fulfillment," something remains "left over" in our existence. According to Simmel, this surplus is something which "we feel, or at least always can feel, as the unformed, the nonfinite among our finite instants" (*VoL*, 76). It is in the reality of such a "shadow realm of unresolved possibilities of ourselves" that Simmel discovers an argument for immortality (*VoL*, 76). For, in his view, the immortality of the soul is tied to the reality of possible selves beyond the actual one. By constantly affirming the contingency of his existence, that is, an individual is believed to be capable of uncovering a layer of meaning that is not absorbed by what is actualized and thereby deserves to be called infinite and immortal. "From the reaching out of the life process beyond each one of its identifiable contents arises the general feeling of an eternity of the soul, a feeling that will not be reconciled with its mortality. Furthermore, this feeling extends significantly beyond instances that we experience as particulars. Within every person reside innumerable possibilities to become another person than he has actually become" (*VoL*, 76). Making the immortality of the soul dependent on an experience of the contingency of its actual existence allows Simmel to disconnect it from the belief in a form of "eternal life" (a concept that he categorizes as a "logical naivet[y]"). In Simmel's view, in order to gain immortality a soul does not require the immortality of a human life, but only a migration into a different form of existence. One could argue that this is precisely what Rembrandt's late self-portrait manages to do: it both clearly captures the contingency and finitude of his actual existence *and* transposes it to a wholly different reality (the painting) that, despite its inorganic nature, does preserve some of its reality.

Chapter 3

1. This letter has been lost. Most likely, it was kept in a folder that, together with the other belongings of Simmel's son Hans Simmel, was confiscated by the Gestapo in 1941. These belongings were bought by an auction house but were destroyed by "the impact of war" (*Kriegseinwirkung*) on June 18, 1944. The folder also included letters from, among other acquaintances, Henri Bergson, Rainer Maria Rilke, and Stefan George (*GSG 23*, 1111–12; see also *GSG 22*, 510–11).

2. See *GSG 22*, 558–59; *GSG 23*, 480; and *GSG 13*, 307. The earliest encounter that is known between Simmel and Rilke is dated October 1897, when, after Rilke's arrival in Berlin, he was introduced to Simmel by Lou Andreas-Salomé (*GSG 22*, 271). For the context of Simmel's contacts with Rodin, see J. A. Schmoll Gen. Eisenwerth, "Simmel und Rodin," in *Ästhetik und Soziologie um die Jahrhundertwende: Georg Simmel*, 18–38.

3. "ma vénération pour le plus grand artiste de notre temps" (*GSG 22*, 559, my translation). Simmel repeats this formula in a letter to Isaak Benrubi in May 1909 (*GSG 22*, 697).

4. [*fesselte uns an die bloße Gegebenheit der Dinge*] [*einer Formung des Stoffes . . . durch die dieser einen rein anschaulichen Reiz . . . gewinnt*].

5. [*nicht die unmittelbare einzelne Wirklichkeit, sondern das von dieser gerade überdeckte eigentliche Wesen, ein nur innerlich geschautes Ideal*].

6. [*ein kontinuierliches Gleiten ohne feste Ausschlagspole und Haltpunkte . . . , weniger ein Wechseln zwischen dem Ja und dem Nein, als eine Gleichzeitigkeit von Ja und Nein*].

7. For the same claim, see Faath, *Mehr-als-Kunst*, 220–24.

8. [*sind die Rodinschen Wesen von innen her ausgeliefert, sie sind bis zu ihrem tiefsten Kern vergewaltigt*].

9. [*etwas im tiefsten Grunde Selbstsicheres*] [*von etwas Gewaltigerem als dem bloß persönlichen Schicksal*] [*das den Raum überhaupt und damit auch ihren eigenen erfüllt und damit ganz von selbst auch ihr Verhängnis geworden ist*].

10. [*der festumrissenen Persönlichkeit*] [*einem festeren, beharrenden, dem Fluktuieren entzogenen Kern oder Umfang*].

11. [*von [Stein] umfangen*] [*das Sichherausheben der Figur aus dem Stein*] [*die unmittelbare Versinnlichung des Werdens*] [*der Sinn ihrer Darstellung*] [*auf einer Station eines unendlichen Weges erfaßt*] [*nur in schwer erkennbaren Umrissen aus dem Block herausragt*]. A clear example of this impression that Rodin's figures are always to a certain extent swallowed up by the material out of which they arise is his rendering of Orpheus and Eurydice (1887–93). This work, tellingly, does not depict the moment *before* Orpheus turns around for a glimpse of his beloved but the moment immediately *after*, when Eurydice's body is mercilessly reclaimed by the underworld and a despairing Orpheus comes to realize the outcome of his action. Similarly, in *Fugit Amor* (1885–87), the girl who, in Bernard Champigneulle's words, is "gliding like a fish beneath the supine body of youth" cannot any longer be held back or saved from the material from which she was carved (see Bernard Champigneulle, *Rodin*, trans. J. Maxwell Brownjohn [London: Thames and Hudson, 1986], 151). Leon Trotski, who participated in a lecture by Simmel on Rodin in Vienna in 1911, was very skeptical about the suggestion that the modern subject participates in an eternal and aimless movement. He wrote a seemingly ironic review about Simmel's lecture in *Pravda* (May 27, 1911); see Schmoll Gen. Eisenwerth, "Simmel und Rodin," 36–38.

12. See Gilles Deleuze, "Postscript on the Societies of Control," in *Negotiations, 1972–1990*, trans. Martin Joughin (New York: Columbia University Press, 1995), 177–82. See also John Marks, "Control Society," in *The Deleuze Dictionary*, ed. Adrian Parr (Edinburgh: Edinburgh University Press, 2005), 55–56.

13. [*die Auflösung der festen Inhalte in das flüssige Element der Seele*] [*aus der alle Substanz herausgeläutert ist, und deren Formen nur Formen von Bewegungen sind*].

14. Simmel notes that the incompleteness of Rodin's works invites a gaze that seeks to "repeat the process of creation for itself" and the "suggestion of the fancy that the incomplete itself can be completed" (*GSG* 7, 99–100).

15. [*ein neues Maß von Bewegung in die Figur gebracht*] [*eine neue Biegsamkeit der Gelenke, ein neues Eigenleben und Vibrieren der Oberfläche . . . ein neues Fühlbahrmachen der Berührungsstellen zweier Körper oder eines Körpers in sich, . . . eine neue Ausnutzung des Lichts, . . . eine neue Art, wie die Flächen aneinanderstoßen, sich bekämpfen oder zusammenfließen*] [*die innere Lebendigkeit das ganzen Menschen, mit allem Fühlen, Denken, Erleben*].

16. This argument runs parallel to Rilke's, who wrote his own essay on Rodin only a mere couple of months (in 1903) after Simmel published his first article on the topic (September 1902). In Rilke's opinion, Rodin "saw only innumerable

living surfaces, only life. . . . Rodin seized upon the life that was everywhere about him. He grasped it in its smallest details; he observed it and it followed him; he awaited it at the cross-roads where it lingered; he overtook it as it ran before him, and he found it in all places equally great, equally powerful and overwhelming. There was not one part of the human body that was insignificant or unimportant: it was alive." In Rainer Maria Rilke, *Auguste Rodin*, trans. Jessie Lemont and Hans Trausil (London: Pallas Athena, 2006), 29. For a further elaboration of this idea, see Jacques Rancière, "Master of Surfaces (Paris, 1902)," in *Aesthesis: Scenes from the Aesthetic Regime of Art*, trans. Paul Zakir (London: Verso, 2013), 155–70.

17. See chapter 1 and Simmel, "The Aesthetic Significance of the Face."

18. [*die Gesichter Figuren sind oft wenig ausgeprägt und individuell, und alle seelische Bewegtheit . . . die sonst am Gesicht den Ort ihrer Äußerung fand, werd in dem Sichbiegen und Sichstrecken des Leibes offenbar*] [*Zittern und Erschauern, das über seine Oberfläche rinnt*] [*den Erschütterungen*] [*das Krümmen oder Aufschnellen*]. For Rilke, as well, Rodin captures a life that is "receding from the stage of the face" and is "manifested in bodies" where it is "more dispersed, greater, more mysterious and everlasting" (Rilke, *Auguste Rodin*, 29). See also Geoff Dyer's remark that Rodin's works are marked by "the sense of the surface brimming with what is within," in Geoff Dyer, "The Awakening of Stones: Rodin," in *Working the Room* (Edinburgh: Canongate Books, 2010), 107.

19. [*diesen Teil allein in seiner Bewegung halte er im Ton fest, ohne den übrigen Körper*].

20. For the same idea, be it without reference to Simmel, see Rancière, "Master of Surfaces," 157: "Bodies do not act; from now on, actions constitute bodies." See also J. A. Schmoll Gen. Eisenwerth, "Zur Genesis des Torso-Motivs und zur Deutung des fragmentarischen Stils bei Rodin," in *Rodin-Studien: Persönlichkeit, Werke, Wirkung, Bibliographie* (Munich: Prestel Verlag, 1983), 143–60.

21. In a similar vein, Rodin's severed hands gain a force of expression that is absent in a "normal" hand, and the series where hands have become all-encompassing universes in themselves (*The Hand of God* [1902], *The Hand of the Devil Holding Woman* [1903], *The Cathedral* [1908], and *The Hand Emerging from the Tomb* [1914]) rightly counts as one of Rodin's masterpieces.

22. Rilke, *Auguste Rodin*, 47. The aesthetics of the fragment and the concomitant sensibility for a not yet exhausted potential for (self-)renewal underlies a large part of Rilke's artistic output, most notably, the famous poem "Archaic Torso of Apollo" (1908) and its final line, "You must change your life." For an interesting development of these issues, see Ulrich Baer, *The Rilke Alphabet*, trans. Andrew Hamilton (New York: Fordham University Press, 2014), especially "T for Tower" (162–70).

23. [*von der Kontinuität der Lebensbewegung abgeschnürt*] [*dieses Moment ist das Ganze—das Ganze Schicksal*].

24. Rilke, *Auguste Rodin*, 43.

25. Ibid.

26. [*[i]n dem fruchtbaren Moment liegt immer nur vieles, in der Rodinschen Geste liegt alles*]. Compare with Benjamin's and Agamben's views on gesture, in which the interruptive moment is not simply overcome by an ultimate restoration of the supposed continuity of life's movement. For Benjamin's ideas on

gesture, see, for example, the essay "What Is the Epic Theatre?" (1939), esp. *SW* 4, 305. For Agamben's views on gesture, see his "Kommerell, or on Gesture," in *Potentialities: Collected Essays in Philosophy*, ed. and trans. Daniel Heller-Roazen (Stanford, Calif.: Stanford University Press, 1999), 77–85. For the most comprehensive and insightful interpretation of these ideas, see Samuel Weber, "Citability—of Gesture," in *Benjamin's -abilities* (Cambridge, Mass.: Harvard University Press, 2008), 95–114.

27. [*von diesem Komplex ihres inneren Erlebens*] [*die Verhängnisse, die Dunkelheiten und Seligkeiten*] [*das klingt nicht aus diesen Menschen heraus*].

28. [*eine Richtung und eine Höhe, die man kosmisch nennen kann*]. See also Simmel's essays "Germanic and Classical Romanic Style" and "Individualism," *Theory, Culture & Society* 24, no. 7/8 (2007): 47–52, 66–71.

29. See also Rilke, *Auguste Rodin*, 58: *The Thinker* "sits absorbed and silent, heavy with thought: with all the strength of an acting man he thinks. His whole body has become head and all the blood in his veins has become brain."

30. Georg Simmel, "On the Psychology of Money" (*SoC*, 233–43). The quotation is taken from p. 239. See also Hans Blumenberg's suggestion that in Simmel's work money is the "proto-metaphor" for the flux of life as such (Hans Blumenberg, "Money or Life: Metaphors of Georg Simmel's Philosophy," in *Theory, Culture & Society* 29, no. 7/8 [2012]: 249–62).

31. Georg Simmel, "Metropolis and Mental Life" (*SoC*, 176). See also Simmel's claim that "the same factors which have thus coalesced into the exactness and minute precision of the form of life have coalesced into a structure of the highest impersonality; on the other hand, they have promoted a highly personal subjectivity" (*SoC*, 178). See also Donald N. Levine, "Simmel as Educator: On Individuality and Modern Culture," *Theory, Culture & Society* 8, no. 3 (1991): 99–117.

32. [*viel labiler, in ihren Stimmungen*]. See also Simmel's short text "La Duse," a "snapshot" (*Momentbild*) written for the journal *Jugend* (May 8, 1901) ("The essence of the soul is movement") reprinted in Georg Simmel, "Selections from Simmel's Writings for the Journal *Jugend*," *Theory, Culture & Society* 29, no. 7/8 (2009): 276–77. For more on the idea that the essence of modernity lies in the relentless transformation of the self, see Charles Barbour, "The Maker of Lies: Simmel, Mendacity and the Economy of Faith," *Theory, Culture & Society* 29, no. 7/8 (2012): 218–36; and Deena Weinstein and Michael Weinstein, *Postmodern(ized) Simmel* (London: Routledge, 1993).

33. [*die Liebe überhaupt, die Verzweiflung überhaupt, die Versenkung überhaupt*].

34. See also Frisby, *Fragments of Modernity*, 63: "Simmel's admiration for Rodin's sculpture stems both from its embodiment of modernity and its resolution of modernity's contradiction." See also Frisby's "The Aesthetics of Modern Life: Simmel's Interpretation," *Theory, Culture & Society* 8, no. 3 (1991): 73–93.

35. [*der Gedanke, daß sie sich auch anders bewegen könnten*] [*der seelische Vorgang, sozusagen der Satz, den die Bewegung aussagt*].

36. [*die Notwendigkeit, mit der alle Theile zusammengehören, ein organisches Wachstum, dessen innere Zielsicherheit jeden Zufall ausschließt*].

37. [*ein definitives*] [*Durchgangspunkt*] [*einer aus dem Unbestimmten kommenden und ins Unbestimmte gehenden Wanderung*] [*die Wege ohne Ziele . . . und die Ziele ohne Wege*].

38. [*Indem er uns unser tiefstes Leben noch einmal in der Sphäre der Kunst erleben läßt, erlöst er uns von eben dem, wie wir es in der Sphäre der Wirklichkeit erleben*].

39. [*dient dem Ausdruck am vollkommensten*].

40. [*geht auch den Weg zu einer neuen Monumentalität—der des Werdens, der Bewegtheit*] [*der Bewegung eine zeitlose Bedeutung zu geben*].

41. See Nelly Silagy Benedek, *Auguste Rodin: The Burghers of Calais, A Resource for Educators* (New York: Metropolitan Museum of Art, 2000), 11; and Rilke, *Auguste Rodin*, 79–82. See also Ruth Butler, *Rodin: The Shape of Genius* (New Haven, Conn.: Yale University Press, 1993), 199–213.

42. Geoff Dyer puts it like this: "The gravity of what they have inflicted on themselves causes the sky to bear down on them with atrocious force. Called on to make a gesture—of self-sacrifice—the ennobling ideal of martyrdom is undermined and betrayed by their gestures," Dyer, "The Awakening of Stones: Rodin," 113.

43. A comparison with Aloïs Riegl's interpretation of *The Nightwatch* in the context of his study of the Dutch group portrait (1902) seems called for and is promising. Like Simmel, Riegl emphasizes the internal nature of the unity of the painting (in the first place, by virtue of the physical activity of the militiamen and the psychological coordination between the depicted figures). However, unlike Simmel, Riegl also mentions an external unity (related to the captain's outstretched hand, directing the troops to march toward the beholder and to the chiaroscuro which connects the depicted figures with "free" space). See Aloïs Riegl, *The Group Portraiture of Holland*, trans. Evelyn M. Kain and David Britt (Los Angeles: Getty Research Institute for the History of Art and the Humanities, 1999), 264–79. See also Benjamin Binstock, "Postscript: Aloïs Riegl in the Presence of 'The Nightwatch,'" *October* 74 (1995): 36–44.

44. In this regard, it is not insignificant that only four of the six citizens can be historically identified, Froissart's account having left out two names.

45. Dyer, "The Awakening of Stones: Rodin," 113.

46. Rilke puts it as follows: "[They] do not touch one another," they "stand side by side like the last trees of a hewn-down forest" and they are united only by "the surrounding atmosphere." In Rilke, *Auguste Rodin*, 86.

47. Dyer, "The Awakening of Stones: Rodin," 114.

48. See Hannah Arendt, "The Decline of the Nation-State and the End of the Rights of Men," in *The Origins of Totalitarianism* (San Diego, Calif.: Harcourt, 1976), 267–302. For the further development of this theme, see Giorgio Agamben, *Homo Sacer: Sovereign Power and Bare Life*, trans. Daniel Heller-Roazen (Stanford, Calif.: Stanford University Press, 1998), 1–12 and 126–35.

49. Rilke, *Auguste Rodin*, 83.

Introduction to Part II

1. According to Hans Simmel, his father voted for either the Liberal or the Social Democratic parties, but in the latter case only when its candidates seemed without a chance (in Hans Simmel, "Auszüge aus den Lebenserinnerungen," 260). Benjamin's relationship with communism was mixed and nuanced; see, for example, Eiland and Jennings, *Walter Benjamin: A Critical Life*, 447–48.

2. See also Theodor Adorno's remark that "Simmel . . . was, for all his psychological idealism, the first to accomplish the return of philosophy to concrete

subjects." In Theodor W. Adorno, "The Handle, the Pot, and Early Experience," in *Notes To Literature, Volume 2*, ed. Rolf Tiedemann, trans. Shierry Weber Nicholson (New York: Columbia University Press, 1991), 213. See also Elizabeth Goodstein, "Style as Substance: Georg Simmel's Phenomenology of Culture," *Cultural Critique* 52 (2002): 209–34.

3. See also Benjamin's plea for "a fight for the crude and material things without which no refined and spiritual things could exist" (*SW 4*, 390).

4. For an extensive analysis of Simmel's views on the metropolis, see, for example, David Frisby, *Cityscapes of Modernity: Critical Explorations* (Cambridge: Polity, 2001), 100–158.

5. For an excellent study of the connections between the philosophy of life (and movement) and fascism, see Nitzan Lebovic, *The Philosophy of Life and Death: Ludwig Klages and the Rise of a Nazi Biopolitics* (New York: Palgrave Macmillan, 2013). For a similar discussion, applied to the medium of dance, see Lilian Karina, Marion Kant, and Jonathan Steinberg, *Hitler's Dancers: German Modern Dance and the Third Reich* (New York: Berghahn Books, 2004). For the view that Simmel was a precursor of contemporary critics of capitalism, see Austin Harrington and Thomas M. Kemple, "Introduction: Georg Simmel's 'Sociological Metaphysics': Money, Sociality, and Precarious Life," *Theory, Culture & Society* 29, no. 7/8 (2012): 7–25; and the contributions of Darmon and Frade, Dodd, Fitzi, and Barbour in the same journal issue.

6. "To move along with rhythm [*im Rhythmus schwingen*] means to be moved and included by the pulse of life [*ergriffen sein vom Pulsschlag des Lebens*]," in Ludwig Klages, "Von Wesen des Rhythmus: Auszug aus dem Vortrage," *Sudhoff's Archiv für Geschichte der Medizin und der Naturwissenschaften* 27, no. 3/4 (1934): 228. See also ibid., 224 and 225. For these issues and the relation between Klages and Benjamin, see Stéphane Symons, "The Creature That Can Still Survive: Walter Benjamin on Mickey Mouse and Rhythmic Movement," in *Telos* 176 (Fall 2016): 165-86.

7. The reference to "primal phenomenon" in Klages can be found in "Von Wesen des Rhythmus," 225.

8. Ernst Bloch, quoted in David Frisby, "Introduction to the Translation," in *PhoM*, 22.

9. Georg Lukács, *History and Class Consciousness: Studies in Marxist Dialectics*, trans. Rodney Livingstone (Cambridge, Mass.: MIT Press, 1971), 95.

10. Karl Mannheim, quoted by David Frisby, "Introduction to the Translation," in *PhoM*, 33; and Horkheimer, "Lebensphilosophie: Bergson, Simmel, Dilthey," 288.

11. Kracauer, "Georg Simmel," in *The Mass Ornament*, 241 and 251. See also Jürgen Habermas, "Georg Simmel on Philosophy and Culture: Postscript to a Collection of Essays," *Critical Inquiry* 22, no. 3 (1996): 408 and 413. Habermas, as well, considers Simmel's metaphysics "dubious" and robbed of "the power and courage of political-practical conclusions." In Habermas's view Simmel had a "yearning for undifferentiated, overseeable totalities" (413).

12. Georg Simmel, "The Handle," in "Two Essays," *The Hudson Review* 11, no. 3 (1958): 371.

13. Ibid., 374.

14. Ibid., 373.

15. Ibid., 376.

16. Ibid.
17. Adorno, "The Handle, the Pot, and Early Experience," 214.
18. Ibid., 213–14.
19. Ibid., 214. See also Adorno's critical remarks about Benjamin's reference to Simmel in his essays on Baudelaire ("The materialist determination of cultural characteristics is possible only when mediated through the *process as a whole*"; *SW* 4, 101).
20. Adorno, "The Handle, the Pot, and Early Experience," 213.
21. Ibid., 215.
22. Ibid.
23. For an analysis that focuses on the similarities between Simmel and Benjamin's views on modern experience and the metropolis, see, for instance, Paolo Jedlowski, "Simmel on Memory," in *Georg Simmel and Contemporary Sociology*, ed. Michael Kaern, Bernard S. Phillips, and Robert S. Cohen (Dordrecht: Kluwer Academic, 1990), 131–54.
24. For one out of many interesting discussions of these issues in Simmel, see Birgitta Nedelmann, "On the Concept of 'Erleben' in Georg Simmel's Sociology," in *Georg Simmel and Contemporary Sociology*, ed. Kaern, Phillips, and Cohen, 225–42.
25. Adorno, "The Handle, the Pot, and Early Experience," 213.

Chapter 4

1. To my knowledge, so far almost no attention has been given to the specific meaning and philosophical weight of the concept of *unscheinbar* in Benjamin's essays and books. This is very surprising for two different reasons. The first one has, quite simply, to do with the enormous number of essays, articles, books, conferences, and—recently—even artworks that are devoted to this still somewhat strange and unfamiliar figure of twentieth-century, Continental philosophy. Despite all the attention, scholarly and non-scholarly, given to Benjamin, the word *unscheinbar* itself seems to have escaped most people's attention. The second reason why this is surprising is that this one word brings together some of the key elements in his thinking, and an in-depth analysis of it can illuminate a unity in his philosophy that is all too often overlooked. For two very interesting essays that do mention the concept and have prepared the way for this chapter, see Sigrid Weigel, "Bildwissenschaft aus dem Geiste wahrer Philologie," in *Walter Benjamin: Die Kreatur, das Heilige, die Bilder* (Frankfurt am Main: Fischer Taschenbuch Verlag, 2008), 237–50 (the reference to "die Bedeutung des 'Unscheinbaren' " is on p. 246); and Liliane Weissberg, "Circulating Images: Notes on the Photographic Exchange," in *Writing the Image after Roland Barthes*, ed. Jean-Michel Rabaté (Philadelphia: University of Pennsylvania Press, 1997), 109–31 (the reference to the "*unscheinbare Stelle*" is on p. 110).
2. See also Benjamin's statements that "knowledge is possession" (*O*, 29) and that it "is open to question but truth is not" (*O*, 30) and the definition of truth as an "intentionless state of being" and as "the death of intention" (*O*, 36). For more information on this important distinction between truth and knowledge, see, for example, Beatrice Hanssen, "Philosophy at Its Origin: Walter Benjamin's Prologue to the *Ursprung des deutschen Trauerspiels*," *MLN* 110, no. 4 (1995): 809–33; and the chapter "Language" in Friedlander, *Walter Benjamin*, 9–27.

3. See, for example, the statement that "the representational impulse of truth is the refuge of beauty as such" (*O*, 31).

4. For a brief but clear discussion of the relationship between these ideas and intuitions in Benjamin and Heidegger, see Rolf Tiedemann, *Studien zur Philosophie Walter Benjamins* (Frankfurt am Main: Suhrkamp Verlag, 1973), 90–91. In Tiedemann's opinion, Benjamin's ideas regarding this theme of *Seinsvergessenheit* are even more extreme than Heidegger's in that they are ultimately "irreconcilable with such [i.e., Heidegger's] flowing back into the originary, [irreconcilable] with the retreat into being, into 'the' event ['*das' Ereignis*]" (90). A more elaborate analysis of the similarities and differences between Benjamin's and Heidegger's views on this issue can be found in Willem van Reijen, *Der Schwarzwald und Paris: Heidegger und Benjamin* (Munich: Wilhelm Fink Verlag, 1998), especially in the chapter "Sprache," 142–65.

5. See, for example, Beatrice Hanssen, "Portrait of Melancholy (Benjamin, Warburg, Panofsky)," *MLN* 114, no. 5 (1999): 991–1013; and, especially, the chapter "*Trauerspiel* and Melancholy Subjectivity," in *Melancholy Dialectics: Walter Benjamin and the Play of Mourning*, by Max Pensky (Amherst: University of Massachusetts Press, 2001).

6. See, for example, Andrew Benjamin, "The Absolute as Translatability," 116: "The Fall becomes the moment staging the presence of the Absolute in terms that are, in the end, proper to it: namely, the necessary impossibility of the Absolute's actualization. With the Fall there is a retention of the Absolute."

7. See also the statement that "the thing in itself has no word, being created from God's word and known in its name by a human word" (*SW 1*, 69). For the most substantial discussion of Benjamin's views on language, see Winfried Menninghaus, *Walter Benjamins Theorie der Sprachmagie* (Frankfurt am Main: Suhrkamp Verlag, 1995).

8. For more background about this discussion, see Rodolphe Gasché, "Saturnine Vision and the Question of Difference: Reflections on Walter Benjamin's Theory of Language," in *Benjamin's Ground: New Readings of Walter Benjamin*, ed. Rainer Nägele (Detroit: Wayne State University Press, 1986), 83–104; and Bettine Menke, "'However One Calls into the Forest . . .' Echoes of Translation," in *Walter Benjamin and Romanticism*, 83–97.

9. See, for example, Miriam Hansen's claim that "superimposed upon the historical-materialist trajectory of decline is a less linear—though no less pessimistic—sense of belatedness, indebted to the temporality of Jewish Messianism," in Miriam Bratu Hansen, "Benjamin, Cinema and Experience: 'The Blue Flower in the Land of Technology,'" *New German Critique* 40 (1987): 190.

10. For such readings that focus on the nostalgic and mournful element in Benjamin's views on modernity, see, for example, Andrew Benjamin, "Boredom and Distraction: The Moods of Modernity"; Wohlfarth, "Et Cetera: The Historian as Chiffonnier"; and Comay, "The Sickness of Tradition: Between Melancholia and Fetishism."

11. This argument about a *negative* ability runs parallel to and was inspired by Giorgio Agamben's ideas on potentiality as put forward in the essay "On Potentiality," in *Potentialities*, 177–84. See, for example, his reading of Aristotle's *Metaphysics*, the statement that "all potentiality is [also] impotentiality" (181) and his views on a "potential not to be" (182): "If a potentiality to not-be

originally belongs to all potentiality, then there is truly potentiality only where the potentiality to not-be does not lag behind actuality but passes fully into it as such" (183). For other elaborations of similar intuitions in Agamben's work, see, for example, the paragraph "Vocation and Revocation," in *The Time That Remains: A Commentary on the Letter to the Romans*, trans. Patricia Dailey (Stanford, Calif.: Stanford University Press, 2005), 23–26; and the essay "Bartleby, or On Contingency," in *Potentialities*, 243–71.

12. Samuel Weber, "Introduction," in *Benjamin's -abilities*, 7. See also his "Impart-ability: Language as Medium," in *Benjamin's -abilities*, 40: "Benjamin's–*barkeiten* . . . do not simply define their own virtuality in terms of the *absence* of what they name, but rather in terms of its radical alteration."

13. As has often been noted, Aby Warburg's concept of *Nachleben* (afterlife) was highly influential. See, for example, Weber's *Benjamin's -abilities*; and Weigel, "Bildwissenschaft aus dem Geiste wahrer Philologie."

14. In taking Benjamin's theologically inspired ideas to be complementary to his (Marxist) views on modernity, my reading of his work is in line with what Michael Löwy has called the "fourth approach," that is, an alternative to the "materialist school," the "theological school," and the "school of contradiction." See Michael Löwy, *Fire Alarm: Reading Walter Benjamin's "On the Concept of History"* (London: Verso, 2005), 20. Despite the conflicting views of noteworthy friends and later scholars like Scholem, Brecht, or Adorno, there are many passages in Benjamin's work that back up this view that there is an essential and not a merely arbitrary relationship between his theologically inspired ideas and the sociopolitical ones. See, for example, his claim that "'historical materialism' is to win all the time" and that it can "easily be a match for anyone" but only on the condition that it "enlists the services of theology" (*SW 4*, 389). See also the statements that his "thinking is related to theology as blotting pad is related to ink. It is saturated with it. Were one to go by the blotter, however, nothing of what is written would remain" and that it is forbidden "to conceive of history as fundamentally atheological, little as it may be granted us to try to write it with immediately theological concepts" (*AP*, 471).

15. Like Confucius, Lao-tzu never founded a formal school. For that reason, movement and wandering belong to the most crucial characteristics of his thinking. See, for example, Lao-tzu's saying that "a good traveler has no fixed plans, and is not intent on arriving," which lies surprisingly close to Benjamin's own statement that "not to find one's way around a city does not mean much. But to lose one's way in a city, as one loses one's way in a forest, requires some schooling" (*SW 3*, 352).

16. This intuition that there is a specific importance attached to people who pass on a truth or wisdom that is not otherwise available places the essay on Brecht in the same framework as the one on Kafka that was written one year earlier. Both essays, that is to say, revolve around a realization that "the consistency of truth has been lost" and the subsequent (deeply paradoxical) feeling that one has to "g[i]ve [it] up so that [one] could hold on to its transmissibility" (*SW 3*, 326).

17. See footnote 17, written by Edmund Jephcott: "*Unversieglich* literally means 'inexhaustible,' 'everflowing' " (*SW 2*, 250).

18. For a very interesting reading of this passage, see Eli Friedlander's chapter "Rescue" in *Walter Benjamin: A Philosophical Portrait*, 157–89, for example,

the statement that "recognizing the stakes of history would be bringing the present into a critical state" (169). See also the tension that Friedlander constructs around the concepts of empathy and melancholy on the one hand ("deadening the past . . . making every moment of it similarly powerless to affect the present" [164]), and a presence of mind to and construction of the past on the other ("a unique opportunity for transforming the present" [167]). For the closest reading of Benjamin's theses on the philosophy of history and the difference with historicism, see Löwy, *Fire Alarm*, especially 86–102.

19. For more on this idea about an irreducible distance that is preserved in the very moment of commemoration, and for an analysis of the criticism of the notion of empathy that it entails, see Löwy, *Fire Alarm*, 46–49.

20. For only one out of many illustrations of this double form of disenchantment, see Benjamin's statement that "human actions were deprived of all value. Something new arose: an empty world" (O, 139). For an extensive analysis of the religious and cultural background of this idea (and for the historical background of Benjamin's own interpretations), see Jane O. Newman, *Benjamin's Library: Modernity, Nation, and the Baroque* (Ithaca, N.Y.: Cornell University Press, 2011), especially the third chapter, "Melancholy Germans: War Theology, Allegory and the Lutheran Baroque," 138–84. For in-depth analyses of the antinomies between life and faith and Benjamin's concept of melancholy, and for a comparison with the ideas of Aby Warburg, see, for example, Jochen Becker, "Ursprung so wie Zerstörung: Sinnbild und Sinngebung bei Warburg und Benjamin," in *Allegorie und Melancholie*, ed. Willem van Reijen (Frankfurt am Main: Suhrkamp Verlag, 1992), 64–89; Hanssen, "Portrait of Melancholy (Benjamin, Warburg, Panofsky)"; and, especially, the chapter "*Trauerspiel* and Melancholy Subjectivity," in Max Pensky, *Melancholy Dialectics*.

21. See, for example, Jane O. Newman's statement in *Benjamin's Library*, 167: "The melancholy Baroque man is imprisoned in [a] 'satanic' melancholic paralysis."

22. One could add two remarks to this idea. The first one is that a large part of Benjamin's *own* cultural, artistic, philosophical, and sociological interests is steeped in this same, baroque love for phenomena that make a show out of being *non*-real. In my opinion, at least three different instances of *non*-reality can be distinguished in his work. A first thematic line in Benjamin's interests runs through numerous forms of ostentation, theatricality, and the phenomenon of dramatic alienation. For more on this, see, for example, Samuel Weber, "Storming the Work: Allegory and Theatricality in Benjamin's *Origin of the German Mourning Play*," in *Theatricality as Medium* (New York: Fordham University Press, 2004), 160–80 (the concept of "inauthentic simultaneity" [p. 173] is very relevant here); and Rainer Nägele, *Theater, Theory, Speculation: Walter Benjamin and the Scenes of Modernity* (Baltimore: Johns Hopkins University Press, 1991). A second thematic interest goes out to activities that are real but that nevertheless retain a sense of autonomy from ordinary life, for example, children's games and toys and the concept of play/room-for-play (*Spielraum*). For more on this, see the work of Miriam Bratu Hansen, especially "Play-Form of Second Nature," in *Cinema and Experience: Siegfried Kracauer, Walter Benjamin, and Theodor W. Adorno* (Berkeley: University of California Press, 2012), 183–204; and Hansen, "Room-for-Play: Benjamin's Gamble with Cinema," *October* 109 (2004): 3–45. A third thematic interest revolves around the inclination to withdraw from

ordinary reality and to study it in books rather than actively engage with it. See, for example, Benjamin's description of the "gate to justice" as "the law which is studied but no longer practiced" (*SW* 2, 815). For more on this, see Samuel Weber, "Violence and Gesture: Agamben Reading Benjamin Reading Kafka Reading Cervantes . . . ," in *Benjamin's -abilities*, 195–210; and Friedlander, *Walter Benjamin: A Philosophical Portrait*, 212–21.

A second remark revolves around the idea that theatricality, play, and study denote, each in their own way, not a mere *suspension* of the attachment to the outside world but an alternative manner of *relating* to it. What is at stake for Benjamin is the ability to not disrupt one's investment in reality despite the awareness that it cannot in itself be regarded as meaningful. One could therefore claim that what is *non*-real according to Benjamin is not opposed to what is real but only to the *absence* of reality (theatricality, play, and study all presuppose an exteriority that is being related to). For a similar argument, see the reference to *non*-sense later in the text and Deleuze's statement that non-sense is not the opposite of sense but the opposite of the absence of sense.

23. Similar to the remark in the previous note, this baroque love for alternative processes of signification can be understood as the source of Benjamin's *own* interest in the human ability to "read what was never written" (Hofmannsthal, cited in both *SW* 2, 722 and *SW* 4, 405) and in signs that have a distinct physical and visual presence (baroque emblems, advertising signs, physiognomy, etc.). See also the references to allegory later in the text.

24. On the issue of meaning understood as a *remains* or *residue*, see different texts written by Giorgio Agamben, for example, "The Assistants," in *Profanations*, trans. Jeff Fort (New York: Zone Books, 2007), 29–35 ("The unfulfilled is what remains," p. 34); Agamben, *Remnants of Auschwitz: The Witness and the Archive*, trans. Daniel Heller-Roazen (New York: Zone Books, 1999), 164 ("The remnants of Auschwitz—the witnesses—are neither the dead nor the survivors, neither the drowned nor the saved. They are what remains between them"); and Agamben, *The Time That Remains*.

25. On Aby Warburg's reading of melancholy's "consoling, humanistic message of liberation [*humanistischen Trostblatt*] from the fear of Saturn," see his "Pagan-Antique Prophecy in Words and Images in the Age of Luther," in *The Renewal of Pagan Antiquity: Contributions to the Cultural History of the European Renaissance*, ed. and trans. David Britt (Los Angeles: Getty Research Institute for the History of Art and the Humanities, 1999), 644.

26. For these ideas on the link between meaning and contingency (and for the further development of the argument), I am heavily indebted to intuitions put forward by Roland Breeur. See, for example, his essays on Proust and "Over het voor-en nadeel van het leven voor de geschiedenis" ["On the Use and Disadvantages of Life for History"], in *De tijd bestaat niet: Essays over domheid, vrijheid en emoties* (Nijmegen: Uitgeverij Vantilt, 2012), 211–36.

27. See Samuel Weber, "Storming the Work," for example, 174: "Allegory is the traditional means of investing a manifestation with a signification that it cannot possibly have in terms of a purely immanent, self-contained structure. It thereby brings the signifying potential traditionally associated with a generalized transcendence to bear upon the claims of a localizable and individualizable secular immanence."

28. See Willem van Reijen, "Innerlichkeit oder Begriffsarbeit? Die Barockrezeption W. Benjamins und Th. W. Adornos," in *Allegorie und Melancholie*, 19: "The experience of the absolute depravity [*Hinfälligkeit*] of our life and its meaning becomes the starting point of the idea of salvation" (my translation).

29. See Benjamin's essay on Proust and his ideas on the *souvenir involontaire*'s "rejuvenating force [*verjüngenden Kraft*] which is a match for the inexorable process of aging" (*SW 2*, 244; *GS II-1*, 320). Contrary to the ideas that will be presented in the following paragraphs, however, in some places Benjamin likens the *souvenir involontaire* to the experience of an aura and thus implicitly opposes it to the allegorical gaze that I will deem more important. See, for example, the Baudelaire essay where Benjamin states that "to experience the aura of an object we look at means to invest it with the ability to look back at us. This ability corresponds to the data of *mémoire involontaire*" (*SW 4*, 338). In Proust's own text, however, the descriptions of the *souvenir involontaire* often *do* clearly refer to that type of experience which, in Benjamin's work, would be termed *non*-auratic. *Souvenirs involontaires*, that is to say, come together with a physical *directness* or bodily *shock* (in opposition to the duration, distance, and the "inapproachability" that mark the aura), and they reveal the *fragmentized* nature of the past (in opposition to the semblance of unity [*Schein*] that marks the aura). For a similar reading of the *souvenir involontaire* and an alternative way of understanding aura (focusing on disjunction rather than unity), see Miriam Bratu Hansen, *Cinema and Experience*, 109–13. In addition to this, it is striking that important passages in Proust's *Recherche do* recount what Benjamin would term an auratic experience, but these describe moments in which a *souvenir involontaire* seems *blocked* and does *not* fully present itself to the self. Such experiences trigger a feeling of distance, loss, and ambiguity of meaning (the most important characteristics of the auratic experience) but, as such, they do *not* deliver the sudden return of a past moment. The most famous one is the experience of the three mysterious but ultimately *un*revealing trees on the carriage ride back from Carqueville, related in Marcel Proust, *Within a Budding Grove*, in *Remembrance of Things Past, Volume 1*, trans. C. K. Scott Moncrieff (New York: Random House, 1932), 543–44.

30. The original passage is: "No sooner had I touched the topmost button than my bosom swelled, filled with an unknown, a divine presence, I shook with sobs, tears streamed from my eyes. The person who came to my rescue, who saved me from barrenness of spirit, was the same who, years before, in a moment of identical distress and loneliness, in a moment when I was no longer in any way myself, had come in, and had restored me to myself, for that person was myself and more than myself." In Marcel Proust, *Cities of the Plain*, in *Remembrance of Things Past, Volume 2*, trans. C. K. Scott Moncrieff (New York: Random House, 1932), 113.

31. In the famous passage on the madeleine cake at the end of the "Overture" to the *Recherche*, Proust opposes the "*forms* of things" to the "*smell* and *taste* of things" (my emphasis). Unlike the former, which "have lost the power of expansion which would have allowed them to resume their place in [his] consciousness," the latter are described as "remain[ing] poised a long time" and as "ready to remind [him], waiting and hoping for their moment." This ability of the smell and taste of things to "survive" into the present is an illustration of what Benjamin would call *Unscheinbarkeit* in that they are described as both "more

fragile" *and* "more vital" at the same time and as both "more unsubstantial" *and* "more persistent." Moreover, the *souvenir involontaire* is to be termed *unscheinbar* for a second reason as well. As I will describe in the second half of the chapter, Benjamin understands what is *unscheinbar* as a fragment that makes visible an unexpected and refracted unity that is different from the unity the former "naturally" or "logically" belongs to. It is along these lines that Proust describes the taste of the madeleine cake. See the tension between "ruins" and "essence" and between "rest" and "vast structure" in the following sentence: "The smell and taste of things remain poised a long time . . . amid the ruins of all the rest [*la ruine de tout le reste*]; and bear unfaltering, in the tiny and almost impalpable drop of their essence [*leur gouttelette presque impalpable*], the vast structure of recollection [*l'édifice immense du souvenir*]," in Marcel Proust, *Swann's Way*, in *Remembrance of Things Past, Volume 1*, 36.

32. Gilles Deleuze, *Proust and Signs*, trans. Richard Howard (Minneapolis: University of Minnesota Press, 2000), 11–13.

33. See Benjamin's important statement in the Proust essay where he distinguishes the concepts of identity and similarity and marks the latter with a proto-Derridean dynamic of *différance*: "The similarity of one thing to another which we are used to, which occupies us in a wakeful state, reflects only vaguely the deeper similarity of the dream world in which everything that happens appears not in identical but in similar disguise [*nie identisch, sondern ähnlich*], opaquely similar to itself [*sich selber undurchschaubar ähnlich*]" (*SW* 2, 239; *GS II-1*, 314). See also Roland Breeur, "Proust: Herinnering in stijl" ["Proust: Recollection in Style"], in *De tijd bestaat niet*, for example, 181: "[Affective] memory preserves in Proustian terms what is most 'universal' in given situations: the impressions. But this universal is evoked by a detail. Such a detail gives us a universal impression of an event from the past, like the piece of wall that reveals the true art of Vermeer. . . . But this detail does not on first view have anything to do with the whole that it evokes." See also, further on the same page, the statement that "the detail derives its significance from a whole in which it does not fully disappear. . . . The meaning of the involuntary memory thus lies somewhere 'in between' " (my translations).

34. See Proust, *Swann's Way*, 35: "I decide to attempt to make it reappear. I retrace my thoughts to the moment at which I drank the first spoonful of tea. I find again the same state, illumined by no fresh light."

35. Gilles Deleuze, "Eleventh Series of Nonsense," in *Logic of Sense*, ed. Constantin V. Boundas, trans. Mark Lester and Charles Stivale (New York: Continuum, 2004), 79. An ordinary sign, on the contrary, does *not* "say its own sense" because it does not display its own role in the process of signification: it is a *mere* sign in that it remains somehow transparent vis-à-vis its referent or derives its meaning from the difference with other signs.

36. Ibid., 80.

37. Ibid., 83: "Nonsense does not have any particular sense, but is opposed to the absence of sense rather than to the sense that it produces in excess—without ever maintaining with its product the simple relation of exclusion to which some people would like to reduce them."

38. From this perspective, the term *souvenir involontaire* is misleading because it seems to connect the former self with the fullness of a presence that it never

had and the past with an impulse of self-revelation that is lacking. In this regard, it is crucial to understand the paradox that the past that returns in a *souvenir involontaire* did not in fact preexist this moment of return: it is a past that differs from any former "present" (it was never fully experienced) and which is *actualized* only at the moment of recollection itself. See the description of the *souvenir involontaire* as a moment of "creation" where the seeking mind "is face to face with something which does not so far exist, to which it alone can give reality and substance [*quelque chose qui n'est pas encore et que seul il peut réaliser*], which it alone can bring into the light of day," in Proust, *Swann's Way*, 36. See also Deleuze's ideas on the "pure past" in *Proust and Signs*, 59; and Breeur, "Proust: Herinnering in stijl," 185–86.

39. See also Roland Breeur, "De tijd bestaat niet" ["Time Does Not Exist"], in *De tijd bestaat niet*, 88: "Perhaps, what affects and moves the most in memories is not so much the fact that we develop ourselves as a unity, but that we, despite this development, nevertheless preserve something of the child we once were. If, still, we are touched by that past, it [is] rather [connected to] the awareness that it has disappeared forever and that it does no longer match who we are now. The past touches us as loss and not as the confirmation of a deep unity and continuity" (my translation).

40. For what follows, an earlier mentioned essay on Proust was very influential: Roland Breeur, "Proust: Herinnering in stijl," especially 180–87.

41. See Henri Bergson, *Matter and Memory*, trans. Nancy Margaret Paul and W. Scott Palmer (New York: Zone Books, 1991), 34: "Memory . . . covering as it does with a cloak of recollections a core of immediate perception, and also contracting a number of external moments into a single internal moment, constitutes the principal share of individual consciousness in perception."

42. See ibid., 138: "My body is a center of action, the place where the impressions received choose intelligently the path they will follow to transform themselves into movements accomplished."

43. See Roland Breeur's analysis of the difference between an organic and an atomic model of memory and the statement that "the essential that is evoked [by the *souvenir involontaire*] transcends the past that is revived: it is not identical to it. For that reason, all the memories that I recall cannot satisfy or suspend the desire that motivates my memory in its quest. What is recalled through the detail touches me on account of the awareness of a form of 'forgetfulness' that no memory can overcome"; in Breeur, "Proust: Herinnering in stijl," 186. For more on the signifying power of the detail, see Samuel Weber, "God and the Devil—In Detail," in *Benjamin's -abilities*, for example, 244: "The detail is that which detaches itself from what would otherwise be the pure self-sufficiency of the simple and unitary monad, and what, as detached, becomes capable of 'mirroring' or representing that from which the monad has separated itself: other monads and the more complex substances they compose. The internal detachment of the *detail* thus introduces into the windowless monad the possibility of its representing the diversity 'outside' it."

44. For interesting analyses of these conceptual personae, see the work of Irving Wohlfarth and Susan Buck-Morss. See most notably, Wohlfarth, "Et Cetera? The Historian as Chiffonnier," 142–68 and the statement that "the *chiffonnier* would represent [a] monad, an incisive particular which, like a well-cut crystal (or rough

diamond), mirrors the whole. Cutting the crystal does not mean cutting corners or smoothing rough edges in order to produce some well-rounded microcosm: the pieces of the mosaic fit together as parts of the whole, and as *pars pro toto*, only if their essential asperities are accentuated" (144). See also Irving Wohlfarth, "Perte d'Auréole: The Emergence of the Dandy," *MLN* 85, no. 4 (1970): 529–71 (what is at stake in, for example, Baudelaire's poetry is the "negativity of modern experience . . . made aesthetically productive" [535]). For more background on the significance of the figure of the ruin in Benjamin's work (in both the *Trauerspiel* book and the *Arcades Project*) and for an analysis of its political relevance, see the chapter "Historical Nature: Ruin" in Buck-Morss, *The Dialectics of Seeing*, 159–201.

45. See the famous last paragraph of the *Trauerspiel* book: "In the ruins of great buildings the idea of the plan speaks more impressively than in lesser buildings, however well preserved they are; and for this reason the German *Trauerspiel* merits interpretation. In the spirit of allegory it is conceived from the outset as ruin, a fragment. Others may shine resplendently as on the first day; this form preserves the image of beauty to the very last" (O, 235). About this idea and how it is connected to the concept of "origin," see Weber, "Genealogy of Modernity," in *Benjamin's -abilities*, 131–63, for example, 134: "Origin, in short, qua *Ursprung*, has nothing to do with taking a stand, going upright, with acquiring a certain stature, status or stability. Origin is springing, a leap, an offspring that springs from the alternation of becoming and passing away, of coming and going."

46. For more on this relational and dislocated nature of a meaning "in between" objects, experiences, or images, see the earlier mentioned Weber, "Genealogy of Modernity," 131–63, for example, 136: "The 'totality' of which Benjamin speaks does not signify the overcoming of originary incompleteness, but rather the deployment of the possibilities of differential relations that define the idea." For an extensive analysis of similar intuitions in the work of Aby Warburg, see Georges Didi-Huberman, *L' Image survivante: Histoire de l' art et temps des fantômes selon Aby Warburg* (Paris: Les Éditions de Minuit, 2002), especially the chapter "Le Montage Mnemosyne: Tableaux, fusées, détails, intervalles," 452–505. For more on the concept of meaning as a *Zwischenraum* ("l'espace entre"), see 496–505.

47. For the clearest out of many illustrations, see the statement that it is important to "carry over the principle of montage into history. That is, to assemble large-scale constructions out of the smallest and most precisely cut components. Indeed, to discover in the analysis of the small individual moment the crystal of the total event" (*AP*, 461). See also the statements that a "resolute refusal of the concept of 'timeless truth' is in order" and that "truth is . . . bound to a nucleus of time lying hidden within the knower and the known alike." For this reason, "the eternal . . . is far more the ruffle on a dress than some idea" (*AP*, 463).

48. For similar interpretations of Benjamin's essays on mechanically (re)produced images that do not, however, look at the concept of *unscheinbar*, see, for example, Ariella Azoulay, "[Death's] Display Showcase: Walter Benjamin," in *Death's Showcase: The Power of Image in Contemporary Democracy*, trans. Danieli Ruvik (Cambridge, Mass.: MIT Press, 2001), 33: "[Benjamin] is interested in photography—and in looking at photographs—as practices that make possible

the recuperation of experience and its transmission, which make possible in turn the recuperation of an ethical stance in the age of mechanical reproduction." Azoulay's readings are, unlike mine, focused on the ethico-political dimension of the empowerment of the spectator's gaze; see Ariella Azoulay, *The Civil Contract of Photography* (New York: Zone Books, 2008) and statements such as the following: "The realization of the contract [Azoulay's term to denote the social relationship between photographer, photographed, and spectator that is actualized by every photographic image] is not something only subsisting in the photographic act, between photographer and photographed, but draws most of its strength and validity from the very fact that it is inexhaustible and does not flow merely in expected directions" (127). For similar political stakes, see W. J. T. Mitchell, "Benjamin and the Political Economy of the Photograph," in *The Photography Reader*, ed. Liz Wells (London: Routledge, 2003), 53–58.

49. In this case, the non-sensical nature of the connection between the photograph and the future death of the fiancée can be taken quite literally, since scholars have argued that Benjamin's identification of the woman in the photograph was mistaken (she is not Dauthendey's first wife, who committed suicide, but his second). See the reference to André Gunthert in Ariella Azoulay, "The [Aesthetic] Distance: Benjamin and Heidegger," in *Death's Showcase*, 36.

50. For extensive analyses of what such "active" responses entail (and for the essential role of the body in such a response), see Susan Buck-Morss's views on a "synaesthetic system" that revolved a form of "sense-consciousness, decentered from the classical subject, wherein external sense-perceptions come together with the internal images of memory and anticipation," in "Aesthetics and Anaesthetics: Walter Benjamin's Artwork Essay Reconsidered," *October* 62 (1992): 13. For an analysis of this shattering of an original unity and the response to such a multiplicity of meaning, see also Howard Eiland, "Reception in Distraction," *boundary 2* 30, no. 1 (2003): 51–66; and Gertrud Koch, "Cosmos in Film: On the Concept of Space in Walter Benjamin's 'Work of Art' Essay," in Benjamin and Osborne, eds., *Walter Benjamin's Philosophy: Destruction and Experience*, 205–15. For the way in which this relates to, among other things, the phenomenon of mimicry and gendered spectatorship, see also Miriam Bratu Hansen, "Benjamin, Cinema and Experience: 'The Blue Flower in the Land of Technology,' " for example, 217–19.

51. Roland Barthes, *Camera Lucida: Reflections on Photography*, trans. Howard Richard (New York: Farrar, Straus and Giroux, 1982), 27.

52. Ibid., 42. It is very remarkable that, despite the profound differences between Benjamin's and Barthes's views on the significance of the "detail" in photographs, almost all commentaries only focus on the similarities without looking any further. For some examples of this, see Miriam Bratu Hansen, *Cinema and Experience*, 156; Ariella Azoulay, "[Death's] Display Showcase: Walter Benjamin," 38; and Margaret Iversen, "The Art Seminar," in *Photography Theory*, ed. James Elkins (New York: Routledge, 2007), 157: "I find it quite useful to put the *punctum* in relation to Benjamin's 'Little History of Photography,' where he talks about the double portrait of Dauthendey and his wife." The only important reference to the *difference* between Benjamin's and Barthes's views that we could find is in Weissberg, "Circulating Images: Notes on the Photographic Exchange," 110: "In Barthes a particular detail like a shoe can evoke the appropriation of the

image as memory. He can recall the past. For Benjamin, however, the *unscheinbare Stelle* should draw the photograph into the here and now, give evidence of its present currency. Memory is experienced in these seemingly invisible places not as a referent to the past, moreover, but to the future." My own views are fully in line with Weissberg's.

53. Barthes, *Camera Lucida*, 55.

54. Ibid., 49.

55. Ibid., 55, my emphasis.

56. Ibid., 79. See also the following sentence: "What life remained would be absolutely and entirely unqualifiable (without quality)," ibid., 75.

57. Ibid., 90–91.

58. See in this regard Benjamin's dictum that "the cracking open of natural teleology" is an "article" of his "politics" (*AP*, 631).

59. For a clear elaboration of some of the key features of Benjamin's concepts of fate, myth, and guilt, see Friedlander, *Walter Benjamin: A Philosophical Portrait*, 112–38, especially 114–18 ("Life and Meaning") and the statement that "where meaningful forms of life disintegrate, the entanglement in life, namely the ambiguity of myth, takes over" (117). For the main features of the concept of myth in Benjamin's writings, see the introduction to Graeme Gilloch, *Myth and Metropolis: Walter Benjamin and the City* (Cambridge: Polity, 1996), in particular 9–13. Gilloch writes that myth "appears to have at least a fourfold significance for [Benjamin]: as fallacious thought, as compulsion, as tyranny, and as metaphorical device" (9).

60. In this context, see also Friedlander's analysis of the important difference between tragedy (myth, Fate) and *Trauerspiel* (history): "Tragedy . . . is not only an artistic form but also a mode of conceiving of the fulfillment of meaning in history as what makes it possible to bring an order to the contingencies of historical time," in Friedlander, *Walter Benjamin: A Philosophical Portrait*, 125. See also the statement that "in [tragedy] is realized the possibility of the closure of meaning, beyond all intention, or conscious use of language by its speakers. . . . In contrast, the essential experience of the *Trauerspiel* is the failure of language to attain closure or fulfillment in meaning," ibid., 128.

61. See also Benjamin's statement that Fate has no "autonomous time" and that its time "is parasitically dependent on the time of a higher, less natural life. It has no present, for fateful moments exist only in bad novels, and it knows past and future only in curious variations" (*SW 1*, 204).

62. See the statement in the Goethe essay that, for this reason, "no work of art may seem wholly alive, in a manner free of spell-like enchantment, without becoming mere semblance and ceasing to be a work of art. The life undulating in it must appear petrified and as if spellbound in a single moment" (*SW 1*, 340).

Chapter 5

1. See http://airminded.org/2010/09/26/thursday-26-september-1940/.

2. See http://ww2today.com/26th-september-1940-1300-killed-in-london-alone-this-week.

3. See Anson Rabinbach, "Between Enlightenment and Apocalypse: Benjamin, Bloch and Modern German Jewish Messianism," *New German Critique* 34 (1985): 78–124.

4. [*die Windrose zur Bestimmung*] [*dem menschlichen Dasein ihr Spiel treiben*] [*den Ort völliger Indifferenz von Erfolg und von Mißerfolg*].
5. [*eingewurzeltes Vorurteil*].
6. [*wie dieses Dasein in das Weltgefüge eingreift*].
7. [*daß beide hinter seinem Rücken sich verständigten*].
8. This internal change of the experience of contingency explains why Benjamin does not simply write that success is "the deepest expression *of* the contingencies of this world" but that it is "the deepest expression *for* the contingencies for this world," thus highlighting that the very expression of contingency *adds* something to it and does not simply represent it.
9. [*Die Hand hat sich der Sache angenommen und im Handumdrehn ist sie einig mit ihr geworden*].
10. Sigrid Weigel's concept of "double reference" was important in putting together these ideas on the "disparity" of the world, which will underlie a big part of this chapter. See Weigel, *Walter Benjamin: Images, the Creaturely, and the Holy*, 27–29.
11. For this paragraph, I borrow from the chapter on myth in Eli Friedlander, *Walter Benjamin: A Philosophical Portrait*, 112–38.
12. Simmel, "the Problem of Fate," 83.
13. [*der ihm vertrauten, eigenen und eingebannten*].
14. [*ein erstes und letztes [Opfer] zugleich*] [*neue Inhalte des Volkslebens*].
15. [*die Dichtung in die Lehre zu überführen*].
16. [*für die es vielleicht Hoffnung gibt*].
17. For a further discussion of Benjamin's *Trauerspiel* book along these lines, see also Weber, "Storming the Work."
18. See Eli Friedlander's discussion of this topic in his *Walter Benjamin: A Philosophical Portrait*, 125–31.
19. [*sie fragt nach Schicksal, Mythos und Verhängnis überhaupt nicht*].
20. [*das unzähliger Versehen*] [*die endlich, infolge eines letzten kleinen Fehlers, doch das genaue Resultat ergeben*].
21. [*ein Schelm, ein Tropf, ein Narr, ein armer Schlucker*] [*was sie auch sei: diese Welt paßt ihr wie angegossen*].
22. [*Ihr Schlüssel ist eine mathematische Figur*].
23. See also Siegfried Kracauer's statement that "to be sure, the minor triumphs of Buster Keaton or Chaplin's Tramp over destructive natural forces, hostile objects, and human brutes were sometimes due to feats of acrobatic skill. Yet unlike most circus productions, film comedy did not highlight the performer's proficiency in braving death and surmounting impossible difficulties; rather it minimized his accomplishments in a constant effort to present successful rescues as the outcome of sheer chance," in Siegfried Kracauer, *Theory of Film: The Redemption of Physical Reality* (Princeton, N.J.: Princeton University Press, 1997), 62.
24. David Robinson, *Chaplin: His Life and Art* (London: Penguin Books, 2001), 117. Siegfried Kracauer, however, has a different view on this matter, writing that "from early slapstick to Chaplin's full-length films, the visuals in a measure retained the character of snapshots. They were matter of fact records rather than expressive photographs. . . . Their concern [of the comedy makers] was alienated physical existence," in "Silent Film Comedy," in *Siegfried Kracauer's American Writings: Essays on Film and Popular Culture*, ed. Johannes

von Moltke and Kristy Rawson (Berkeley: University of California Press, 2012), 216. See also Henri Michaux's statement about Chaplin: "We no longer have emotions. But we still move" (quoted in Peter Conrad, "Arms and Mankind," in *Modern Times, Modern Places: Life and Art in the 20th Century* [London: Thames and Hudson, 1998], 223). Kracauer's argument testifies to his overall agenda to understand film as an inherently redemptive medium on account of its supposedly immediate rendition of reality. See, for instance, his reference to the "camera's inborn curiosity and function as a ragpicker," an example of which he finds in Chaplin's *A Dog's Life*, in *Theory of Film*, 54.

25. For the opposite view, see, for instance, the reference to "Chaplin's lowbrow, even kitschy sentimentalism" in Tace Hedrick, *Mestizo Modernism: Race, Nation and Identity in Latin American Culture, 1900–1940* (New Brunswick, N.J.: Rutgers University Press, 2003), 153.

26. [*dem femininen Einschlag des Verelendeten*] [*soviel Glanz um so viel Schäbigkeit*].

27. Slavoj Žižek's analysis of *City Lights* revolves around a similar destruction of the classical idea of teleology, using a Lacanian framework to indicate that the final scene is "far from realizing a predestined telos" and "marks the intrusion of a radical openness in which every ideal support of our existence is suspended," in "Why Does a *Letter* Always Arrive at Its Destination?" in *Enjoy Your Symptom! Jacques Lacan in Hollywood and Out* (New York: Routledge, 1992), 9.

28. [*stellen sie sie mit steigender Kraßheit dar*].

29. Friedlander, *Walter Benjamin: A Philosophical Portrait*, 121.

30. [*Maske des Unbeteiligtseins*].

31. [*die von außen her ihnen den richtigen Akzent verleihen*].

32. Robinson, *Chaplin: His Life and Art*, 117.

33. [*[e]in wacher Sinn . . . für das Extreme, Komische, Private oder Überraschende der Lage*].

34. [*die Grausamkeit des Streits*].

35. [*von allen Tugenden vielleicht die einzige, welche sie unverwandelt übernimmt*].

36. [*nichts weniger als rigorose Sittenvorschrift*] [*nur Repräsentation der außer Kraft gesetzten*].

37. [*Repräsentation von seiner Unentschiedenheit*].

38. [*all jene Kräfte und Instanzen, die er ausschloß, als Helfer, Mittler und Versöhner einläßt*].

39. [*Er spielt dem, der ihn übt, die Regie der Unterhandlung, am Ende aber auch die der Interessen zu*].

40. [*tritt die wahre Höflichkeit in Kraft*].

41. [*dem Unterliegenden die nächste Chance*].

42. Henri Bergson, "La Politesse," in *Mélanges*, ed. André Robinet (Paris: Presses Universitaires de France, 1972), 326.

43. [*qui fait que la charité, se doublant de pénétration, manœuvre sans peine à travers les mille détours des susceptibilités, des amours-propres*], ibid., 328.

44. [*une espèce de souplesse intellectuelle*], ibid., 322.

45. Ibid., 328–29.

46. [*prolongerait la justice et la charité au-delà du monde tangible*] [*les grands conciliateurs des esprits et des cœurs*], ibid., 329.

47. [*sort naturellement de l'accord et de la camaraderie des intelligences*], ibid., 329, my emphasis.

48. [*de nous laisser croire qu'il ne serait pas le même pour tout le monde*] [*le propre de cet homme très poli est de préférer chacun de ses amis aux autres, et de réussir ainsi à les aimer tous également*], ibid., 322.

49. "Goodness, like all that is beautiful and alive on this earth, grows from a germ and develops itself but it is not created [*sort d'un germe et se développe mais ne se crée pas*]," ibid., 326. See also the reference to "a great natural goodness" [*une grande bonté naturelle*], ibid., 326.

50. Ibid., 332.

51. [*une république idéale*] [*véritable cité des esprits*], ibid., 327–28.

52. For an overview of this topic, see Samuel Weber, "Citability—Of Gesture," in *Benjamin's -abilities*, 95–115.

53. This is, of course, one of the possible ways to interpret the phrase that "Chaplin is the living embodiment of Goethe's *aperçu*: Man would not be the noblest on earth if he were not too noble for it" (*SW* 2, 199, translation modified).

54. For a further discussion of the concept of *Spielraum*, see Miriam Bratu Hansen, "Play-Form of Second Nature," in *Cinema and Experience*, 183–204.

55. Gilles Deleuze, *Cinema 2: The Time-Image*, trans. Hugh Tomlinson and Robert Galeta (London: Athlone, 1989), 155.

56. Ibid., 152. One statement in Chaplin's memoires is particularly relevant here. "I neither believe nor disbelieve in anything. That which can be imagined is as much an approximation to truth as that which can be proved by mathematics. One cannot always approach truth through reason; it confines us to a geometric cast of thought that calls for logic and credibility. We see the dead in our dreams and accept them as living, knowing at the same time they are dead. And although this dream mind is without reason, has it not its own credibility?" in Charles Chaplin, *My Autobiography* (New York: Simon and Schuster, 1964), 291. See also the paragraph "False Opposition," in Béla Balázs's book *The Spirit of Film*, where he mentions that "in watching the grotesque and fantastic scenes in Chaplin's films it is hard to avoid the impression of truth," in Béla Balázs, *Early Film Theory: Visible Man and the Spirit of Film*, ed. Erica Carter, trans. Rodney Livingstone (New York: Berghahn Books, 2010), 223. Siegfried Kracauer's interpretation of such scenes runs counter to these statements; see, for instance, his *Theory of Film*, 86: "Their very staginess denotes that they spring from a primary concern for physical reality." Still, a couple of pages further on, Kracauer does mention that "Chaplin's dream interludes not only accentuate the actual misery of the tramp but anticipate freedom from strictures and positive happiness. There is a touch of utopia about these challenges to space, time, and gravitation" (88).

57. [*Diskontinuierliche Bilder lösen in kontinuierlicher Folge einander ab*].

58. [*seine einzigartige Bedeutung besteht darin, daß er den Menschen seinem Gestus . . . nach in den Film einmontiert*].

59. [*es ist immer dieselbe ruckartige Abfolge kleinster Bewegungen, die das Gesetz der filmischen Bilderfolge zum Gesetze der menschlichen Motorik erlebt*].

60. See, for instance, Kevin Brownlow, *The Search for Charlie Chaplin* (London: UKA, 2010), 91.

61. [*Jede einzelne seiner Bewegungen setzt sich aus seiner Folge abgehackter Bewegungsteilchen zusammen*].

62. [*im Prozeß der Consumption durch das Filmband vertreten*].

63. In this context, Jacques Rancière's essay on Charlie Chaplin is very relevant. Interpreting Chaplin's interaction with the machine in the context of the Russian avant-garde, Rancière associates Chaplin's mechanized manner of acting with the revolutionary dream of turning the power of the machine against itself. What matters most in Chaplin's choreography is, therefore, the "perfect equality of the functional response and its unforeseeable consequences": "At the exact juncture of vulgar reaction with ideal choreography, there is a mechanical precision of movement." See Jacques Rancière, "The Machine and Its Shadow (Hollywood, 1916)," in *Aesthesis*, 191–206 (the quotations are from pp. 201–2). William Rothman's analysis runs counter to the views of both Benjamin and Rancière. Discussing *City Lights*, Rothman understands the essence of Chaplin's cinema as a drive to *overcome* the mechanic condition and *overstep* the boundaries of film (which are, in his opinion, a metaphor for a more fundamental separation from the world): "Not despair but a passionate wish and a palpable terror are at the heart of Chaplin's films: the wish and terror of overcoming the barrier for which film is a metaphor, the wish and terror of making or allowing a dream to become real"; William Rothman, "The Ending of *City Lights*," in *The "I" of the Camera: Essays in Film Criticism, History, and Aesthetics* (Cambridge: Cambridge University Press, 2004), 46.

64. For a very extensive discussion of this topic, see Miriam Bratu Hansen, *Cinema and Experience*, 132–62.

65. [*Chaplin zeigt die Komik von Hitlers Ernst*].

66. See also Miriam Bratu Hansen's discussion of this issue in her *Cinema and Experience*, 130.

67. Though undeveloped, a similar duality underlies Theodor Adorno's short text about Chaplin (on the occasion of Chaplin's 75th birthday). Adorno draws attention to the significance of a certain form of cruelty in his work and also connects this with a redemptive quality: "All the laughter he brings about is so near to cruelty; solely in such proximity to cruelty does it find its legitimation and its element of the salvational," in "Chaplin Times Two," in *The Essential Chaplin: Perspectives on the Life and Art of the Great Comedian*, ed. Richard Schickel (Chicago: Ivan R. Dee, 2006), 272.

68. [*[s]eine Kleider sind imprägniert gegen alle Schicksalsschläge*].

69. For an interesting development of a similar intuition, see André Bazin, "Charlie Chaplin," in *The Essential Chaplin*, especially 92–94. In Bazin's opinion as well, "the very category of the sacred does not exist [for Chaplin]" (93). See also Kracauer's (undeveloped) idea that "behind many nonsolutions, including those of the old Chaplin comedies, there lurks, perhaps, a desire to exalt the power of resistance of the seeming weak who time and again cheat destiny," Kracauer, *Theory of Film*, 270 (see also p. 281).

70. See also Elie Faure's statement that "[Chaplin's] innocence and his malice go hand in hand, and by means of his malice he reveals his innocence," in "The Art of Charlie Chaplin," in *The Essential Chaplin*, 83.

71. This externality of guilt and the important difference between guilt and shame might explain why Emmanuel Levinas discusses the Tramp's behavior (and the scene from *City Lights* in which he has swallowed a whistle) in the context of a discussion of shame. Since shame, unlike guilt, involves the experience of

the inappropriability of one's own body and the acknowledgment of the presence of other people, this connection does indeed make much sense. See Emmanuel Levinas, *On Escape*, trans. Bettina Bergo (Stanford, Calif.: Stanford University Press, 2003), 65.

72. [*um die Herrenkaste beim Wort zu nehmen*].

73. [*die große unabgesetzte und doch höchst differenzierte Resonanz von Volk zu Volk*].

74. [*Der Mensch wäre nicht der Vornehmste auf der Erde, wenn er nicht zu vornehm für die ware*]. See also Andrew Sarris's statement that "Chaplin's timing is so remarkably precise . . . that the white rose of his romanticism seems to flower in the base soil of his earthiness," Andrew Sarris, "The Most Harmonious Comedian," in *The Essential Chaplin*, 56.

75. Deleuze, *Cinema 1: The Movement-Image*, 171.

76. Ibid., 172.

77. For such criticism, see, for instance, Richard Schickel's interpretation of these two scenes in his "Introduction: The Tramp Transformed," in *The Essential Chaplin*, 32–35. Peter Conrad, however, turns this argument around and, rather than regarding the speech in *The Great Dictator* as a proclamation of humanism and pacifism, considers it to be a form of irony. In his understanding, Chaplin was not interested in proclaiming a belief in the ultimate possibility of peace and universal understanding but, to the contrary, sought to expose such ideals as mere illusions. "Chaplin's double role in *The Great Dictator* hints that the demagogue is resident within the little man, whose grudges he articulates. The docile, sweet-natured barber may have been a mask worn by the despot, just as Hitler allegedly adopted Chaplin's mustache as an endearing camouflage." Peter Conrad, "The Chapliniad," in *Modern Times, Modern Places*, 438.

78. In his text on *Monsieur Verdoux*, Jacques Rivette develops a similar line of thought. To the question "What is the goal of cinema?" he replies: "That the real world, such as it is offered on the screen would also be an idea of the world. We must see the world as an idea, we must think it concretely." Rivette sees Chaplin as an artist whose films do not just originate in the attempt to represent the actual world (this does not bring about any form of understanding), nor in the aim to express a mere idea or ideal (this leads to sterile and cerebral cinema), but in the awareness that what is truly important *to* the world is not a mere given that is present *within* it. Chaplin's art is, therefore, "a dynamic figure" and "the preciseness of its movement, of its internal dialectic recreates, step by step, under our eyes, a concrete world: other and explicated, yet all the more ambiguous for being at once an incarnated idea [*idée incarnée*] and a real shot through with meaning [*réel transpercé de sens*]." Jacques Rivette, "Revoir Verdoux," in *Cahiers du Cinéma* 143 (1963): 42–43, my translation.

Two Concluding Remarks

1. Klages, "Von Wesen des Rhythmus," 225–28.

2. Georg Simmel, "The Stranger," in *The Sociology of Georg Simmel*, ed. and trans. Kurt Wolff (New York: Free, 1950), 407–8.

3. Georg Simmel, "The Sociology of Secrecy and Secret Societies," trans. Albion W. Small, *The American Journal of Sociology* 11, no. 4 (1906): 448. See also the claim that a "reciprocal concealment" is a "necessity" for a lively society, ibid.,

448. For these issues (and the concept of self-deception that is related to it), see Barbour, "The Maker of Lies." See also Gregor Fitzi, "A 'Transnormative' View of Society Building: Simmel's Sociological Epistemology and Philosophical Anthropology of Complex Societies," *Theory, Culture & Society* 29, no. 7/8 (2012): 177–96.

4. Georg Simmel, "The Poor," in *Social Problems* 12, no. 2 (1965): 135.

5. See also the following statement: "The boundary is unconditional in that its existence is constitutive of our given position in the world but . . . no boundary is unconditional since every one can in principle be altered" (*VoL*, 2). See also Georg Simmel, "The Social Boundary," *Theory, Culture & Society* 24, no. 7/8 (2007): 53–56. For the idea that Simmel's views on society are determined by metaphysical presuppositions, see, for example, Scott Lash, "*Lebenssoziologie*: Georg Simmel in the Information Age," *Theory, Culture & Society* 22, no. 3 (2005): 1–23.

6. The first part of the sentence comes from Simmel, "The Poor," 139, the second part from *VoL*, 5, my emphasis.

7. Benjamin also notes that it is likely that the very first text he composed all by himself was engaged with precisely this issue, namely with the story of a poorly paid man who distributes leaflets that nobody is interested in and who ultimately decides to throw them all away (*SW 3*, 404).

8. Aristotle, "De Memoria et Reminiscentia (On Memory and Reminiscence)," in *The Basic Works of Aristotle*, ed. Richard McKeon, trans. J. I. Beare (New York: Random House, 1941), 607 (449b).

9. Ibid., 607–8 (449b-450a).

10. Ibid., 610 (450b).

11. Ibid.

12. Johann Peter Hebel, "Unverhofftes Wiedersehen," in *Hebels Werke in Einem Band* (Berlin: Aufbau Verlag, 1978), 206.

13. Aristotle, "De Memoria et Reminiscentia (On Memory and Reminiscence)," 612 (451b).

14. For the reference to the "knowing contemplation" of mnemonic tokens, see, for example, ibid., 610 (450b), translation modified.

15. For the reference to "investigation," see ibid., 616 (453a). For the reference to "think together," see ibid., 616 (453a), translation modified.

16. For the reference to "deliberation," see ibid., 616 (453a).

17. Ibid., 613–14 (451b-452a).

18. Hebel, "Unverhofftes Wiedersehen," 207.

19. Ibid., 207.

BIBLIOGRAPHY

Adorno, Theodor. "Chaplin Times Two." In *The Essential Chaplin: Perspectives on the Life and Art of the Great Comedian*, edited by Richard Schickel, 267–72. Chicago: Ivan R. Dee, 2006.

———. "Exchange with Theodor W. Adorno on 'The Paris of the Second Empire in Baudelaire.'" In *SW 4*, 99–115.

———. "The Handle, the Pot, and Early Experience." In *Notes to Literature, Volume 2*, edited by Rolf Tiedemann, translated by Shierry Weber Nicholson, 211–19. New York: Columbia University Press, 1991.

———. "A Portrait of Walter Benjamin." In *Prisms*, translated by Samuel Weber and Shierry Weber, 227–41. Cambridge, Mass: MIT Press, 1997.

Agamben, Giorgio. *Homo Sacer: Sovereign Power and Bare Life*. Translated by Daniel Heller-Roazen. Stanford, Calif.: Stanford University Press, 1998.

———. "Kommerell, or on Gesture." In *Potentialities: Collected Essays in Philosophy*, edited and translated by Daniel Heller-Roazen, 77–85. Stanford, Calif.: Stanford University Press, 1999.

———. "On Potentiality." In *Potentialities: Collected Essays in Philosophy*, edited and translated by Daniel Heller-Roazen, 177–84. Stanford, Calif.: Stanford University Press, 1999.

———. *Profanations*. Translated by Jeff Fort. New York: Zone Books, 2007.

———. *Remnants of Auschwitz: The Witness and the Archive*. Translated by Daniel Heller-Roazen. New York: Zone Books, 1999.

———. *The Time That Remains: A Commentary on the Letter to the Romans*. Translated by Patricia Dailey. Stanford, Calif.: Stanford University Press, 2005.

Arendt, Hannah. "The Decline of the Nation-State and the End of the Rights of Men." In *The Origins of Totalitarianism*, 267–302. San Diego, Calif.: Harcourt, 1976.

Aristotle. "De Memoria et Reminiscentia (On Memory and Reminiscence)." In *The Basic Works of Aristotle*, edited by Richard McKeon, translated by J. I. Beare, 607–17. New York: Random House, 1941.

Azoulay, Ariella. *The Civil Contract of Photography*. New York: Zone Books, 2008.

———. *Death's Showcase: The Power of Image in Contemporary Democracy*. Translated by Ruvik Danieli. Cambridge, Mass.: MIT Press, 2001.

Bachelard, Gaston. *La Dialectique de la durée*. Paris: Presses Universitaires de France, 2006.

Baer, Ulrich. *The Rilke Alphabet*. Translated by Andrew Hamilton. New York: Fordham University Press, 2014.

Balázs, Béla. *Early Film Theory: Visible Man and the Spirit of Film*. Edited by Erica Carter, translated by Rodney Livingstone. New York: Berghahn Books, 2010.

Barbour, Charles. "The Maker of Lies: Simmel, Mendacity and the Economy of Faith." *Theory, Culture & Society* 29, no. 7–8 (2012): 218–36.

Barthes, Roland. *Camera Lucida: Reflections on Photography*. Translated by Richard Howard. New York: Farrar, Straus and Giroux, 1982.

Bazin, André. "Charlie Chaplin." In *The Essential Chaplin: Perspectives on the Life and Art of the Great Comedian*, edited by Richard Schickel, 85–95. Chicago: Ivan R. Dee, 2006.

Becker, Jochen. "Ursprung so wie Zerstörung: Sinnbild und Sinngebung bei Warburg und Benjamin." In *Allegorie und Melancholie*, edited by Willem van Reijen, 64–89. Frankfurt am Main: Suhrkamp Verlag, 1992.

Benedek, Nelly Silagy. *Auguste Rodin: The Burghers of Calais, a Resource for Educators*. New York: Metropolitan Museum of Art, 2000.

Benjamin, Andrew. "The Absolute as Translatability: Working through Walter Benjamin on Language." In *Walter Benjamin and Romanticism*, edited by Beatrice Hanssen and Andrew Benjamin, 109–22. New York: Continuum, 2002.

———. "Boredom and Distraction: The Moods of Modernity." In *Walter Benjamin and History*, edited by Andrew Benjamin, 156–70. London: Continuum, 2005.

Benjamin, Walter. "Berliner Kindheit um Neunzehnhundert" (1934). In *GS IV*, 235–304. Translated into English as "Berlin Childhood around 1900 (1934 Version)." In *SW 3*, 344–413.

———. "Brief an Gershom Scholem" (1938). In *Gesammelte Briefe VI, 1938–1940*, edited by Christoph Gödde and Henri Lonitzs, 105–14. Frankfurt am Main: Suhrkamp Verlag, 2000. Translated into English as "Letter to Gershom Scholem on Franz Kafka." In *SW 3*, 322–29.

———. "Briefwechsel Theodor W. Adorno und Walter Benjamin" (1938). In *Briefwechsel, 1928–1940*, 364–86. Frankfurt am Main: Suhrkamp Verlag, 1994. Translated into English as "Exchange with Theodor W. Adorno on 'The Paris of the Second Empire in Baudelaire.'" In *SW 4*, 99–115.

———. "Chaplin" (1928 or 1929). In *GS VI*, 137–38. Translated into English as "Chaplin." In *SW 2*, 199–200.

———. *The Correspondence of Walter Benjamin, 1910–1940*. Translated by Manfred R. Jacobson and Evelyn M. Jacobson. Chicago: University of Chicago Press, 1994.

———. "Das Leben der Studenten" (1915). In *GS II*, 75–87. Translated into English as "The Life of Students." In *SW 1*, 37–47.

———. "Das Paris des Second Empire bei Baudelaire" (1938). In *GS I*, 511–604. Translated into English as "The Paris of the Second Empire in Baudelaire." In *SW 4*, 3–92.

———. "Das Passagen-Werk." In *GS V-6*. Translated into English as *The Arcades Project*. Translated by Howard Eiland. Cambridge, Mass: Harvard University Press, 2002.

———. "Der Autor als Produzent" (1934). In *GS II*, 683–701. Translated into English as "The Author as Producer." In *SW 2*, 768–82.

———. "Der Begriff der Kunstkritik in der Deutschen Romantik" (1919). In *GS I*, 7–122. Translated into English as "The Concept of Criticism in German Romanticism." In *SW 1*, 116–200.

———. "Der destruktive Charakter" (1931). In *GS IV*, 396–98. Translated into English as "The Destructive Character." In *SW 2*, 541–42.
———. "Der Erzähler" (1936). In *GS II*, 438–65. Translated into English as "The Storyteller." In *SW 3*, 143–66.
———. "'Der Idiot' von Dostojewskij" (1917). In *GS II*, 237–41. Translated into English as "Dostoevsky's *The Idiot*." In *SW 1*, 78–81.
———. "Der Sürrealismus" (1929). In *GS II*, 295–310. Translated into English as "Surrealism." In *SW 2*, 207–21.
———. "Die Aufgabe des Übersetzers" (1921). In *GS IV*, 9–21. Translated into English as "The Task of the Translator." In *SW 1*, 253–63.
———. "Die Bedeutung der Zeit in der moralischen Welt" (1921). In *GS VI*, 97–98. Translated into English as "The Meaning of Time in the Moral Universe." In *SW 1*, 286–87.
———. "Die Bedeutung des schönen Scheins . . ." (1936). In *GS VII*, 667–68. Translated into English as "The Significance of Beautiful Semblance." In *SW 3*, 137–38.
———. "Die Formel in der die dialektische Struktur des Films . . ." (1935). In *GS I*, 1040. Translated into English as "The Formula in Which the Dialectical Structure of Film Finds Expression." In *SW 3*, 94–95.
———. "Franz Kafka" (1934). In *GS II*, 409–38. Translated into English as "Franz Kafka." In *SW 2*, 794–818.
———. "Goethes Wahlverwandtschaften" (1924-25). In *GS I*, 123–201. Translated into English as "Goethe's Elective Affinities." In *SW 1*, 297–360.
———. "Hitlers herabgeminderte Männlichkeit . . ." (1934). In *GS VI*, 103–4. Translated into English as "Hitler's Diminished Masculinity." In *SW 2*, 792–93.
———. "Ibizenkische Folge" (1932). In *GS IV*, 402–9. Translated into English as "Ibizan Sequence." In *SW 2*, 587–94.
———. "Johann Peter Hebel (I)" (1926). In *GS II*, 277–80. Translated into English as "Johann Peter Hebel (I)." In *SW 1*, 428–31.
———. "Kleine Geschichte der Photographie" (1931). In *GS II*, 368–85. Translated into English as "Little History of Photography." In *SW 2*, 507–30.
———. "Kommentare zu Gedichten von Brecht" (1939). In *GS II*, 539–72. Translated into English as "Commentary on Poems by Brecht." In *SW 4*, 215–50.
———. "Das Kunstwerk im Zeitalter seiner technischen Reproduzierbarkeit, Das 'Dritte Fassung'" (1939). In *GS I*, 471–508. Translated into English as "The Work of Art in the Age of Its Technological Reproducibility: Third Version." In *SW 4*, 251–83.
———. "Das Kunstwerk im Zeitalter seiner technischen Reproduzierbarkeit, Das 'Zweite Fassung'" (1936). In *GS VII*, 350–84. Translated into English as "The Work of Art in the Age of Its Technological Reproducibility: Second Version." In *SW 3*, 101–33.
———. "Metaphysik der Jugend" (1914). In *GS II*, 91–104. Translated into English as "Metaphysics of Youth." In *SW 1*, 6–17.
———. "Paris, die Hauptstadt des XIX. Jahrhunderts" (1935). In *GS V*, 45–59. Translated into English as "Paris, the Capital of the Nineteenth Century." In *SW 3*, 32–49.
———. "Robert Walser" (1929). In *GS II*, 324–28. Translated into English as "Robert Walser." In *SW 2*, 257–61.

———. "Rückblick auf Chaplin" (1929). In *GS III*, 157–59. Translated into English as "Chaplin in Retrospect." In *SW 2*, 222–24.
———. "Schicksal und Charakter" (1919). In *GS II*, 171–79. Translated into English as "Fate and Character." In *SW 1*, 201–6.
———. "Schönheit und Schein" (1921). In *GS VI*, 129. Translated into English as "Beauty and Semblance." In *SW 1*, 283.
———. "Sokrates" (1916). In *GS II*, 129–32. Translated into English as "Socrates." In *SW 1*, 52–54.
———. "Theologisch-Politisches Fragment" (1921). In *GS II*, 203–4. Translated into English as "Theological-Political Fragment." In *SW 3*, 305–6.
———. "Trauerspiel und Tragödie" (1916). In *GS II*, 133–37. Translated into English as "*Trauerspiel* and Tragedy." In *SW 1*, 55–57.
———. "Über das Programm der kommenden Philosophie" (1918). In *GS II*, 157–71. Translated into English as "On the Program of the Coming Philosophy." In *SW 1*, 100–110.
———. "Über den Begriff der Geschichte" (1940). In *GS I*, 691–704. Translated into English as "On the Concept of History." In *SW 4*, 389–400.
———. "Über einige Motive bei Baudelaire" (1939). In *GS I*, 605–53. Translated into English as "On Some Motifs in Baudelaire." In *SW 4*, 313–55.
———. "Über 'Schein' " (1920). In *GS I*, 831–33. Translated into English as "On Semblance." In *SW 1*, 223–25.
———. "Über Sprache überhaupt und über die Sprache des Menschen" (1916). In *GS II*, 140–57. Translated into English as "On Language as Such and on the Language of Man." In *SW 1*, 62–74.
———. *Ursprung des Deutschen Trauerspiels* (1925). In *GS I*, 203–430. Translated into English as *The Origin of German Tragic Drama*. Translated by John Osborne. London: Verso Books, 1998.
———. "Was ist das epische Theater? (2)" (1939). In *GS II*, 532–39. Translated into English as "What Is the Epic Theater? II." In *SW 4*, 302–9.
———. "Zum Bilde Prousts" (1929). In *GS II*, 310–24. Translated into English as "On the Image of Proust." In *SW 2*, 237–47.
———. "Zur Kritik der Gewalt" (1921). In *GS II*, 179–203. Translated into English as "Critique of Violence." *In SW 1*, 236–52.
———. "Zwei Gedichte von Friedrich Hölderlin" (1915). In *GS II*, 105–26. Translated into English as "Two Poems by Friedrich Hölderlin." In *SW 1*, 18–36.
Bergson, Henri. *Creative Evolution*. Translated by Arthur Mitchell. Whitefish, Mont.: Kessinger, 2003.
———. *The Creative Mind. An Introduction to Metaphysics*. Translated by Mabelle L. Andinson. New York: Dover Books, 2007.
———. "La Politesse." In *Mélanges*, edited by André Robinet, 317–32. Paris: Presses Universitaires de France, 1972.
———. *Matter and Memory*. Translated by Nancy Margaret Paul and W. Scott Palmer. New York: Zone Books, 1991.
Binstock, Benjamin. "Postscript: Aloïs Riegl in the Presence of 'The Nightwatch.' " *October* 74 (1995): 36–44.
Blankert, Albert. "Looking at Rembrandt, Past and Present." In *Rembrandt: A Genius and His Impact*, edited by Albert Blankert, 32–59. Melbourne: National Gallery of Victoria, 1997.

Bleicher, Josef. "From Kant to Goethe: Georg Simmel on the Way to 'Leben.'" *Theory, Culture & Society* 24, no. 6 (2007): 139–58.

———. "Leben." *Theory, Culture & Society* 23, no. 2–3 (2006): 343.

Blumenberg, Hans. "Money or Life: Metaphors of Georg Simmel's Philosophy." *Theory, Culture & Society* 29, no. 7–8 (2012): 249–62.

Breeur, Roland. *De tijd bestaat niet: Essays over domheid, vrijheid en emoties*. Nijmegen: Uitgeverij Vantilt, 2012.

Brownlow, Kevin. *The Search for Charlie Chaplin*. London: UKA, 2010.

Buck-Morss, Susan. "Aesthetics and Anesthetics: The Artwork Essay Reconsidered." *October*, no. 62 (1992): 3–41.

———. *The Dialectics of Seeing: Walter Benjamin and the Arcades Project*. Cambridge, Mass: MIT Press, 1989.

Butler, Ruth. *Rodin: The Shape of Genius*. New Haven, Conn.: Yale University Press, 1993.

Button, Robert William. "Fate, Experience and Tragedy in Simmel's Dialogue with Modernity." *Theory, Culture & Society* 29, no. 7–8 (2012): 53–77.

Champigneulle, Bernard. *Rodin*. Translated by J. Maxwell Brownjohn. London: Thames and Hudson, 1986.

Chaplin, Charles. *My Autobiography*. New York: Simon and Schuster, 1964.

Comay, Rebecca. "The Sickness of Tradition: Between Melancholia and Fetishism." In *Walter Benjamin and History*, edited by Andrew Benjamin, 88–101. New York: Continuum, 2005.

Conrad, Peter. "Arms and Mankind." In *Modern Times, Modern Places: Life and Art in the 20th Century*, 203–27. London: Thames and Hudson, 1998.

———. "The Chapliniad." In *Modern Times, Modern Places: Life and Art in the 20th Century*, 421–39. London: Thames and Hudson, 1998.

Coser, Lewis. "The Stranger in the Academy." In *Georg Simmel*, edited by Lewis A. Coser, 29–39. Englewood Cliffs, N.J.: Prentice-Hall, 1965.

d'Andrea, Fabio. "Redemption in a Fragment: Simmel and Benjamin." *Simmel Studies* 14 (2004): 39–55.

Darmon, Isabelle, and Carlos Frade. "Beneath and Beyond the Fragments: The Charms of Simmel's Philosophical Path for Contemporary Subjectivities." *Theory, Culture & Society* 29, nos. 7–8 (2012): 197–217.

Deleuze, Gilles. *Cinema 1: The Movement-Image*. Translated by Hugh Tomlinson and Barbara Habberjam. London: Athlone, 1986.

———. *Cinema 2: The Time-Image*. Translated by Hugh Tomlinson and Robert Galeta. London: Athlone, 1989.

———. *Logic of Sense*. Edited by Constantin V. Boundas, translated by Mark Lester and Charles Stivale. New York: Continuum, 2004.

———. "Postscript on the Societies of Control." In *Negotiations 1972–1990*, translated by Martin Joughin, 177–82. New York: Columbia University Press, 1995.

———. *Proust and Signs*. Translated by Richard Howard. Minneapolis: University of Minnesota Press, 2000.

Deleuze, Gilles, and Félix Guattari. *A Thousand Plateaus: Capitalism and Schizophrenia*. Translation and foreword by Brian Massumi. Minneapolis: University of Minnesota Press, 1998.

Didi-Huberman, Georges. *L' Image survivante: Histoire de l' art et temps des fantômes selon Aby Warburg*. Paris: Les Éditions de Minuit, 2002.

Dodd, Nigel. "Simmel's Perfect Money: Fiction, Socialism and Utopia in *The Philosophy of Money*." *Theory, Culture & Society* 29, no. 7–8 (2012): 146–76.

Dyer, Geoff. "The Awakening of Stones: Rodin." In *Working the Room*, 103–15. Edinburgh: Canongate Books, 2010.

Eiland, Howard. "Reception in Distraction." *boundary 2* 30, no. 1 (2003): 51–66.

Eiland, Howard, and Michael W. Jennings. *Walter Benjamin: A Critical Life*. Cambridge, Mass: Harvard University Press, 2014.

Faath, Ute. *Mehr-als-Kunst: Zur Kunstphilosophie Georg Simmels*. Würzburg: Königshausen und Neumann, 1998.

Faure, Elie. "The Art of Charlie Chaplin." In *The Essential Chaplin: Perspectives on the Life and Art of the Great Comedian*, edited by Richard Schickel, 76–84. Chicago: Ivan R. Dee, 2006.

Fenves, Peter. *The Messianic Reduction: Walter Benjamin and the Shape of Time*. Stanford, Calif.: Stanford University Press, 2011.

Fitzi, Gregor. *Soziale Erfahrung und Lebensphilosophie: Georg Simmels Beziehung zu Henri Bergson*. Konstanz: UVK Verlagsgesellschaft, 2002.

———. "A 'Transnormative' View of Society Building: Simmel's Sociological Epistemology and Philosophical Anthropology of Complex Societies." *Theory, Culture & Society* 29, no. 7–8 (2012): 177–96.

Freud, Sigmund. "Triebe und Triebschicksale." In *Gesammelte Werke*, volume 10, *Werken aus den Jahren 1913–1917*, 209–32. Frankfurt am Main: Fischer Taschenbuch Verlag, 1999.

Friedlander, Eli. *Walter Benjamin: A Philosophical Portrait*. Cambridge, Mass.: Harvard University Press, 2012.

Frisby, David. "The Aesthetics of Modern Life: Simmel's Interpretation." *Theory, Culture & Society* 8, no. 3 (1991): 73–93.

———. *Cityscapes of Modernity: Critical Explorations*. Cambridge: Polity, 2001.

———. *Fragments of Modernity: Theories of Modernity in the Work of Simmel, Kracauer and Benjamin*. Cambridge: Polity, 1985.

———. "Introduction to the Translation." In Georg Simmel, *The Philosophy of Money*, edited by David Frisby, translated by Tom Bottomore and David Frisby, 1–49. London: Routledge, 2004.

———. "Preface to the Third Edition." In Georg Simmel, *The Philosophy of Money*, edited by David Frisby, translated by Tom Bottomore and David Frisby, xiv–xlv. London: Routledge, 2004.

———. *Simmel and Since: Essays on Georg Simmel's Social Theory*. London: Routledge, 1992.

———. *Sociological Impressionism: A Reassessment of Georg Simmel's Social Theory*. London: Routledge, 2013.

Gasché, Rodolphe. "Saturnine Vision and the Question of Difference: Reflections on Walter Benjamin's Theory of Language." In *Benjamin's Ground: New Readings of Walter Benjamin*, edited by Rainer Nägele, 83–104. Detroit: Wayne State University Press, 1986.

Gassen, Kurt, and Michael Landmann. "Bausteine zur Biographie." In *Buch des Dankes an Georg Simmel*, edited by Kurt Gassen and Michael Landmann, 11–33. Berlin: Duncker und Humblot, 1958.

Gilloch, Graeme. "The Faces of Amsterdam: Rembrandt, Simmel and the Painting of Modern Lives." *Episteme*, no. 4 (2010): 233–58.

———. *Myth and Metropolis: Walter Benjamin and the City*. Cambridge: Polity, 1996.

Goodstein, Elizabeth. "Style as Substance—Georg Simmel's Phenomenology of Culture." *Cultural Critique*, no. 52 (2002): 209–34.

Habermas, Jürgen. "Georg Simmel on Philosophy and Culture: Postscript to a Collection of Essays." *Critical Inquiry* 22, no. 3 (1996): 403–14.

Hall, James. *Michelangelo and the Reinvention of the Human Body*. New York: Farrar, Straus and Giroux, 2005.

Hansen, Miriam Bratu. "Benjamin, Cinema and Experience: 'The Blue Flower in the Land of Technology.'" *New German Critique* 40 (1987): 179–224.

———. *Cinema and Experience: Siegfried Kracauer, Walter Benjamin, and Theodor W. Adorno*. Berkeley: University of California Press, 2012.

———. "Room-for-Play: Benjamin's Gamble with Cinema." *October* 109 (2004): 3–45.

Hanssen, Beatrice. "Philosophy at Its Origin: Walter Benjamin's Prologue to the *Ursprung des Deutschen Trauerspiels*." *MLN* 110, no. 4 (1995): 809–33.

———. "Portrait of Melancholy (Benjamin, Warburg, Panofsky)." *MLN* 114, no. 5 (1999): 991–1013.

———. *Walter Benjamin's Other History: Of Stones, Animals, Human Beings, and Angels*. Berkeley: University of California Press, 2000.

Harrington, Austin, and Thomas M. Kemple. "Introduction: Georg Simmel's 'Sociological Metaphysics': Money, Sociality, and Precarious Life." *Theory, Culture & Society* 29, no. 7–8 (2012): 7–25.

Hebel, Johann Peter. "Unverhofftes Wiedersehen." In *Hebels Werke in Einem Band*, 205–7. Berlin: Aufbau Verlag, 1978.

Hedrick, Tace. *Mestizo Modernism: Race, Nation and Identity in Latin American Culture, 1900–1940*. New Brunswick, N.J.: Rutgers University Press, 2003.

Heidegger, Martin. *Being and Time*. Foreword by Dennis J. Schmidt, translated by Joan Stambaugh. Albany: State University of New York Press, 1996.

Hirst, Michael. *Michelangelo and His Drawings*. New Haven, Conn.: Yale University Press, 1988.

Hirst, Michael, and Jill Dunkerton. *The Young Michelangelo: Making and Meaning*. London: National Gallery, 1994.

Horkheimer, Max. "Lebensphilosophie: Bergson, Simmel, Dilthey." In *Gesammelte Schriften*, volume 10: *Nachgelassene Schriften 1914–1931*, edited by Alfred Schmidt, 267–98. Frankfurt am Main: Fischer Taschenbuch Verlag, 1990.

Hughes, Anthony. *Michelangelo*. Translated by Sophie Behr and Pierre Clertant. London: Phaidon, 1997.

Iversen, Margareth. "The Art Seminar." In *Photography Theory*, edited by James Elkins, 129–203. New York: Routledge, 2007.

Jameson, Fredric. "The Theoretical Hesitation: Benjamin's Sociological Predecessor." *Critical Inquiry* 25, no. 2 (1999): 267–88.

Jedlowski, Paolo. "Simmel on Memory." In *Georg Simmel and Contemporary Sociology*, edited by Michael Kaern, Bernard S. Phillips, and Robert S. Cohen, 131–54. Dordrecht: Kluwer Academic, 1990.

Karina, Lilian, Marion Kant, and Jonathan Steinberg. *Hitler's Dancers: German Modern Dance and the Third Reich*. New York: Berghahn Books, 2004.

Kemple, Thomas M. "A Chronology of Simmel's Works in English." *Theory, Culture & Society* 29, no. 7–8 (2012): 317–23.

Kettler, David. "Introduction to 'Soul and Culture.'" *Theory, Culture & Society* 29, no. 7–8 (2012): 279–85.

Klages, Ludwig. "Vom Wesen des Rhythmus: Auszug aus dem Vortrage." *Sudhoffs Archiv für Geschichte der Medizin und der Naturwissenschaften* 27, no. 3/4 (1934): 223–28.

Koch, Gertrud. "Cosmos in Film: On the Concept of Space in Walter Benjamin's 'Work of Art' Essay." In *Walter Benjamin's Philosophy: Destruction and Experience*, edited by Andrew Benjamin and Peter Osborne, 205–15. London: Routledge, 1994.

Kölbl, Alois. *Das Leben der Form: Georg Simmels kunstphilosophischer Versuch über Rembrandt.* Vienna: Böhlau, 1998.

Kösser, Uta. "Simmels Rembrandt." *Simmel Studies* 13, no. 2 (2003): 439–83.

Kracauer, Siegfried. "Georg Simmel." In *The Mass Ornament. Weimar Essays*, edited and translated by Thomas Y. Levin, 225–57. Cambridge, Mass.: Harvard University Press, 1995.

———. "Silent Film Comedy." In *Siegfried Kracauer's American Writings: Essays on Film and Popular Culture*, edited by Johannes von Moltke and Kristy Rawson, 213–17. Berkeley: University of California Press, 2012.

———. *Theory of Film: The Redemption of Physical Reality.* Princeton, N.J.: Princeton University Press, 1960.

Kraus, Karl. *The Last Days of Mankind.* Translated by Fred Bridgham and Edward Timms. New Haven, Conn.: Yale University Press, 2015.

Lang, Karen. "Simmel's *Rembrandt* and *The View of Life*." In *New Approaches to Neo-Kantianism*, edited by Nicolas de Warren and Andrea Staiti, 186–202. Cambridge: Cambridge University Press, 2015.

Langbehn, Julius. *Rembrandt als Erzieher.* Weimar: Alexander Duncker Verlag, 1943.

Lash, Scott. "Lebenssoziologie: Georg Simmel in the Information Age." *Theory, Culture & Society* 22, no. 3 (2005): 1–23.

Lebovic, Nitzan. *The Philosophy of Life and Death: Ludwig Klages and the Rise of a Nazi Biopolitics.* New York: Palgrave Macmillan, 2013.

———. "Simmel's Apple: The Image of Living Time." In *Georg Simmel in Translation: Interdisciplinary Border Crossings in Culture and Modernity*, edited by David Kim, 189–212. Cambridge: Cambridge Scholars, 2009.

Lechner, F. J. "Simmel on Social Space." *Theory, Culture & Society* 8, no. 3 (1991): 195–201.

Lee, Monica, and Daniel Silver. "Simmel's Law of the Individual and the Ethics of the Relational Self." *Theory, Culture & Society* 29, no. 7/8 (2012): 124–45.

Lehmann, Ulrich. *Tigersprung: Fashion in Modernity, Ulrich Lehmann.* Cambridge, Mass.: MIT Press, 2000.

Lehtonen, Turo-Kimmo, and Olli Pyyhtinen. "On Simmel's Conception of Philosophy." *Continental Philosophy Review* 41, no. 3 (2008): 301–22.

le Rider, Jacques. "Rembrandt de Langbehn à Simmel: Du clair-obscur de l'âme allemande aux couleurs de la modernité." *Société* 44 (1994): 145–55.

Levinas, Emmanuel. *On Escape.* Translated by Bettina Bergo. Stanford, Calif.: Stanford University Press, 2003.

Levine, Donald. N. "Simmel as Educator: On Individuality and Modern Culture." *Theory, Culture & Society* 8, no. 3 (1991): 99–117.
———. "*Soziologie* and *Lebensanschauung*: Two Approaches to Synthesizing 'Kant' and 'Goethe' in Simmel's Work." *Theory, Culture & Society* 29, no. 7–8 (2012): 26–52.
Löwy, Michael. *Fire Alarm: Reading Walter Benjamin's "On the Concept of History."* London: Verso, 2005.
Lukács, Georg. "Georg Simmel." *Theory, Culture & Society* 8, no. 3 (1991): 145–50.
———. *History and Class Consciousness: Studies in Marxist Dialectics*. Translated by Rodney Livingstone. Cambridge, Mass.: MIT Press, 1971.
Mannheim, Karl. "Georg Simmel als Philosoph." In *Georg Lukács, Karl Mannheim und der Sonntagskreis*, edited by Eva Karádi and Erzsesbet Vezér, 150–53. Frankfurt am Main: Vervuert, 1985.
———. "Soul and Culture." *Theory, Culture & Society* 29, no. 7–8 (2012): 286–301.
Marian, Micko. *Walter Benjamin und Georg Simmel*. Wiesbaden: Harrassowitz Verlag, 2010.
Marks, John. "Control Society." In *The Deleuze Dictionary*, edited by Adrian Parr, 55–56. Edinburgh: Edinburgh University Press, 2005.
Martinez, Ann T. "Walter Benjamin: A Sociologist in the Path of Simmel." *Humboldt Journal of Social Relations* 12, no. 1 (1984–85): 114–31.
McCole, John. "Georg Simmel and the Philosophy of Religion." *New German Critique*, no. 94 (2005): 8–35.
Menke, Bettine. "'However One Calls into the Forest . . .'; Echoes of Translation." In *Walter Benjamin and Romanticism*, edited by Beatrice Hanssen and Andrew Benjamin, 83–97. New York: Continuum, 2002.
Menninghaus, Winfried. *Walter Benjamins Theorie der Sprachmagie*. Frankfurt am Main: Suhrkamp Verlag, 1995.
Meyer, Ingo. "Benjamin, Adorno und in Hintergrund der Dritte." *Simmel Studies* 15 (2005): 63–115.
Mitchell, W. J. T. "Benjamin and the Political Economy of the Photograph." In *The Photography Reader*, edited by Liz Wells, 53–58. London: Routledge, 2003.
Nägele, Rainer. *Theater, Theory, Speculation: Walter Benjamin and the Scenes of Modernity*. Baltimore: Johns Hopkins University Press, 1991.
Nedelmann, Birgitta. "On the Concept of 'Erleben' in Georg Simmel's Sociology." In *Georg Simmel and Contemporary Sociology*, edited by Michael Kaern, Bernard S. Phillips, and Robert S. Cohen, 225–42. Dordrecht: Kluwer Academic, 1990.
Newman, Jane O. *Benjamin's Library: Modernity, Nation, and the Baroque*. Ithaca, N.Y.: Cornell University Press, 2011.
Osborne, Peter. "Small-Scale Histories, Large-Scale Defeats: Walter Benjamin's Politics of Time." In *Walter Benjamin's Philosophy: Destruction and Experience*, edited by Andrew Benjamin and Peter Osborne, 59–109. London: Routledge, 1994.
Pensky, Max. *Melancholy Dialectics: Walter Benjamin and the Play of Mourning*. Amherst: University of Massachusetts Press, 2001.

Proust, Marcel. *Remembrance of Things Past, Volume 1*. Translated by C. K. Scott Moncrieff. New York: Random House, 1932.

———. *Remembrance of Things Past, Volume 2*. Translated by C. K. Scott Moncrieff. New York: Random House, 1932.

Pyyhtinen, Olli. "Life, Death and Individuation: Simmel on the Problem of Life Itself." *Theory, Culture & Society* 29, no. 7–8 (2012): 78–100.

Rabinach, Anson. "Between Enlightenment and Apocalypse: Benjamin, Bloch and Modern German Jewish Messianism." *New German Critique* 34 (1985): 78–124.

Rammstedt, Otthein. "On Simmel's Aesthetics: Argumentation in the Journal *Jugend*, 1897–1906." *Theory, Culture & Society* 8, no. 3 (1991): 125–44.

Rancière, Jacques. "The Machine and Its Shadow (Hollywood, 1916)." In *Aesthesis: Scenes from the Aesthetic Regime of Art*, translated by Paul Zakir, 191–206. London: Verso, 2013.

———. "Master of Surfaces (Paris, 1902)." In *Aesthesis: Scenes from the Aesthetic Regime of Art*, translated by Paul Zakir, 155–70. London: Verso, 2013.

Raulet, Gerard. "Simmel et ses héritiers." *Information sur les Sciences Sociales* 25, no. 4 (1986): 845–59.

Riegl, Aloïs. *The Group Portraiture of Holland*. Translated by Evelyn M. Kain and David Britt. Los Angeles: Getty Research Institute for the History of Art and the Humanities, 1999.

Rilke, Rainer Maria. *Auguste Rodin*. Translated by Jessie Lemont and Hans Trausil. London: Pallas Athena, 2006.

Rivette, Jacques. "Revoir Verdoux." *Cahiers du Cinéma* 143 (1963): 42–43.

Robinson, David. *Chaplin: His Life and Art*. London: Penguin Books, 2001.

Rothman, William. "The Ending of *City Lights*." In *The "I" of the Camera: Essays in Film Criticism, History, and Aesthetics*, 44–54. Cambridge: Cambridge University Press, 2004.

Santner, Eric L. *On Creaturely Life: Rilke, Benjamin, Sebald*. Chicago: University of Chicago Press, 2006.

Sarris, Andrew. "The Most Harmonious Comedian." In *The Essential Chaplin: Perspectives on the Life and Art of the Great Comedian*, edited by Richard Schickel, 45–58. Chicago: Ivan R. Dee, 2006.

Schama, Simon. *Rembrandt's Eyes*. Knopf: New York, 1999.

Schickel, Richard. "Introduction: The Tramp Transformed." In *The Essential Chaplin: Perspectives on the Life and Art of the Great Comedian*, edited by Richard Schickel, 3–43. Chicago: Ivan R. Dee, 2006.

Schmoll Gen. Eisenwerth, J. A. "Simmel und Rodin." In *Ästhetik und Soziologie um die Jahrhundertwende: Georg Simmel*, edited by Hannes Böhringer and Karlfriend Gründer, 18–38. Frankfurt am Main: Vittorio Klostermann, 1976.

———. "Zur Genesis des Torso-Motivs und Zur Deutung des Fragmentarischen Stils bei Rodin." In *Rodin-Studien: Persönlichkeit, Werke, Wirkung, Bibliographie*, 143–60. Munich: Prestel Verlag, 1983.

Scholem, Gershom. *Walter Benjamin: The Story of a Friendship*. Translated by Harry Zohn. London: Faber and Faber, 1982.

Schwartz, Gary. *Het Rembrandt boek*. Translated by Loekie Schwartz and Paul Van Calster. Antwerp: Mercatorfonds, 2006.

Simmel, Georg. "Aesthetik des Porträts" (1905). In *GSG 7*, 321–32.

———. "Böcklins Landschaften" (1895). In *GSG 5*, 96–104.
———. "Das Geheimnis und die geheime Gesellschaft" (1908). In *GSG 11*, 383–455. Translated into English as "The Sociology of Secrecy and Secret Societies." *The American Journal of Sociology* 11, no. 4 (1906): 441–98.
———. "Das individuelle Gesetz" (1913/1918). In *Lebensanschauung, GSG 16*, 346–425. Translated into English as "The Law of the Individual." In *VoL*, 99–154.
———. "Das Problem der Historischen Zeit" (1916). In *GSG 15*, 287–304. Translated into English as "The Problem of Historical Time." In *Essays on Interpretation in Social Science*, edited and translated by Guy Oakes, 127–44. Manchester: Manchester University Press, 1980.
———. "Das Problem des Schicksals" (1913). In *GSG 12*, 483–92. Translated into English as "The Problem of Fate." *Theory, Culture & Society* 24, no. 7–8 (2007): 78–84.
———. "Der Begriff der Kultur" (1900). In *GSG 6*, 617–22. Translated into English as "The Concept of Culture." In *SoC*, 36–40.
———. "Der Begriff und die Tragödie der Kultur" (1911/1912). In *GSG 12*, 194–223. Translated into English as "The Concept and Tragedy of Culture." In *SoC*, 55–75.
———. "Der Bildrahmen: Ein ästhetischer Versuch" (1902). In *GSG 7*, 101–8. Translated into English as "The Picture Frame: An Aesthetic Study." *Theory, Culture & Society* 11, no. 1 (1994): 11–17.
———. "Der Konflikt der modernen Kultur" (1918). In *GSG 16*, 181–208. Translated into English as "The Conflict of Modern Culture." In *SoC*, 75–90.
———. "Der Henkel" (1911). In *GSG 14*, 278–87. Translated into English as "The Handle," in "Two Essays." *The Hudson Review* 11, no. 3 (1958): 371–78.
———. "Deutschlands innere Wandlung" (1914). In *GSG 15*, 273–85.
———. "Die ästhetische Bedeutung des Gesichts" (1901). In *GSG 7*, 36–42. Translated into English as "The Aesthetic Significance of the Face." In *Georg Simmel: 1858–1919*, edited by Kurt Wolff, translated by Lore Ferguson, 276–81. Columbus: Ohio State University Press, 1959.
———. "Die beiden Formen des Individualismus" (1901). In *GSG 7*, 49–56.
———. "Die Gegensätze des Lebens und die Religion" (1904). In *GSG 7*, 295–303.
———. "Die Großstädte und das Geistesleben" (1903). In *GSG 7*, 116–31. Translated into English as "The Metropolis and Mental Life." In *SoC*, 174–85.
———. "Die Krisis der Kultur" (1916). In *GSG 13*, 190–201. Translated into English as "The Crisis of Culture." In *SoC*, 90–101.
———. "Die Kunst Rodins und das Bewegungsmotiv in der Plastik" (1909). In *GSG 12*, 28–36.
———. "Die Transzendenz des Lebens" (1918). In *Lebensanschauung, GSG 16*, 212–35. Translated into English as "Life as Transcendence." In *VoL*, 1–17.
———. "Die Wendung zur Idee" (1918). In *Lebensanschauung, GSG 16*, 236–96. Translated into English as "The Turn Toward Ideas." In *VoL*, 19–61.
———. "Einführung Philosophische Kultur" (1911). In *GSG 14*, 162–67. Translated into English as "Introduction to Philosophical Culture." In *SoC*, 33–36.
———. "Erinnerung an Rodin" (1917). In *GSG 13*, 307–12.
———. *Essays on Religion*. Edited and translated by Horst Jürgen Helle and Ludwig Nieder. New Haven, Conn.: Yale University Press, 1997.

———. "Exkurs über den Fremden" (1908). In *GSG 11*, 764–71. Translated into English as "The Stranger." In *The Sociology of Georg Simmel*, edited and translated by Kurt Wolff, 402–8. New York: Free, 1950.

———. "Exkurs über die soziale Begrenzung" (1908). In *GSG 11*, 698–702. Translated into English as "The Social Boundary." *Theory, Culture & Society* 24, no. 7–8 (2007): 53–56.

———. "Germanischer und Klassisch-Romanischer Stil" (1918). In *GSG 13*, 313–20. Translated into English as "Germanic and Classical Romanic Style." *Theory, Culture & Society* 24, no. 7–8 (2007): 47–52.

———. "Goethe" (1912/1913). In *GSG 15*, 7–270.

———. "Goethe und die Jugend" (1914). In *GSG 13*, 98–104. Translated into English as "Goethe and Youth." *Theory, Culture & Society* 24, no. 7–8 (2007): 85–90.

———. "Henri Bergson" (1914). In *GSG 13*, 53–69.

———. "Individualismus" (1917). In *GSG 13*, 299–306. Translated into English as "Individualism." *Theory, Culture & Society* 24, no. 7–8 (2007): 66–71.

———. "L'art pour L'art" (1914). In *GSG 13*, 9–15.

———. "Michelangelo als Dichter" (1889). In *GSG 2*, 37–48.

———. "Michelangelo: Ein Kapitel zur Metaphysik der Kultur" (1910/1911). In *GSG 12*, 111–36 and *GSG 14*, 304–29.

———. "Philosophie der Landschaft" (1913). In *GSG 12*, 471–82. Translated into English as "The Philosophy of Landscape." *Theory, Culture & Society* 24, no. 7–8 (2007): 20–29.

———. *Philosophie des Geldes* (1900). In *GSG 6*. Translated into English as *The Philosophy of Money*. Edited by David Frisby, translated by Tom Bottomore and David Frisby. London: Routledge, 2004.

———. *Rembrandt: Ein kunstphilosophischer Versuch* (1916). In *GSG 15*, 305–515. Translated into English as *Rembrandt: An Essay in the Philosophy of Art*. Edited and translated by Alan Scott and Helmut Staubmann. London: Routledge, 2005.

———. "Rembrandts religiöse Kunst" (1914). In *GSG 13*, 70–89. Translated into English as "Rembrandt's Religious Art." In *Essays on Religion*, edited and translated by Horst Jürgen Helle and Ludwig Nieder, 77–97. New Haven, Conn.: Yale University Press, 1997.

———. "Rodin (mit Einer Vorbemerkung über Meunier)" (1911). In *GSG 14*, 330–48.

———. "Rodins Plastik und die Geistesrichtung der Gegenwart" (1902). In *GSG 7*, 92–100.

———. "Sechzehn Vorlesungen gehalten an der Berliner Universität." In *GSG 9*, 8–226.

———. "Selections from Simmel's Writings for the Journal *Jugend*." *Theory, Culture & Society* 29, no. 7–8 (2012): 263–78.

———. "Soziologische Aesthetik" (1896). In *GSG 5*, 197–214. Translated into English as "Sociological Aesthetics." In *The Conflict in Modern Culture and Other Essays*, translated and edited by K. P. Etzkorn, 68–80. New York: Teachers, 1968.

———. "Tod und Unsterblichkeit" (1918). In *Lebensanschauung, GSG 16*, 297–345. Translated into English as "Death and Immortality." In *VoL*, 63–97.

———. "Vom Realismus in der Kunst" (1908). In *GSG 8*, 404–15.

———. "Vom Wesen der Kultur" (1908). In *GSG 8*, 363–73. Translated into English as "On the Essence of Culture." In *SoC*, 40–45.

———. "Zum Problem des Naturalismus" (1923). In *GSG 20*, 220–48.

———. "Zur Metaphysik des Todes" (1910/1911). In *GSG 12*, 81–96.

———. "Zur Psychologie der Frauen" (1887–90). In *GSG 2*, 66–102.

———. "Zur Psychologie des Geldes" (1889). In *GSG 2*, 49–65. Translated into English as "On the Psychology of Money." In *SoC*, 233–43.

———. "Zur Soziologie der Armut" (1906). In *GSG 8*, 24–57. Translated into English as "The Poor." *Social Problems* 12, no. 2 (1965): 118–40.

Simmel, Hans. "Auszüge aus den Lebenserinnerungen." In *Ästhetik und Soziologie um die Jahrhundertwende: Georg Simmel*, edited by Hannes Böhringer and Karlfried Gründer, 247–68. Frankfurt am Main: Vittorio Klostermann, 1976.

Staiti, Andrea. *Husserl's Transcendental Phenomenology: Nature, Spirit, and Life*. Cambridge: Cambridge University Press, 2014.

Symons, Stéphane. "The Creature That Can Still Survive: Walter Benjamin on Mickey Mouse and Rhythmic Movement." *Telos* 176 (Fall 2016): 165-86.

———. "Walter Benjamin and the 'Highly Productive Use of the Human Being's Self-Alienation.'" In *The Aesthetic Ground of Critical Theory: New Readings of Benjamin and Adorno*, edited by Nathan Ross, 99–110. Lanham, Md.: Rowman and Littlefield, 2015.

Tiedemann, Rolf. *Studien zur Philosophie Walter Benjamins*. Frankfurt am Main: Suhrkamp Verlag, 1973.

Van Reijen, Willem. *Der Schwarzwald und Paris: Heidegger und Benjamin*. Munich: Wilhelm Fink Verlag, 1998.

———. "Innerlichkeit Oder Begriffsarbeit? Die Barockrezeption W. Benjamins und Th.W. Adornos." In *Allegorie und Melancholie*, edited by Willem van Reijen, 17–31. Frankfurt am Main: Suhrkamp Verlag, 1992.

Warburg, Aby. "Pagan-Antique Prophecy in Words and Images in the Age of Luther." In *The Renewal of Pagan Antiquity: Contributions to the Cultural History of the European Renaissance*, edited and translated by David Britt, 597–697. Los Angeles: Getty Research Institute for the History of Art and the Humanities, 1999.

Watier, Patrick. "The War Writings of Georg Simmel." *Theory, Culture & Society* 8, no. 3 (1991): 219–33.

Weber, Samuel. *Benjamin's -abilities*. Cambridge, Mass.: Harvard University Press, 2008.

———. "Storming the Work: Allegory and Theatricality in Benjamin's *Origin of the German Mourning Play*." In *Theatricality as Medium*, 160–80. New York: Fordham University Press, 2004.

Weigel, Sigrid. "The Artwork as Breach of a Beyond: On the Dialectic of Divine and Human Order in Walter Benjamin's 'Goethe's Elective Affinities.'" In *Walter Benjamin and Romanticism*, edited by Beatrice Hanssen and Andrew Benjamin, 197–206. New York: Continuum, 2002.

———. "Bildwissenschaft aus dem Geiste wahrer Philologie." In *Walter Benjamin: Die Kreatur, Das Heilige, Die Bilder*, 237–50. Frankfurt am Main: Fischer Taschenbuch Verlag, 2008.

———. *Body- and Image-Space: Re-Reading Walter Benjamin*. London: Routledge, 1996.

———. *Walter Benjamin: Images, the Creaturely, and the Holy*. Translated by Chadwick Smith. Stanford, Calif.: Stanford University Press, 2013.

Weingartner, Rudolph Herbert. *Experience and Culture: The Philosophy of Georg Simmel*. Middletown, Conn.: Wesleyan University Press, 1960.

Weinstein, Deena, and Michael A. Weinstein. "Georg Simmel: Sociological Flâneur Bricoleur." *Theory, Culture & Society* 8, no. 3 (1991): 151–68.

———. *Postmodern(ized) Simmel*. London: Routledge, 1993.

Weissberg, Liliane. "Circulating Images: Notes on the Photographic Exchange." In *Writing the Image after Roland Barthes*, edited by Jean-Michel Rabaté, 109–31. Philadelphia: University of Pennsylvania Press, 1997.

Wohlfarth, Irving. "Et Cetera? The Historian as Chiffonnier." *New German Critique*, no. 39 (1986): 143–68.

———. "Perte d'Auréole: The Emergence of the Dandy." *MLN* 85, no. 4 (1970): 529–71.

Žižek, Slavoj. *Enjoy Your Symptom! Jacques Lacan in Hollywood and Out*. New York: Routledge, 1992.

INDEX